This book is concerned with the eth
of law. Professor Burton analyzes the grounds, content, and
force of a judge's legal and moral duties to uphold the law.
He defends two primary theses. The first is the good faith
thesis, whereby judges are bound in law to uphold the law,
even when they have discretion, by acting only on reasons
warranted by the conventional law as grounds for judicial
decisions. The good faith thesis counters the common view
that judges are not bound by the law when they exercise
discretion. The second is the permissible discretion thesis,
whereby, when exercised in good faith, judicial discretion is
compatible with the legitimacy of adjudication in a constitutional democracy under the Rule of Law. The permissible
discretion thesis counters the view that judges can fulfill
their duty to uphold the law only when the law yields determinate results.

Together, these two theses provide an original and powerful theory of adjudication in sharp contrast both to conservative theories that would restrict the scope of adjudication
unduly, and to leftist critical theories that would liberate
judges from the Rule of Law.

Judging in good faith

Cambridge Studies in Philosophy and Law

GENERAL EDITOR: JULES COLEMAN (YALE LAW SCHOOL)

ADVISORY BOARD

David Gauthier (University of Pittsburgh)
David Lyons (Cornell University)
Richard Posner (Judge of the Seventh Circuit Court of Appeals, Chicago)
Martin Shapiro (University of California, Berkeley)

This exciting new series will reflect and foster the most original research currently taking place in the study of law and legal theory by publishing the most adventurous monographs in the field as well as rigorously edited collections of essays. It will be a specific aim of the series to traverse the boundaries between disciplines and to form bridges between traditional studies of law and many other areas of the human sciences. Books in the series will be of interest not only to philosophers and legal theorists but also to political scientists, sociologists, economists, psychologists, and criminologists.

Other books in the series

Jeffrie G. Murphy and Jean Hampton: *Forgiveness and mercy*
Stephen R. Munzer: *A theory of property*
R. G. Frey and Christopher W. Morris (eds.): *Liability and responsibility: Essays in law and morals*
Robert F. Schopp: *Automatism, insanity, and the psychology of criminal responsibility*
Jules Coleman: *Risks and wrongs*

Judging in good faith

STEVEN J. BURTON

WILLIAM G. HAMMOND PROFESSOR OF LAW
UNIVERSITY OF IOWA

CAMBRIDGE
UNIVERSITY PRESS

Published by the Press Syndicate of the University of Cambridge
The Pitt Building, Trumpington Street, Cambridge CB2 1RP
40 West 20th Street, New York, NY 10011-4211, USA
10 Stamford Road, Oakleigh, Melbourne 3166, Australia

First published 1992

First paperback edition 1994

Library of Congress Cataloging-in-Publication Data
Burton, Stephen J.
Judging in good faith / Steven J. Burton
p.   cm. – (Cambridge Studies in philosophy and law)
Includes index.
ISBN 0-521-41994-8 (hardback)
ISBN 0-521-47740-9 (paperback)
1. Law – Philosophy. 2. Jurisprudence. 4. Judicial process – Moral
and ethical aspects. I. Title. II. Series.
K237.B87   1992
340'.112 – dc20   91-47159
CIP

A catalog record for this book is available from the British Library.

ISBN 0-521-41994-8 hardback
ISBN 0-521-47740-9 paperback

Transferred to digital printing 2004

For Serena, Daryn, Max, and Sam

Contents

vii

Contents

Contents

Preface

This book is about the ethics of judging in courts of law. At the core of such an ethics is the judge's duty to uphold the law. That there is such a duty in principle is largely uncontroversial within jurisprudence and judicial practice. The ground of the duty, its specific content, and its force, however, generally are left unanalyzed as the duty is taken for granted. In my view, this is a mistake, leading to much confusion on a matter of central importance in a democracy like the United States. Different conceptions of judicial duty support markedly different ideas of proper adjudication in courts of law. Too simple an understanding of this key duty can lead to both undue constrictions of legitimate adjudication and misplaced criticism of the Rule of Law. Constitutional democracies, by contrast with totalitarian, authoritarian, socialist, and communitarian political regimes, insist that uses of governmental power be within the law. Judges are supposed to uphold the law when they say whether others have acted within the law and when they take action themselves, implementing the Rule of Law and protecting individuals from oppression. The stakes are great. We should get it straight.

I will develop and defend a view of judicial duty – the "good faith thesis" – that permits a meaningful scope for adjudication under law within a constitutional democracy. Briefly, my thought is that the familiar jurisprudential treatments of adjudication share a common and undefended commitment to what I call the "determinacy condition." This condition holds that judges cannot fulfill their duty to uphold the law unless they reach the single right result determined by the law. The problem is that the conventional law – the Constitution, statutes, administrative rules, and the common law – is indeterminate to a significant extent, leaving judges discretion in some cases, including many of the most important cases that come before the highest appellate courts. Accepting the determinacy condition implies that these cases are not decided under the law (unless the concept of law is expanded beyond conventional recognition). Thus, some would restrict the scope of proper adjudication to cases in which the conventional law determines the result, transforming adjudication into a far more conservative institution than it has been in the United States in recent decades. Others would allow an expansive scope for adjudication by treating the law as a matter of moral and political principles that determine right results, leaving judges inadequately constrained by convention to satisfy most observers. Yet others would maintain that the law determines results in a narrow range of cases and, at the same time, permits a broad scope for adjudication, allowing judges discretion otherwise to go outside the law for the grounds of their decisions, again leaving judges inadequately constrained by convention.

The good faith thesis abandons the determinacy condition completely. It understands the law as a provider of legal reasons, not necessarily results. It understands the legitimacy of adjudication to depend on respect for the reasons, not agreement with the results, in cases. The good faith thesis claims that judges are bound in law to uphold the conventional law, even when they have discretion, by acting only on reasons warranted by that law as grounds for judicial decision. A companion thesis – the "permissible discretion thesis" – claims that, when exercised in good faith, judicial discretion is compatible with the legitimacy of adjudication in a constitutional democracy. Together, the good faith and permissible discretion theses allow a meaningful scope for adjudication while maintaining that the law is conventional and that judges are constrained to interpret and apply it in all cases within their jurisdiction.

Legal scholars, who increasingly place their legal work in the context of another discipline, face a dilemma. Most of us want to speak primarily to legal scholars, judges, lawyers, legislators, and others concerned with justice and the legal system. At the same time, we want to draw on other disciplines in a capable way that enhances the quality of our legal work while earning the respect of professionals in other fields. The dilemma deepens with the increasingly specialized and interdisciplinary focus of current legal scholarship. Reaching the legal audience often seems possible only at the cost of treating another discipline's insights superficially; mastering another discipline often leads to esoteric legal scholarship of little interest to most lawyers. Many efforts to build bridges simply fail, especially those that do not take sufficient care to understand the materials of another field in their own terms or that allow central questions of the other field to supplant those of special concern to the law. Great admiration is due to such scholars in analytical jurisprudence as Ronald Dworkin and H. L. A. Hart, who succeed regularly with both legal and philosophical audiences.

This book is an effort to understand adjudication in law using analytical techniques and philosophical arguments while speaking primarily to the intellectual interests of non-philosophers concerned with the law. My thesis perhaps could be explained and defended in shorter compass using a technical philosophical discourse. I have chosen, however, to try reaching a much larger part of the legal community, including other legal scholars and teachers, judges, litigating lawyers, and others who study courts. One consequence of this choice is that the project became a book rather than a long journal article. Other consequences of this choice are that I pass over some points that are controversial among philosophers of law in particular and, more so, philosophers in general; time is taken to explain some ideas that would need no explanation in a work intended for a specialized audience; whole chapters respond to contrary positions of a philosophical sort that are popular in legal circles but of little interest to professional philosophers; and many citations and some textual passages are included in the footnotes, primarily for those who want to verify my claims or to pursue matters further.

It is important, in my view, for an author to make the nature of his project clear at the outset. As the reader will see, I believe that much confusion in jurisprudence is generated by a tendency to mix up different kinds of scholarly claims – general philosophical claims about legal systems with claims about the law or adjudication in the local legal system, claims about how things came to be as they are with claims about whether the current practice is justified, and claims that are conceptual, descriptive, or normative. We need not start with the naive assumption that each participant in the discussion is agreeing or disagreeing significantly with each other participant. Green can be interested in practical reason while Black wonders at the metaphysics of law, Gray cares about the justification of coercion, and Brown is fascinated by the law's genesis. They make claims that sound as though they are in disagreement, and sometimes they are. But at other times they will be focusing on different questions. Each probably thinks that his or her own question is the most important, and they may well disagree about that. But only rarely will that be the topic of the discussion, and more rarely will that discussion be fruitful. I will cut against recent trends, in one of many ways, by suggesting that there is less genuine disagreement here than meets the eye.

Analytical jurisprudence, in my view, encompasses three main projects. General jurisprudence concerns centrally the theory of legal systems and the nature of legal rights and duties. The theory of legal systems, for example, focuses on the conditions for the existence of a legal system and for the identification of its laws, ideally in all possible worlds. This project is exemplified by H. L. A. Hart's famous thesis that a mature legal system exists only if there is, as a matter of fact, a rule of recognition in force among officials, with which the law is identified. By contrast, particular jurisprudence concerns the law within one legal system (or perhaps a small cluster of related legal systems). It might focus on the content of the rule of recognition in the U.S. legal system and consider, for example, whether moral criteria for cruelty are a part of the law due to the Eighth Amendment's prohibition on cruel and unusual punishment. The theory of adjudication is the third main project. It concerns the decision of particular cases under the law within one legal system. The rule of recognition may be used by judges to identify the law, but adjudication involves additionally the interpretation and application of that law in concrete cases. This book presents and defends the core of a theory of adjudication within the U.S. legal system.

A theory of adjudication can be carried out theoretically or practically. A theoretical understanding of adjudication would proceed from outside the practice in a scientific spirit, taking into account only such things as the objective behavior of individual judges or the observable regularities in judicial practice, and forming descriptive and explanatory theories about what is happening. In his academic writings, Oliver Wendell Holmes, Jr., for the most part offered theoretical understandings while seeking to banish mental and normative elements of practice. My project also proceeds from the outside, but with resolute sensitivity to how the law appears to and functions for persons on the inside. To judges, I will argue crucially, the law appears as a set of reasons for action in various circumstances. No theory of adjudication can be complete unless it is mindful of the role of reasons in adjudication by judicial agents. Accordingly, I refer to the venture as a "practical understanding of adjudication." "Practical" signifies only that it is oriented to judicial action understood with regard for the actor's stand-point in real-world circumstances. This should be contrasted with a theory of judicial behavior as it is seen from a strict observer's standpoint. As an understanding of "adjudication," it must get down to cases. This should be contrasted with an abstract theory that might be fine in principle but would flounder in practice.

A practical understanding of adjudication can be developed conceptually, descriptively, and normatively. This book emphasizes both conceptual and normative elements. It makes a descriptive claim that the law appears to judges as a set of reasons for action; accordingly, thoughtful judges should be able to recognize in my account an ideal version of what they are trying to do. No claim is made, however, that judges typically act in accordance with my thesis or explain themselves in its terms (though I suspect the good faith thesis captures much of the practice). My sense is that something has gone haywire in the most important kinds of adjudication in the United States. It is not only that the judiciary is making decisions with which I disagree. As judicial craft, I find opinions like Justice Brennan's opinion in *Patterson v. McLean Credit Union*, discussed at Sections 3.2 and following, as wanting as Justice Scalia's opinion in the Peyote Case, discussed at Section 4.3. Rather, mine is a sense that parts of American judicial practice are straying far from what is distinctively *legal*, as required by the tenets of democratic government under the Rule of Law. Some theorists celebrate the restriction of important adjudication to definitional and historical plumbing work, and others might praise the wanderlust into at-large social engineering or cultural management. I have a good centrist's conviction that there is something distinctively legal that can guide judges significantly and that, far from requiring them to turn a blind eye to justice, can help them better to do justice under the law. This conceptual and normative project is an effort to develop and defend a practicable and attractive ethic of judging in a judicious spirit.

Preface

Many persons were generous with their time and talents in helping me to bring this book to completion. For their comments and criticisms on various iterations of the manuscript, the author thanks former Attorney General Edward H. Levi, Justice Howard A. Levine, former Justice Mark MacCormick, Judge Richard A. Posner, and Professors Eric G. Andersen, John Bell, Ronald Dworkin, Lakshman Guruswamy, Ken Kress, Joseph Raz, Bonnie Steinbock, John Stick, and Serena Stier, and several anonymous reviewers. For their help in preparing the manuscript, I thank Douglas Greene and Herbert Sitz. I owe a special debt to the works of Joseph Raz and to his personal generosity during my stay in Oxford in 1987. I also owe a special debt to Edward H. Levi, whose encouragement and gentle guidance were invaluable. And, as usual, I owe the greatest debt to my wife, Serena. I also thank participants in faculty workshops held on portions of this project at the Philosophy Department, State University of New York at Albany, the Benjamin Cardozo School of Law of Yeshiva University, the New York University School of Law, the Duke Law School, and the University of Edinburgh.

I have been exceptionally lucky in receiving generous funding, which permitted me an embarrassing amount of time free of teaching and administrative duties. The University of Iowa in 1986 made me a University Faculty Scholar, giving me the equivalent of three semester-long research leaves over the next four years together with extraordinary technical and financial support. This made it possible for me to spend a semester at Oxford University, where the ideas in this book began to take primitive shape even while a great many bad ideas were being buried. In addition, the Fulbright Program was generous in supporting my research at Oxford by making me a Fulbright Scholar. University College was kind enough to give me a professional home there. Additional funding was made available by the Burlington-Northern Foundation, through a Faculty Achievement Award for excellence in teaching at the University of Iowa. Dean N. William Hines and the University of Iowa College of

xvii

Law were ever ready to backstop these other funding sources, not the least by arranging for my courses to be covered while I was on leave.

Part I

The good faith thesis

Chapter 1

Stubborn indeterminacy

1.1. THE DETERMINACY PROBLEM

The problem of legal indeterminacy has moved to the center of jurisprudential debate in the United States since Oliver Wendell Holmes, Jr., proclaimed:

> The life of the law has not been logic: it has been experience. The felt necessities of the time, the prevalent moral and political theories, intuitions of public policy, avowed or unconscious, even the prejudices which judges share with their fellow-men, have had a good deal more to do than the syllogism in determining the rules by which men should be governed. The law embodies the story of a nation's development through many centuries, and it cannot be dealt with as if it contained only the axioms and corollaries of a book of mathematics.[1]

Holmes's foil was Christopher Columbus Langdell, the famous father of legal education by Socratic dialogue.[2] The lore is that Langdell supposed the law to be a consistent and complete body of dogmatic rules. For him, the law was objective in that it was rooted in timeless concepts each of which had an essential nature. It was neutral in that it stood apart

---

1 Oliver Wendell Holmes, *The Common Law*, ed. Mark D. Howe (Boston: Little, Brown & Co., 1963), p. 5.
2 See [Oliver Wendell Holmes], "Book Notice," *American Law Review*, 14 (1880): 233–5 [reviewing Christopher C. Langdell, *A Selection of Cases on the Law of Contracts*, 2d ed. (Boston: Little, Brown & Co., 1879)].

from the contingent empirical context and might be invoked
by persons with disparate opportunities to enjoy their legal
rights or perform their legal duties. The law was determinate
in that it dictated single right results in all possible cases. For
convenience, this understanding of the law will be called
"determinate-formalism."[3]

Langdell's effort to create a determinate-formalist science
of law is a now undisputed object lesson.[4] Holmes's attack
inspired successive waves of criticism that in time became
the "determinacy critique," which denies that the law produces determinate results and, therefore, also that it is neutral or objective. By emphasizing the multiple causes of the
law and judicial decisions, focusing on historical and social
forces outside the corpus of official legal rules, Holmes
sought to understand the law theoretically without under-
estimating the complexity and variability of its genesis. He
defined the law as "[t]he prophecies of what the courts will
do in fact, and nothing more pretentious."[5] Similarly, he
treated legal rights and duties as predictions of judicial behavior, seeking to substitute a scientific foundation for
"empty words."[6] Many of the legal realists in the 1920s and

---

3 See Thomas C. Grey, "Langdell's Orthodoxy," *University of Pittsburgh Law Review*, 45 (1983): 1–53. See also Duncan Kennedy, "The Structure of Blackstone's Commentaries," *Buffalo Law Review*, 28 (1979): 209–382.
4 Those who recently have defended versions of legal formalism do not claim that the law must dictate particular results in all cases. See Frederick Schauer, "Formalism," *Yale Law Journal*, 97 (1988): 509–48, at 544–8; Ernest J. Weinrib, "Legal Formalism: On the Immanent Rationality of Law," *Yale Law Journal*, 97 (1988): 949–1016, at 953–7, 1008–12. See also Roberto M. Unger, *The Critical Legal Studies Movement* (Cambridge: Harvard University Press, 1986), pp. 1–14 (criticizing a broad conception of legal formalism).
5 Oliver Wendell Holmes, "The Path of the Law," in *Collected Legal Papers* (New York: Harcourt, Brace and Howe, 1920): pp. 167–202, at 173.
6 Oliver Wendell Holmes, "Law in Science and Science in Law," in ibid.: pp. 210–43, at 229. See also Holmes, "Natural Law," in ibid.: pp. 310–16, at 313 ("But for legal purposes a right is only the hypostasis of a prophecy – the imagination of a substance supporting the fact that the public force will be brought to bear upon those who do things said to contravene it – just as we talk of the force of gravitation accounting for the conduct of bodies in space."); Holmes, "The Path of

4

1930s continued the Holmesian project by redefining law as the observable regularities in aggregate official behavior.[7] They employed social scientific methods to describe and explain those regularities to enhance the predictability of the law while continuing to debunk determinate-formalism in law. Others, disaffected with positivistic social science and the maldistribution of effective legal power in society, more recently have adapted the project of understanding law theoretically to draw on social theory, literary theory, and history while trying to soften up the law for change, abandoning the goal of prediction.[8] Throughout, the salience of claims that the law is indeterminate mushroomed as the determinacy critique deepened.

In my view, much too much is made of the indeterminacy of legal results. The determinacy critique stems broadly from the riveting clash between Langdell and Holmes, both of whom in their legal theories made determinacy of results a central requirement for law. Contemporary versions of the determinacy critique, in particular, express skepticism due to the failure of the Holmesian project to provide both a determinate theoretical understanding of the law and a determi-

---

the Law," at 169 ("[A] legal duty so called is nothing but a prediction that if a man does or omits certain things he will be made to suffer in this or that way by judgment of the court; and so of a legal right.").

7 For example, Karl N. Llewellyn, *The Bramble Bush* (New York: Oceana Publications, 1951), pp. 12–13 (*"What these officials do about disputes is, to my mind, the law itself. . . .* And so to my mind the main thing is seeing what officials do, do about disputes, or about anything else; and seeing that there is a certain regularity in their doing – a regularity which makes possible prediction of what they and other officials are about to do tomorrow"); Walter W. Cook, "Scientific Method and the Law," *American Bar Association Journal*, 13 (1927): 303–9, at 308 (rules and principles of law describe past behavior of judges).

8 For example, Clare Dalton, "An Essay in Deconstruction of Contract Doctrine," *Yale Law Journal*, 94 (1985): 997–1114; Robert W. Gordon, "Critical Legal Histories," *Stanford Law Review*, 36 (1984): 57–125; Robert W. Gordon, "Historicism in Legal Scholarship," *Yale Law Journal*, 90 (1981): 1017–56; David M. Trubeck, "Where the Action Is: Critical Legal Studies and Empiricism," *Stanford Law Review*, 36 (1984): 575–622, at 577–9. See also Sanford Levinson, *Constitutional Faith* (Princeton: Princeton University Press, 1988).

nate basis for ensuring a reasonably just legal system. There is, however, a third approach that abandons determinacy of results as a conceptual requirement for law and that has been left largely unattended. I call that approach in general jurisprudence "law as practical reason."[9] A conceptual and normative theory of adjudication within law as practical reason – the "good faith thesis" – will be presented in Chapters 2 and 3 and defended thereafter. Because the thesis breaks out of the dualistic tradition spawned by Langdell and Holmes – logic versus experience – it will be useful first to clarify the central problem of legal indeterminacy and some of the starting assumptions.

1.2. INDETERMINACY CLARIFIED

The yearning for determinacy of results seems ever-present, especially among young law students and frustrated lawyers. A lesson that needs to be relearned in each generation is that the law can appear to be an objective, neutral, and determinate body of rules, but really is situated in a social

9 Steven J. Burton, "Law as Practical Reason," *Southern California Law Review*, 62 (1989): 747–93. The relevant idea of "practical reason" has a long intellectual history, starting with Aristotle and undergoing sometimes important changes as it was developed in the philosophies of St. Thomas Aquinas, Immanuel Kant, and more recently H. L. A. Hart and other important philosophers of the Oxford School. It is not, as is sometimes supposed, just a grab bag of ways of deciding what to do, but a potentially rigorous and constrained intellectual framework for reasoning about action. For a sample of recent treatments of law as practical reason, see John Finnis, *Natural Law and Natural Rights* (Oxford: Clarendon Press, 1982); Neil MacCormick, *Legal Reasoning and Legal Theory* (Oxford: Clarendon Press, 1978): Joseph Raz, *Practical Reason and Norms* (London: Hutchinson, 1975); Katharine T. Bartlett, "Feminist Legal Methods," *Harvard Law Review*, 103 (1990): 828–88; Daniel A. Farber & Philip P. Frickey, "Practical Reason and the First Amendment," *UCLA Law Review*, 34 (1987): 1615–56; Anthony T. Kronman, "Alexander Bickel's Philosophy of Prudence," *Yale Law Journal*, 94 (1985): 1567–616; "The Works of Joseph Raz: A Symposium," *Southern California Law Review*, 62 (1988): 731–1235. For an idiosyncratic approach to practical reason, see Richard A. Posner, *The Problems of Jurisprudence* (Cambridge: Harvard University Press, 1990), pp. 71–8.

context, exposed to political bias, and indeterminate to a significant extent. In a brief and abstract version, the determinacy critique goes something like this: The first principle of adjudication in courts of law is that judges are under a duty to uphold the law.[10] They are required to identify the law of their legal system, to interpret that law, and to apply it in disputes that come before them. The law, however, is not so clear, consistent, and complete that it constrains judges to reach a single legally required outcome in many cases. The law then is indeterminate, and the judge has discretion.[11]

To elaborate, legal indeterminacy is not the same as a lack of clarity in a legal rule or other standard for legal decision making. A formal legal rule, for example, may be vague or ambiguous as formulated, or it may conflict in its terms with another legal rule of the same kind. Such a rule, taken in isolation, is indeterminate with respect to the result in a case.

---

10 American Bar Association, *Model Code of Judicial Conduct*, Canon 3(B)(2) (1990) (a judge "should be faithful to the law and maintain professional competence in it"); § 2.1.

11 "*Discretion* means the power to choose between two or more courses of action each of which is thought of as permissible." Henry M. Hart, Jr. & Albert M. Sacks, *The Legal Process: Basic Problems in the Making and Application of Law*, tent. ed. (Cambridge, Mass.: Harvard Law School, 1958), p. 162. For other general explanations of discretion, see, for example, Aharon Barak, *Judicial Discretion* (New Haven: Yale University Press, 1989), p. 7; Kenneth C. Davis, *Discretionary Justice* (Baton Rouge, La.: Louisiana State University Press, 1969), pp. 4–5; Ronald Dworkin, *Taking Rights Seriously* (Cambridge: Harvard University Press, 1977), pp. 31–9, 68–71; D. Galligan, *Discretionary Powers* (Oxford: Clarendon Press, 1990), pp. 1–107; H. L. A. Hart, *The Concept of Law* (Oxford: Clarendon Press, 1961), pp. 120–32; Neil MacCormick, *Legal Reasoning and Legal Theory*, pp. 246–55; R. Kent Greenawalt, "Discretion and Judicial Decision: The Elusive Quest for the Fetters that Bind Judges," *Columbia Law Review*, 75 (1975): 359–99, at 386; Joseph Raz, "Legal Principles and the Limits of Law," in *Ronald Dworkin and Contemporary Jurisprudence*, ed. Marshall Cohen (Totowa, N.J.: Rowman & Allanheld, 1983): pp. 73–87, at 74; §§ 2.2 and following. Not all discretion results from unintended indeterminacy in the law. Sometimes, it is conferred on judges by the law, as when a trial judge's decision to admit evidence is reversible only when discretion is abused. What is said in this book about judicial discretion applies to discretion resulting from both legal indeterminacy and conferred discretionary powers.

7

The rule, however, exists within a system that includes rules of interpretation, hierarchies of legal authority, and other rules about rules. The rules about rules might resolve the initial lack of clarity, as when a statute contains clear definitional provisions or is made "subject to" another statute. This renders the indeterminacy harmless and uninteresting.[12] As Karl Llewellyn famously demonstrated, however,[13] rules of interpretation and hierarchies of legal authority commonly contain problems of vagueness, ambiguity, and conflict with other rules about rules. So the indeterminacy can be stubborn because it resists resolution as one moves through a legal analysis to deeper levels, no matter how many times one backs up and tries different lines of thought or argument. The law then is indeterminate in a real and important sense.

The legal realists did a good job of highlighting the apparent indeterminacy of formal legal rules.[14] Many of them thought, however, that it was not a great problem because discretion could be exercised on the basis of underlying social policies.[15] Legal process theorists thought similarly that apparent indeterminacy could be resolved on the basis of underlying principles and purposes.[16] More recently, law

12 See Andrew Altman, *Critical Legal Studies: A Liberal Critique* (Princeton: Princeton University Press, 1990), pp. 79–98.

13 Karl N. Llewellyn, "Remarks on the Theory of Appellate Decision and the Rules or Canons About How Statutes are to be Construed," *Vanderbilt Law Review*, 3 (1950): 395–406.

14 See generally, Edward A. Purcell, *The Crisis of American Democratic Theory* (Lexington, Ky.: University of Kentucky Press, 1973), pp. 74–94.

15 See generally, Robert S. Summers, *Instrumentalism and American Legal Theory* (Ithaca, N.Y.: Cornell University Press, 1982).

16 See Benjamin N. Cardozo, *The Nature of the Judicial Process* (New Haven: Yale University Press, 1921), p. 141 (Judge, when free, is to draw his inspiration from consecrated principles); Hart & Sacks, *The Legal Process*, p. 165 (discretionary decisions must be consistent with other established applications of a rule and serve the principles and policies it expresses); Lon L. Fuller, "Positivism and Fidelity to Law – A Reply to Professor Hart," *Harvard Law Review*, 71 (1958): 630–72, at 661–9 (judges should interpret laws in light of the laws' purposes); Herbert Wechsler, "Toward Neutral Principles of Constitutional Law," *Harvard Law Review*, 73 (1959): 1–35 (constitutional decision

and economics theorists have advanced economic efficiency or wealth maximization partly as particular social policies that could solve the jurisprudential problem,[17] and Ronald Dworkin has urged that there is one soundest theory of law that produces one right answer in almost all controversies as a matter of principle.[18] Others have called attention to underlying professional conventions that constrain judges.[19] As critical legal studies scholars have taken great pains to show, however, all such resources might have their own indeterminacies.[20] Policies, purposes, economic analysis, prin-

should be based on general and neutral principles).

17 Richard A. Posner, *Economic Analysis of Law*, 3d ed. (Boston: Little, Brown & Co., 1986).

18 Dworkin, *Taking Rights Seriously*, pp. 81–130; Ronald Dworkin, *A Matter of Principle* (Cambridge: Harvard University Press, 1985), pp. 119–80; Ronald Dworkin, *Law's Empire* (Cambridge: Harvard University Press, Belknap Press, 1986), pp. 266–71. See also Rolf E. Sartorius, *Individual Conduct and Social Norms* (Encino, Calif.: Dickinson Pub. Co., 1975), pp. 181–210; Michael S. Moore, "A Natural Law Theory of Interpretation," *Southern California Law Review*, 58 (1985): 277–398.

19 See Steven J. Burton, *An Introduction to Law and Legal Reasoning* (Boston: Little, Brown & Co., 1985), pp. 95–8, 136–43, 204–8; Melvin A. Eisenberg, *The Nature of the Common Law* (Cambridge: Harvard University Press, 1988); Owen M. Fiss, "Objectivity and Interpretation," *Stanford Law Review*, 34 (1982): 739–63; Owen M. Fiss, "Conventionalism," *Southern California Law Review*, 58 (1985): 177–97.

20 The starting point of the most relevant critical literature is Duncan Kennedy, "Legal Formality," *Journal of Legal Studies*, 2 (1973): 351–98. See generally Mark G. Kelman, *A Guide to Critical Legal Studies* (Cambridge: Harvard University Press, 1987); Roberto M. Unger, *Knowledge and Politics* (New York: Free Press, 1975); Unger, *The Critical Legal Studies Movement*; James Boyle, "The Politics of Reason: Critical Legal Theory and Local Social Thought," *University of Pennsylvania Law Review*, 133 (1985): 685–780; Peter Gabel & Duncan Kennedy, "Roll Over Beethoven," *Stanford Law Review*, 36 (1984): 1–55; Allan C. Hutchinson, "Democracy and Determinacy: An Essay on Legal Interpretation," *University of Miami Law Review*, 43 (1989): 541–76; Duncan Kennedy, "Form and Substance in Private Law Adjudication," *Harvard Law Review*, 89 (1976): 1685–778; Mark G. Kelman, "Trashing," *Stanford Law Review*, 36 (1984): 293–348; Mark G. Kelman, "Interpretive Construction in the Substantive Criminal Law," *Stanford Law Review*, 33 (1981): 591–673; Gary Peller, "The Metaphysics of American Law," *California Law Review*, 73 (1985): 1151–290; Joseph W. Singer, "The Player and the Cards: Nihilism and Legal Theory," *Yale Law Journal*,

ciples, and professional conventions cannot be counted on to produce determinate results.[21] Consequently, it may seem, judges must resolve indeterminacies on the basis of controversial political values – not the law.

Stubborn indeterminacy is real, not apparent. Indeterminacy is most problematic when there is no one right answer to be reached using all of the resources the law provides; it is also troubling when members of the legal community, each using all lawyerly skill in good faith, can disagree about an outcome upon full adjudication of a case. These points deserve emphasis because too many sweeping indeterminacy claims are facile. To negate some possible misunderstandings, it is not only that members of the legal community do not readily agree on the right answer in a case, or that some lawyers might be mistaken when they think they know, or that competing arguments can be made without professional embarrassment. Since bad arguments establish nothing, the law is not significantly indeterminate because incompatible results can be advocated. Even arguments that are good enough for a lawyer to be justified in filing a lawsuit, but not good enough for a judge to justify a judgment, show nothing about the law's indeterminacy. Conflicting judicial decisions, too, do not establish indeterminacy if one of them is mistaken and generally would be recognized as such

94 (1984): 1–70.
21 Some critical scholars seem to say that the law does not produce determinate results in any case whatever. For example, Mark V. Tushnet, *Red, White, and Blue: A Critical Analysis of Constitutional Law* (Cambridge: Harvard University Press, 1988), pp. 191–2 (legal realists showed that legal materials and reasoning "are so flexible that they allow us to assemble diverse precedents into whatever pattern we choose"); Hutchinson, "Democracy and Determinacy," at 543 (the law is irredeemably indeterminate and thoroughly political); Singer, "The Player and the Cards," at 10–11 (legal doctrine "infinitely manipulable"), 20 (legal doctrine "sufficiently ambiguous or internally contradictory to justify any result we can imagine"); sources cited in Ken Kress, "Legal Indeterminacy," *California Law Review*, 77 (1989): 283–337, at 302 n. 67. If that were so, legal indeterminacy would be both stubborn and pervasive. See also Anthony D'Amato, "Can Any Legal Theory Constrain Any Judicial Decision?," *University of Miami Law Review*, 43 (1989): 513–39.

within the legal community. Human fallibility is not the point. Moreover, legal indeterminacy is compatible with highly predictable judicial behavior.[22] The law might seem settled, for a time, because no one with influence asks the hard questions. Such contingent stabilities can be questioned at any time, and the legal community then may lack the resources needed to resolve a dispute. Indeterminacy occurs in a case most notably when the law has incompatible implications for concrete judicial action and, on thorough analysis by impartial and capable lawyers, no standard or set of standards that generates a determinate result within any practicable frame of reference.

Stubborn legal indeterminacy need not be pervasive.[23] On some matters, legal materials that conflict in the abstract will converge to require one answer to a specific legal question, albeit for different reasons. This would be the case if someone were to sue today for a declaratory judgment that slavery is lawful in the United States, or were to defend against a speeding ticket on the ground that existing traffic laws against speeding are unconstitutional. On other matters, the law may be indeterminate at the level of formal rules, but all the relevant rules of interpretation supported by all the vari-

22 Gordon, "Critical Legal Histories," at 125. See also Kelman, *A Guide to Critical Legal Studies*, pp. 13, 258 (internal contradictions do not render daily outcomes wholly unpredictable); David Kairys, "Legal Reasoning," in *The Politics of Law*, ed. David Kairys (New York: Pantheon Books, 1982): 11–17, at 15 (results in cases are not random or wholly unpredictable); Singer, "The Player and the Cards," at 19–25 (outcomes in our legal system are often predictable despite legal indeterminacy).

23 See Burton, *Law and Legal Reasoning*, pp. 94–8, 125–32 (convergence in concrete judgments can produce easy cases despite controversy over abstract standards); Kress, "Legal Indeterminacy," at 295–337 (legal indeterminacy is at most moderate). See also Altman, *Critical Legal Studies*, pp. 90–8; R. Kent Greenawalt, "How Law Can Be Determinate," *UCLA Law Review*, 38 (1990): 1–86; Kenney Hegland, "Goodbye to Deconstruction," *Southern California Law Review*, 58 (1985): 1203–21; Alvin B. Rubin, "Does Law Matter? A Judge's Response to Critical Legal Studies," *Journal of Legal Education*, 37 (1987): 307–14; Frederick Schauer, "Easy Cases," *Southern California Law Review*, 58 (1985): 399–440.

ous political theories may converge to require one result in a case. Again, the rules of interpretation might be indeterminate, but all relevant policies and principles supported by all relevant political moralities may converge on one resolution. Convergence is possible at any level of analysis and might produce determinate results in a case. Determinate cases are not the same as easy cases; it may take a great deal of work before the resolution is recognized.[24] The number and significance of determinate legal questions should not be underestimated just because many of them concern matters that are generally taken for granted and not likely to result in litigation.

Stubborn indeterminacy, however, is common enough to be important. Great legal debate in and out of the academy focuses on the practical implications of indeterminacy and resulting judicial discretion. Consider the implications of taking seriously conclusions that judges are not upholding the law when it is indeterminate and they have discretion. Well-accepted landmark decisions, such as *Brown v. Board of Education*[25] and *Reynolds v. Sims*,[26] along with controversial cases such as *Roe v. Wade*,[27] become open to revision for jurisprudential reasons. Routine decisions on matters as diverse as child custody and material breach of contract similarly become suspect. Generalizing such implications might suggest that the law is indeterminate in so many cases that only radical restrictions of judicial power can avoid discretionary judicial decisions. Alternatively, perhaps discretion is so inevitable, and mandatory third-party dispute settlement so important, that traditional Rule of Law values should be given up and the judicial power expanded considerably.

---

24 See Duncan Kennedy, "Freedom and Constraint in Adjudication: A Critical Phenomenology," *Journal of Legal Education*, 36 (1987): 518–62.
25 347 U.S. 483 (1954) (separate but equal public schools violate constitutional requirement of equal protection of the law).
26 337 U.S. 533 (1964) (one person, one vote).
27 410 U.S. 438 (1973) (Constitution protects woman's right to choose abortion during earlier stages of pregnancy).

1.3. INDETERMINACY AND JUDGING

The main problem with stubborn indeterminacy in the law is that, it seems, disagreements about the law turn out on analysis to be jurisprudential and political. The indeterminacy recurs as one tries in turn to resolve competing analogies with reference to legal rules, competing rules or rule interpretations with reference to more abstract principles and policies, and competing principles and policies with reference to yet more abstract moral and political theories. Seemingly mundane disagreements in legal reasoning thus might turn out to be irresolvable without answering fundamental questions of political morality. Were that so, it would be hard to understand how a legal argument could resolve a legal question: A judge would rely on political positions that have been controversial for centuries and show no prospect for satisfactory resolution soon. It takes only a bit of cynicism then to regard all adjudication as dependent on the judge's politics in the sense of his personal ideology and partisan loyalties. The law in operation then lacks the objectivity and neutrality required by determinate-formalism and, unless an alternative understanding is developed, by the Rule of Law.

Consider, for example, a routine problem in contract law. A consumer signed a contract calling for payment of $525 in monthly installments over three years in return for a set of china. In fine print, the contract indicated that delivery would be upon full payment at the end of the three years. Interest was calculated at a rate of 22 percent from the date of contracting. The buyer paid for fifteen months before seeing a lawyer. On one hand, it can be argued that the contract is unconscionable and unenforceable[28] because the seller treated the buyer as its creditor for three years and charged the creditor-buyer interest even though the buyer had no use of the seller's money for a time, as in the usual consumer credit transaction. On the other hand, it can be argued that people have a duty to read a contract before signing and to consult

28 U.C.C. § 2–302.

13

counsel if they do not understand it, and they are bound by the terms in a contract they sign.[29] There seems to be no determinate legal standard for deciding between these two arguments without recourse to jurisprudential and political considerations. When we go to that level, the two arguments implicate, respectively, a jurisprudence calling on judges to elevate considerations of justice above the agreed terms of a contract and one requiring judges only to implement the agreement of the contract parties. They implicate also political visions of government as the protector of those who do not protect themselves and as a passive referee for a competitive market. We seem unwilling fully to follow either jurisprudential or political philosophy to the exclusion of the other, and unable to compose a legal standard that accommodates each within a determinate domain. The ultimate ground for going one way or the other in an unconscionability case can seem too personal to the judge for a distinction between law and politics to stand.[30]

The slide from law through indeterminacy to politics is disturbing for practical reasons best focused on judging (though it affects any instance of law application). Only obtuse conceptions of the judicial role welcome judges as philosopher-kings who decide fundamentally contested political questions as a matter of discretion, imposing their views on the parties to a case.[31] A key tenet of constitutional democ-

29 See Wilson v. World Omni Leasing, Inc., 540 So. 2d 713 (Ala. 1989) (truck leasing agreement not unconscionable despite surprising obligations to lessee in fine print because the lessee had a fair opportunity to protect herself).
30 See generally Kennedy, "Form and Substance"; Kelman, *A Guide to Critical Legal Studies*, pp. 15–63.
31 This is not a matter of dispute among judges of otherwise widely varying dispositions. See speech by William J. Brennan, Georgetown University (Oct. 12, 1985) ("Justices are not platonic guardians appointed to wield authority according to their personal moral predilections"); Robert H. Bork, "The Constitution, Original Intent, and Economic Rights," *San Diego Law Review*, 23 (1986): 823–72, at 825 ("Not only is moral philosophy typically inadequate to the task but, more fundamentally, there is no legitimating reason that I have seen why the rest of us should be governed by the *judge's* moral visions").

racy requires official power of any kind to be used only when the specific use is justified. Related Rule of Law values require judges, in particular, to use their power only when applying the law (to state one of several requirements). But it is hard to understand how a judge is applying the law when it is indeterminate and the outcome is discretionary. Discretionary judicial decisions can seem indistinguishable in principle from more obvious kinds of domination.

Intellectual controversy at present tends to follow political lines. Some conservative scholars disapprove of liberal decisions when their legal basis is indeterminate, but believe that the problem is not so deep or pervasive that Rule of Law values as such are threatened.[32] Prominent liberal scholars claim that judges do not have any significant discretion because the law in principle provides a single right answer in almost all cases, though it may require superhuman skill to find it.[33] Centrists acknowledge widespread discretion, but seem unbothered by its implications for the legitimacy of judicial practice in a constitutional democracy like the United States.[34] Some radical leftist scholars claim that legal indeterminacy is so deep and pervasive that the legal tradition should be abandoned in favor of nonhierarchical and even arational alternatives.[35] The conversation seems deadlocked. A basic shift of focus is needed to break out of tired and no longer illuminating patterns of thought that, in the aggregate, politicize the discussion unfortunately.

---

32 For example, Robert H. Bork, *The Tempting of America* (New York: Free Press, 1990); Robert H. Bork, "Neutral Principles and Some First Amendment Problems," *Indiana Law Journal*, 47 (1971): 1–35; Edwin Meese, "The Supreme Court of the United States: Bulwark of a Limited Constitution," *Southern Texas Law Review*, 27 (1986): 455–66; Antonin Scalia, "The Rule of Law as a Law of Rules," *University of Chicago Law Review*, 56 (1989): 1175–88.

33 See sources cited, note 18 above.

34 For example, Cardozo, *The Nature of the Legal Process*, pp. 113–15; Hart, *The Concept of Law*, pp. 138–44; Hart, "Introduction," in *Essays in Jurisprudence and Philosophy*, ed. H. L. A. Hart (Oxford: Clarendon Press, 1983): 1–18, at 6–8; Greenawalt, "Discretion and Judicial Decision."

35 See sources cited, note 20 above.

A central and widely shared presupposition shapes the entire matter. It is that judges deciding controversies are constrained by the law only when it determines one correct result in a lawsuit.[36] This presupposition will be called the "determinacy condition" because it is widely thought to be a necessary condition for judges to fulfill their duty to uphold the law and, in turn, for adjudication to be legitimate in a constitutional democracy. The determinacy condition permits just two alternatives: One can, following Langdell, endorse determinate-formalism or, after the failure of the Holmesian theoretical project to generate an attractive alternative, endorse legal skepticism. In either case, the determinacy condition occupies the preeminently privileged position of serving as a primary criterion for evaluating the law and judging. When members of a legal community generally accept the determinacy condition, it is almost guaranteed that any plausible legal argument will prove on thorough analysis to be inadequate. One can always ask "Why?" and think of a counterargument of some kind, however wild. When the idea of law is so weakened, the political diversity of the legal community is ample to generate recalcitrant disagreement in almost any case. An a priori demand for determinate-formalism or the equivalent thus can generate nihilistic legal theories, provoking moderate responses seeking a third alternative to determinate-formalism and legal skepticism.

36 Accordingly, for example, Ronald Dworkin argues centrally that judges are under a duty to reach the single right result determined by Dworkinian principles in both easy and hard cases. Dworkin, *A Matter of Principle*, pp. 119–46. H. L. A. Hart insists that judges have discretion and must decide on nonlegal grounds when "the law is not clearly settled and dictates no results either way." H. L. A. Hart, *Essays on Bentham* (Oxford: Clarendon Press, 1982), p. 161. CLS scholars claim that the law generally does not dictate results, rendering claims that judges are upholding the law mystifying and deceptive. Sources cited, note 20 above. Richard Posner advances a strong form of legal skepticism because many legal questions are indeterminate by the methods of judicial reasoning. Richard A. Posner, *The Problems of Jurisprudence*; Richard A. Posner, "The Jurisprudence of Skepticism," *Michigan Law Review*, 86 (1988): 827–91; §§ 4.2 and following.

The good faith thesis, to be presented in Chapters 2 and 3, offers such a moderate alternative. It rejects determinate-formalism and the like either as a theory of law and judging or, more important, as a legitimate criterion for evaluating such a theory. Specifically, the good faith thesis proposes to supplant the determinacy condition with a requirement of good faith, understood as a part of the judicial duty to uphold the law that rules out abuses of discretion in a particular way. A companion thesis claims that legal indeterminacy and judicial discretion are compatible with legitimate adjudication in a constitutional democracy.[37] Contrary to the determinacy condition, the law can constrain judges and other legal actors without determining a single result. Relative determinacy at most is a desirable feature of some kinds of laws, notably those governing transactions in which the predictability of the law is especially important and reasonably achievable, when the purpose of the law is only to coordinate an activity fairly, or when the law seeks to encourage reliance and someone has relied in a relevant way. Determinacy is not, however, a jurisprudential criterion applicable to law universally, or to all the law in the United States, or to the results of all adjudication under law.

1.4. INDETERMINACY AND CONTEMPORARY JURISPRUDENCE

The slide through indeterminate law to politics also has implications for academic legal theory, which also can devolve into political contests between rival caucuses. American legal scholars of sharply differing viewpoints are currently developing new jurisprudences – economic analysis, neopragmatism, rhetorical or literary jurisprudence, critical legal

---

37 Good faith surely is not sufficient to establish legitimacy. That requires a complex argument in political philosophy beyond the scope of this book. For my earlier thoughts on the general problem, see Burton, *Law and Legal Reasoning*, pp. 165–236; Steven J. Burton, "Law, Obligation, and a Good Faith Claim of Justice," *California Law Review*, 73 (1985): 1956–83.

theory, feminist jurisprudence, and critical race theory. Advocates of these jurisprudences do not doubt that there is in the United States a conventional law consisting mainly of the Constitution, federal and state statutes, administrative rules authorized by statutes, and the common law. Rather, they charge that the indeterminacy of conventional law is pervasive and stubborn, robbing the law of its point. Consequently, some take an interest – perhaps an obsessive interest – in the way the law appears differently to different people. To many conservatives, for example, the conventional law is a formal system of reasonable rules sanctified by tradition. Other conservatives highlight economic principles that, they claim, underlie the conventional law and have more determinate content. To many liberals, the law seems best interpreted as a matter of moral principle. Leftist academic critics think of it as an ideological cloak of legitimacy over the domination of powerless subgroups by a ruling elite. Put otherwise, some now insist that the conventional law looks like an instrument of reason and good sense, with occasional errors, only to privileged white males. It appears, rather, as a reliable instrument of male hegemony to politically committed feminists and simply as "The Man" to many who live in impoverished inner cities.

1.4.1. The priority of power politics. Underlying much of the emphasis on diverse appearances of the conventional law is a jurisprudential claim that, if true, renders academic legal theory just another arena for result-oriented political combat. It is that stubborn and pervasive indeterminacy implies that there is nothing significant about the law except its various appearances. To clarify, the conventional law can be conceived as a collection of ways of "going on," as Ludwig Wittgenstein put it.[38] It might be suggested, for example,

38 Ludwig Wittgenstein, *Philosophical Investigations*, trans. G. E. M. Anscombe (Oxford: B. Blackwell, 1958), § 151. I do not accept the skeptical reading of Wittgenstein that underlies this use of his thought.

18

that the constitutionalism of original intent is one way of continuing the United States' constitutional tradition. Continued reliance on it coexists with reliance on evolving community standards and other strands of the constitutional tradition.[39] Stubborn indeterminacy might be thought to imply that no such strand in a tradition is in any sound sense *better* than any other. None, moreover, can be better than other, "nonlegal" ways of going on, like economic analysis or cultural revolution. Consequently, it might be concluded, the law has no features that legitimately advantage one or a few ways of going on.

The new jurisprudences, insofar as they partake of this view, exclude any role for *justification* (as distinct from self-expression, explanation, description, prediction, or analysis) in the legal conversation. A justification claims to show that one or another way of going on should be advantaged over others. The possibility of this privileging is precisely what the new jurisprudences sometimes seem to deny.[40]

The loss of a central role for justification would be tragic. Conventional understandings within the American tradition emphasize that a principal point of law is to control abuses of power. Judges adjudicate in important part to help assure that official coercive power is used only when justified in law, thereby limiting or avoiding domination by those who happen to have official status.[41] Moreover, effective constraint of the judges stems from argument about the justifications for judicial action within the legal system; the law is not

39 See generally Philip Bobbitt, *Constitutional Fate: A Theory of the Constitution* (New York: Oxford University Press, 1982); Laurence H. Tribe, *American Constitutional Law*, 2d ed. (Mineola, N.Y.: Foundation Press, 1988); Tushnet, *Red, White, and Blue*.

40 The general point emerges most clearly in J. M. Balkin, "Deconstructive Practice and Legal Theory," *Yale Law Journal*, 96 (1987): 743–86. See also "Symposium: The Critique of Normativity," *University of Pennsylvania Law Review*, 139 (1991): 801–1075.

41 Domination should be understood, not as the use of power by one person over another, but rather as the *unjustified* use of power. The United States did not "dominate" Germany by winning World War II, nor does a judge dominate a guilty and properly convicted criminal by sending him to jail.

19

a physical or emotional constraint. Criticism of the law re-volves around the moral and political arguments justifying one legal alternative over another. Without a role for justifi-cation there would be no apparent way for issues to be joined for intellectual discussion, for one of several legal alternatives to be worthy of execution, or for existing laws to be effectively criticized on their merits. Moreover, there would be no role for any conception of judicial *duty*.

By excluding justification, the new jurisprudences seem to accord a priority to power politics over thought. Controver-sies over *what law is,* which are at the center of any jurispru-dential inquiry, do not seem to turn on the arguments, but rather on the political and rhetorical powers of those who advocate jurisprudential positions because of their perceived political repercussions for favored groups. The law conse-quently can become vulnerable to efforts at what might be called "law reform by fell swoop." A writer in this vein might oppose the idea that common law and statutory rules, of the kind that play the central role in conventional law books and judicial opinions, are meaningful enough to be the law at all. The way then is open to replace the conventional under-standing of the law with another understanding generated for political reasons and defended only rhetorically.[42] Some might wish, for example, to substitute a principle of eco-nomic efficiency or wealth maximization. Others might seek to substitute liberal principles of distributive justice. Yet oth-ers might wish to substitute an antisubordination principle, in effect requiring all law cases to be decided in favor of historically or currently subordinated groups. The ramifica-tions in the actual operation of the legal system could be revolutionary if one such view were to prevail, or if each individual were to act on idiosyncratic or parochial jurispru-dential views. Long regarded as an ivory tower academic's

42 See Steven L. Winter, "Indeterminacy and Incommensurability in Constitutional Law," *California Law Review,* 78 (1990): 1441–541, at 1446 ("[a]fter all, the whole idea is to decline to exert a direct influence on current practices . . . and, instead, to undermine or supplant them altogether").

plaything, interest in jurisprudence has burgeoned partly because it might now seem to have profound real-world implications for easy and sweeping law reform.

The last people to throw out concepts of justification, however, should be those who encourage intellectual criticism of the law to enhance change, whatever the particular view of justice they hold. In their more skeptical moods, several of the new jurisprudences are self-marginalizing. Their critical claims – centrally that no way of going on is really better than any other – are two-edged swords that can readily be turned against their own constructive theories and rhetorical efforts to gain supporters for their political programs: The worst rhetoric is to call it all rhetoric.[43] Moreover, a part of the exclusion of justifications involves a denial that those who do not start with the requisite political convictions can have any good reason to support any program not in their narrow self-interest. Those who do start with the favored politics, moreover, have no good reason to act on their views. When pressed, however, advocates of the new jurisprudences often balk at denying that a judge is under legal and moral duties even while the content of judicial duty might be controversial. Indeed, duties make it intelligible for critics to claim that a decision is wrong, unjust, or mistaken.[44] Once duties are admitted, however, concepts of justification have been admitted and the discussion has entered intellectual territory. Intellectual considerations then must take priority over the play of political interests and ideologies that exalt the cause over its value.

The law surely appears differently to people who are situ-

---

43 "After all, is it not *obviously* contradictory to *hold* a point of view while at the same time holding that *no* point of view is more justified or right than any other?" Hilary Putnam, *Reason, Truth, and History* (Cambridge: Cambridge University Press, 1981), p. 119.

44 A judge often has the de facto power to rule in favor of either party in a case. The chances that she will be reversed for a mistake ordinarily are slim, and being thrown out of office for making a mistaken decision is hardly in the cards. But the de facto power to decide for either party is compatible with the judge's duty to favor the party whose claim is better justified.

ated very differently. The important questions concern what sense, if any, we might make of that fact: What *is* the disagreement? Is it intellectual disagreement such that someone might be mistaken? Or is it only power politics cloaked in intellectual garb? I will argue that the intellectual disagreements are not so deep that, from the standpoint of any judge acting in good faith, of whatever political loyalties, gender, race, or religion, the law is nothing but its appearances. I believe that there is a conversation to be had, founded on a particular conception of judicial duty, in which considerations of legal justification play a crucial role in decision making by judges, other legal actors, and their critics. The priority of power politics is rejected in this alternative conversation. Two starting assumptions amount to an ethical requirement of good faith on the part of participants. I call these assumptions "the priority of the intellectual" and "the primacy of reasons."

1.4.2. The priority of the intellectual. Consider the difference between conservatives who see the law as a system of constraining rules and radicals who see it as a cloak of legitimacy over domination. These two views surely are not incompatible. Political domination, as the radical sees it, can be implemented by a system of constraining rules, as the conservative sees it. The recent laws of apartheid present a convenient example. Neither view should be understood to assert naively that law is only a system of rules or only a cloak of legitimacy. Yet there surely is some kind of significant disagreement here. What kind of disagreement is it?

One possibility is that the disagreement is simply political in a particular sense: On this view, law is politics carried out by other means, as politics is war carried out by other means. Those who would defend the existing law because it benefits their favored groups would see it as a system of constraining rules; those who would change it radically to benefit other groups would see it as disguised domination. Each side would fight for control of the rhetoric of law that might shape how the law is conceived in the culture, as a spin doctor seeks to place political events in an advantageous light for his or her candidate.[45] This and similar political explanations provide unsatisfactory answers to the question about the kind of disagreement involved. They give observations *about the people* who disagree about the law, attributing crude motives to them. The political explanations cut off the possibility that *what the people say* might be worthy of endorsement by others. For some purposes, we might want to know about the people who say jurisprudential things. They might be locked in a struggle for power, treating jurisprudence opportunistically as an instrument for advancing their political agendas. We might respond differently to their texts in light of this fact because an intellectual response would be beside the point. On occasion, moreover, we ourselves might have political commitments that tempt us to endorse characterizations that might advance those commitments instrumentally. We might make mistakes when we succumb. Despite the current popularity of political interpretations of just about anything, however, giving a priority to politics over the intellectual is not the only way to understand jurisprudential disagreement.

Crass political and rhetorical explanations do not say anything *about the law* and, therefore, about what it is that competing jurisprudences disagree about. Talk about "systems of constraining rules" and "cloaks of legitimacy over domination" should say something about the features of the law so that we might learn something about it. That is, after all, why we study jurisprudence (or, rather, why we should study jurisprudence). We then might form a view of the law or, better, a web of views that can be deployed as appropriate in various contexts. Accordingly, one might say that law is a system of constraining rules to call attention to some features of the law without thereby approving of those rules as right or good or denying that the law also has other features. The features made salient by that description might

---

45 For a lucid account, see David Luban, "Difference Made Legal: The Court and Dr. King," *Michigan Law Review*, 87 (1989): 2152–224, at 2153–6.

merit attention in some conversations, such as those about
the potential for judges to act like unguided missiles. Similarly, one might say that the law is a cloak of legitimacy over
domination to dramatize the injustice of some rules. That
feature of law might merit attention in discussions about law
reform or civil disobedience. Again, jurisprudential claims
rarely need be understood to say that the law is only this or
only that in a way that summarily diverts or cuts off discussion.[46] We need not aspire to dogmatism in order to say
something from which we can learn about the law even
though, at any time, more remains to be said and learned.

The priority of the intellectual involves a preference for
maintaining the focus of attention on ideas – *what is said* in
jurisprudential discussion – including political ideas. What
is said can be contrasted with three things: the motivation for
saying it, the rhetoric in which it is said, and the consequences of the saying. To be sure, these aspects coexist and
blend with each other in practice. We learn about the prac-

46 Much misunderstanding is spread, I fear, by the tendency of some
    scholars to read statements by others as absolutes when they are
    meant to be, and generally would be understood as, quantified (in
    all cases, . . . ; in some case, . . .) and qualified (all else being
    equal, . . . ; one feature is . . .) statements by fallible speakers. The
    following complaint by Allan Hutchinson is typical of this tendency in
    contemporary critical thought:

    > As a white man, father, husband, worker, property owner,
    > etc., my life is saturated with and organized around different
    > legal ideas. To dismiss them as fictions . . . is wrong. Al-
    > though law works to impoverish the richness of my life by
    > reducing it *merely* to legal relations, it does play a significant
    > role in formulating my own self-image and derivative patterns
    > of consistent behavior.

    Hutchinson, "Democracy and Determinacy," at 553 (emphasis add-
    ed). I do not think that, when the law classifies a person as a father, it
    thereby claims that he is only a father, or only the collection of legal
    classifications in which he is placed, or that fatherhood is only a
    bundle of legal rights and duties. The law does not seek to displace
    frameworks of understanding drawn from one's parents, religious
    tradition, literary musings, moral reflections, or pop-cultural loyalties,
    all of which provide alternative and mostly compatible ways of under-
    standing oneself and others.

tice, however, by isolating one or another aspect for study in turn. We cannot think or speak usefully about everything at once, nor can we reduce all of these things to any one of them.

To elaborate on the first contrast, one might be motivated, consciously or subconsciously, to claim that the law is pervasively indeterminate in order to debunk the official legal structure and pave the way for radical change. Or one might be motivated to claim that the law is a system of constraining rules in order to preserve a status quo in which one enjoys high status. Which motivation moves one to act might be a function in significant part of one's social class, race, gender, and other personal characteristics. In no case, however, does the cause or motivation support what is said – that the law is pervasively indeterminate or a system of meaningful guiding rules. That the speaker is a privileged white male might put him and us on guard to the possibility of bias tending toward apologetics. But the truth of the claim about law depends entirely on considerations other than the characteristics or motivations of the persons who make the assertions. One might even say something that is true while believing it for the wrong motivating reasons. There is no short cut through the obvious characteristics of the speaker, or pop psychology, to the truth of the matter.

To illustrate the second contrast, consider a use of sexist language: "Any person should be sober when he drives a car." The use of the male pronoun has a negative effect on some women, who feel distracted, excluded, neglected, or offended by such a statement. The effect stems from the rhetoric: *how we speak*, not *what is said*. It should be clear, because of an inherited linguistic convention and the absurdity of alternative interpretations, that the speaker is saying that anyone should be sober when she or he drives a car. There are times when it is appropriate to focus on the rhetoric, which may reflect background cultural attitudes deserving of change. But something important is left out if we focus only on how we speak while neglecting what is said. For example, a motorist in most circumstances would better attend to the relationship between sobriety and driving than to the gender of the pronouns in the warning.

The third contrast reflects the simple fact that a true statement can have unfortunate consequences for oneself or others with whom one identifies. Nominee Douglas Ginsburg was kept off the Supreme Court because it was reported that he smoked marijuana with students while a professor of law at Harvard. Denying the truth of those reports might have been tempting to him because they had such unfortunate consequences. Lawyers sometimes do something like that when acting as advocates. In legal theory, naive instrumentalist jurisprudences encourage a similar tendency. But legal theorists should resist the temptation, despite their legal training. In ordinary nonliterary and nonadversarial contexts, we should not say something "is so" unless we at least have good and adequate grounds for believing it is so. Focusing on what is said invites consideration of the conditions under which what is said would be true or warranted for assertion. The consequences of a statement often are distinct from these grounds.

The priority of the intellectual does not deny the importance of political ideas. Some political considerations themselves are a kind of intellectual consideration. Political theory from Plato to John Rawls has been highly intellectual. Such ideas surely should not be excluded from discussions of legislative policy, the justice of the law, its impact on power relationships in society, its capacity to generate obligations to obey, and other matters. Within adjudication under law, the law remains political in the sense that it works out the practical implications of a cluster of prevailing political ideas. Politics in the sense of personal advantage or partisan loyalties, however, are objectionable when privileged in legal theory or adjudication. A litigating lawyer is committed in advance to interpreting the materials of legal research in a way that protects the client's interests, consistent with the ethics of advocacy. A legal scholar (or judge), however, should not similarly be committed in advance to scouring the scholarly materials to glean only the bits that serve a prior political commitment.[47] The temptation is ever present, and ulterior motives at any time can infect a project unnoticed. The priority of the intellectual does not deny these facts about scholarly practices. Rather, it affords the ground for criticizing oneself or others when we take our eyes off the ball or find them wandering unintentionally.

1.4.3. The primacy of reasons. A favorite foil for the new juris-prudences, as for Holmes and the legal realists, is determi-nate-formalism, often said (erroneously[48]) to be crucial to the legal tradition.[49] On that view, only one rule can apply in a case and that rule must be a per se rule. That is, a judge need only find one or a very few easily identifiable and univocal facts in the situation in order for the rule to be applicable. The judge's duty is to find the facts as they are and apply the rules logically.[50] It is easy to make mincemeat of this deter-minate-formalist model of law, and there is no dearth of efforts to make the mince ever so much more microscopic. Indeed, this model of law is so monumental an anathema to some of the new jurisprudences that no part of it is endura-ble. So recent works contain sweeping rejections of abstrac-tions like rules and categories and even dispense with ele-mentary principles of logic like the ban on contradiction.[51]

47 For a sharply different view, see Kennedy, "Freedom and Constraint in Adjudication," discussed in §§ 5.4 and following.
48 See Burton, *Law and Legal Reasoning*, pp. 187–214; Dworkin, *Law's Empire*, pp. 274–5; William Ewald, "Unger's Philosophy: A Critical Study," *Yale Law Journal*, 97 (1988): 665–756; Kress, "Legal Indeter-minacy"; John Stick, "Can Nihilism Be Pragmatic?," *Harvard Law Re-view*, 100 (1986): 332–401; § 5.3.
49 For example, Kelman, *A Guide to Critical Legal Studies*; Hutchinson, "Democracy and Determinacy," at 542–3; Kennedy, "Legal For-mality," at 366–77.
50 Kennedy, "Legal Formality," at 355. Lon Fuller gave the seal at com-mon law as an example that approaches the formal ideal, since a sealed instrument was enforceable upon finding the seal without fur-ther inquiry. See Lon L. Fuller, "Consideration and Form," *Columbia Law Review*, 41 (1941): 799–824, at 802.
51 See Stanley E. Fish, *Doing What Comes Naturally* (Durham, N.C.: Duke

There are babies that should not be thrown out with the determinate-formalist bathwater. The problem with determinate-formalism is not its use of abstract rules or logic; rather, it is the pretence that legal rules, logically applied, dictate the results in all cases governed by the law. Abstract rules, like other legal standards, can be understood in a model of *reasons* rather than necessary results. As we will see further in Chapter 2, a reason in the relevant sense is the combination of a rule or other abstract prescription – paradigmatically, that some act should be done when some generic fact is instantiated – and a concrete fact that invokes it. It has a logical structure. For example, one complete reason might be stated as follows: All motorists should stop on encountering a red traffic light; Michael Motorist encounters a red traffic light; so, Michael Motorist should stop.[52] The plain fact that Michael encounters a red light itself is inert. It has *force* – is a reason for action – when combined with a prescriptive standard of conduct. Such standards are of many kinds, including legal rules, moral principles, promises, relational obligations, and personal desires. (Not all of them pick out the relevant facts as directly as in the simple example.) Consequently, we can speak of reasons of many kinds, including respectively legal reasons, moral reasons, promissory reasons, relational reasons, and personal reasons. It is a mistake to contrast an "immersion in particulars" or "situational judging" with abstract reasoning. A reason for action marries plain fact with abstract standard.[53]

University Press, 1989); Anthony D'Amato, "Aspects of Deconstruction: Refuting Indeterminacy with One Bold Thought," *Northwestern University Law Review*, 85 (1990): 113–18; Ann C. Scales, "The Emergence of Feminist Jurisprudence," *Yale Law Journal*, 95 (1986): 1373–403; Steven L. Winter, *"Bull Durham* and the Uses of Theory," *Stanford Law Review*, 42 (1990): 639–93.

52 See Joseph Raz, *The Authority of Law* (Oxford: Clarendon Press, 1979), pp. 15–35; Raz, *Practical Reason and Norms*, pp. 16–20; Joseph Raz, "Introduction," in *Practical Reasoning*, ed. Joseph Raz (Oxford: Oxford University Press, 1978): 1–17, at 5.

53 Compare Martha Minow, "Foreword: Justice Engendered," *Harvard Law Review*, 101 (1987): 10–95 (advocating immersion in particulars as against abstraction) with Martha Minow & Elizabeth V. Spelman, "In

In a determinate-formalist jurisprudence, the rules of law might be supposed to bind a judge by providing only one relevant reason for judicial action in any possible case, this reason having absolute force. Duncan Kennedy's earliest critique of formalism suggested something like this view: "[I]t is part of the definition of a rule that it is 'absolute' within its scope: if the judge finds such and such to be the case, he either applies (or follows) the rule by doing thus and so, or the rule is no longer in force."[54] A moment's reflection will indicate, however, that we can dispense with the notion of absolute force, and with necessarily determinate results, without tossing out rules, reasons, and reasoning in favor of situational judging. In our everyday lives, we often reason by identifying and considering many reasons that bear on a decision. Some of them stem from rules, including legal rules. Each reason, we understand, may have some but not necessarily absolute force; that is, it is a reason for action to be weighed together with other competing reasons. Michael Motorist has a reason to stop at a red light, but one can imagine circumstances in which Michael ought not to stop because that reason is overridden by other relevant reasons (for example, an ill passenger in dire need of medical attention). A rule does not necessarily do more than contribute a reason to a judicial decision in a manner akin to such everyday experiences.[55] Accordingly, legal rules and other standards can be retained in a jurisprudence of judging that emphasizes that legal reasoning includes a gauging of the weight of the legal reasons invoked by the context of action.

The traditional response to such a claim is to express immediate skepticism that the idea of weighing reasons is in any way enlightening. A fair test of the success of the good

Context," *Southern California Law Review*, 63 (1990): 1597–652 (admitting the need for abstract aspects of reasoning). See § 8.3.2.

54 Kennedy, "Legal Formality," at 355 n. 10.

55 See §§ 6.2 and following. This is not to say that a rule is only a reason. Analytically, on the most abstract model underlying my approach, a rule or other legal standard is the major premise in a practical syllogism whereas the reason consists of the major and minor premises together.

faith thesis is whether it overcomes this doubt. The response of some advocates of the new jurisprudences, however, predictably will be to charge that a discourse of reasons perpetuates a white male tradition of "rationality" that excludes disempowered voices.[56] Consider the recent emphasis on listening intently to the different voices of women and members of racial minority groups.[57] Such persons were indeed excluded from empowered legal, political, and scholarly conversations for too long a time, depriving them of influence and depriving the conversations of their insights. Their life experiences often differ from a white male's in ways that lead them to say things most white males would not say and that white males might dismiss peremptorily due to subtle and not-so-subtle prejudices. Narratives from other standpoints can enlighten us about how the law appears to others in ways that can be surprising and informative. The advice to listen intently seems wise as far as it goes. But now comes the rub: What should one *do* after taking the advice and listening with some success to others who have unfamiliar backgrounds and perhaps different interests?

Three responses are notable. One is to rest content (or disturbed) with the enhanced understanding of life experiences arrived at from listening, as after reading a good novel. That seems beside the point of legal, moral, and political discussions, which in the end should have implications for what someone should do in fact.[58] The focus here on action can be said to be just another white male value, revealing my bias and self-obliviousness. Perhaps so. On the other hand, I am suspicious, and invite the reader to share my suspicion, of the glibness with which *anything* one says can be dismissed as a product of one's indelible characteristics or upbringing, reducing us all to equality in our powerlessness. Even when the causal connection is strong, it should be recalled that the "genetic fallacy" is the mistake of thinking

56 For further discussion, see § 8.3.2.
57 See, for example, Minow, "Justice Engendered."
58 Reasons for treating the law with an action orientation are summarized in § 4.3. See also Burton, "Law as Practical Reason," at 784–90.

that what causes 'someone to say something determines the soundness of what is said. The circumstances from which a view emerges can give us reasons to suspect bias and to investigate further, not taking the person's word for it. Those circumstances, even when very different from our own, do not establish that the proposition is false or groundless. The further question should focus on the conditions for the proposition to be true or warranted, and therefore worthy of endorsement by others. Keeping an eye on those conditions permits significant disagreement, which requires a contradiction between the opposing views – for example, that some condition is or is not satisfied or that the ensemble of satisfied conditions does or does not support the proposition. There is no implication for action in a conversation when each participant describes how the law appears to him or her and learns that the law appears differently to some others. "Changing the subject," as Richard Rorty puts it,[59] is fine as long as you no longer claim to have said something on the prior topic.

A second response is to defer to the historically disadvantaged voice, conferring on it some kind of authority that overrides one's own independent best judgment. It might be argued, for example, that influence over social beliefs should be distributed fairly among groups with different voices. Historically, such influence has been unequally distributed to favor white males. Therefore, deference to historically disadvantaged voices is required to set things aright.[60] It seems mistaken, however, thus to treat intellectual power by analogy to political power in an egalitarian democracy. In the absence of some reason to think that the disadvantaged voice

---

59 Richard Rorty, *Consequences of Pragmatism* (Minneapolis, Minn.: University of Minnesota Press, 1982), p. xiv.
60 I take this foil to be similar to the views expressed in different terms in Mari J. Matsuda, "Pragmatism Modified and the False Consciousness Problem," *Southern California Law Review*, 63 (1990): 1763–82, at 1764–8. For a response, see Scott Brewer, "Pragmatism, Oppression, and the Flight to Substance," *Southern California Law Review*, 63 (1990): 1753–62. See also Catharine MacKinnon, *Toward a Feminist Theory of the State* (Cambridge: Harvard University Press, 1989), pp. 215–37.

has a right to rule or some inside line on truth and justice, it seems frankly immoral to surrender one's own best judgment. Each person bears responsibility for his or her own actions. Deference to the legal, moral, or political views of others evokes a new kind of subservience justifiable only on bizarre, if not antiintellectual, interpretations of affirmative action.

A third response, after listening well, is to treat the view of the unfamiliar voice as a candidate for being a reason for action for oneself. On this approach, the advice to listen intently and be on guard against one's prejudices counsels people who have traditional intellectual habits to broaden the scope of their search for reasons. The tradition may have confined it unduly, so a broadened search is indicated. The fact that one person has an opinion, belief, or feeling, by itself is inert. It has no force for other persons because it is not itself a reason for them to act differently than they otherwise would. The opinions, beliefs, and feelings of other people, however, can be reasons when combined with a standard of conduct or personal desire. We might find, for example, that we care about sufferings of which we were ignorant and then formulate proposals for changing the law to relieve them. Caring about another person's suffering can be a reason for action; it is not excluded by the primacy of reasons. Listening intently can teach us that *our* reasons in fact are not altogether what we thought they were. We then would be enriched by the conversation, not only because we learned something significant that we did not already know. We then might act differently because our reasons for action are different.

The primacy of reasons has a moral and political motivation, though not one committed to specific substantive views. First, it assumes that there is nothing sacred about the current order of things; indeed, it dwells on the need for laws and judicial decisions to be justified in part to open the door to criticism and change when the existing order falls short. Second, it involves a vision of how people in a diverse community can carry on their disagreements with respect for each other. Ronald Dworkin is correct to place the fact of disagreement at the center of jurisprudential discussion.[61] The ideas of law as a "contested concept" and stubborn indeterminacy, however, can too easily be seen as a reflection of recalcitrant disagreement, as though no question whatever could be resolved agreeably without someone caving in from weakness or domination. We can disagree for a variety of benign reasons. We might disagree only on the facts due to their disorderly conduct, weak evidence, or our fallibility. We might disagree on the applicable standards for similar reasons. More significantly, we might disagree only on the weight of relevant reasons. We might disagree as well because reasons for action are not universal; promises and obligations of role imply that, in a given set of circumstances, some people have reasons that other people would not have.[62] We should hesitate before concluding that a disagreement is a product of political conflict so deep that it threatens the continuation of the conversation, inviting a centrifugal flight from the common ground. Focusing on legal reasons highlights far more in common than does the traditional focus on determinate results. Let us hope that, from that common ground, greater respect for differences can be generated even while we live in one political community.

The primacy of reasons accordingly shifts the emphasis away from affirming or denying the law as a determinate

61 Dworkin, *Law's Empire*, pp. 3–15.
62 The obvious examples are promisors or officeholders, who ought not to act as they should act had they not made a promise or undertaken the duties of an office. See §§ 7.2 and following. Each of us has a history that includes various moral commitments – to others and to ourselves – that change our reasons for action as individuals even when we are otherwise in the same circumstances of action, abstracted in a time slice. For example, a lawyer faced with the classic perjuring-client conundrum might, consistent with institutionalized ethical rules, place the client on the stand, allow the perjured testimony, but refuse to refer to that testimony in any way. Another lawyer in the same circumstances, who has devoted a large part of his life to enhancing professional ethics in the interests of professional integrity, serving on many bar committees and the like in the pursuit of these ends, might properly refuse to put the perjuring client on the stand.

system of rules or other standards that dictate results. The law is not in that way Langdellian, and the point no longer is remarkable. The primacy of reasons also shifts the emphasis away from Holmesian theoretical efforts to describe the regularities in aggregate judicial behavior, to give causal explanations of those regularities, and to predict what courts will do. The skepticism implicit in the new jurisprudences results from the failure of both projects to achieve determinacy. As I will argue at length in Part II, however, the determinacy condition itself has no place in a sound jurisprudence of judging.

The primacy of reasons turns attention to the law as a provider of reasons for action, not necessarily results. By contrast with both the determinate-formalist model of rules and the Holmesian projects, the primacy of reasons opens up discussion and argument to all voices that can supply reasons with some force, however modest, for another person. It does not dispense with rules, reasons, and reasoning because they seem necessary for a legal conversation that avoids a fall into solipsism and conflicts of arbitrary power. What we disagree about most importantly, when we accept the priority of the intellectual, is just what reasons the law does or should provide for a judge or other legal actor who upholds the law in good faith. That is, our most important disagreements are substantive, not involving a conflict in the basic framework of reasoning, because they focus on the content of the laws and the relevance of facts. The remainder of this book will focus on a framework of reasoning within which the most important and highly controversial questions can be addressed intelligently by people thinking and conversing in good faith.

Chapter 2

The good faith thesis

2.1. JUDICIAL DUTY

Practical understandings of adjudication may concern how judges can, do, or should decide cases in general. As advanced here, no descriptive claim is made that judges typically decide cases in a particular way. The emphasis is on judicial duty – how judges can and should adjudicate. It is axiomatic that judges in a legal system are under a legal duty to uphold the law. A legal system involves a division of labor or separation of powers among its institutions. Especially in a diverse or pluralistic society, the division of labor would break down rapidly if judges (or other officials) were to pick and choose the laws they will uphold on the basis of individual critical evaluations of them one by one. The very idea of a legal system requires enough consistency in practice for the laws to be unified in operation. So judges do not fulfill their legal duty if they act only on those parts of the law with which they agree. It should be clear, however, that this legal duty does not entail that judges never act properly in disobedience of the law of a legal system. The law of a legal system does not supplant morality even for the judges acting within the system. To understand the relationship between a judge's legal and moral duties requires careful analysis of, among other things, the grounds, content, and force of a judge's duties to uphold the law.

We first will focus conceptually on what a judge's legal duty requires in the abstract – the lawful-making charac-

35

teristics of a judicial decision. We then will turn to what a judge should do "all things considered," or as a matter of moral duty in particular circumstances. Distinguishing in this way between a judge's legal and moral duties is important, though morality surely has the last word. We will explore this distinction at length in Chapter 7, but it will help to forecast two main points right away. The law (understood conventionally[1]) might or might not do justice in a case. Even when the law fails, a judge's legal duty still has a crucial role. A judge may have a moral duty to follow the law. The moral values of a Rule of Law – predictability, coordination, separation of powers, fairness, equal treatment, and the like – may require the judge to follow the law despite the instant injustice. Consequently, a separate understanding of a judge's legal duty is needed in order to identify what the law requires in its own terms, separate from balancing the moral reasons for following the law against the moral reasons for doing something else.

The good faith thesis concerns a judge's legal duty to uphold the law. It will be explained and defended in the next six chapters before we turn to the moral questions in Chapter 7. The good faith thesis maintains, in brief, that the judicial duty to uphold the law requires judges to act on the reasons

1   There is no need to present and defend a complete theory of law in order to accept that the law in the United States consists mainly of the Constitution, federal and state statutes, administrative rules authorized by statutes, and the common law. In thus relying on conventional law, I neither endorse Dworkin's constructions of conventionalism nor exclude all principles implicit in the explicit legal text. See Steven J. Burton, *An Introduction to Law and Legal Reasoning* (Boston: Little, Brown & Co., 1985), p. 142 n. 120; Ronald Dworkin, *Law's Empire* (Cambridge: Harvard University Press, Belknap Press, 1986), pp. 114–50; John Stick, "Literary Imperialism: Assessing the Results of Dworkin's Interpretive Turn in *Law's Empire*," *UCLA Law Review*, 34 (1986): 371–429, at 410. For other understandings of conventions, see Owen M. Fiss, "Objectivity and Interpretation," *Stanford Law Review*, 34 (1982): 739–63 (conventions as disciplining rules); Gerald J. Postema, "Coordination and Convention at the Foundations of Law," *Journal of Legal Studies*, 11 (1982): 165–203 (conventions as solutions to coordination problems). See also notes 38, 55 below; Chap. 3, note 26; Chap. 8, note 4 and accompanying text.

provided by the law and not on reasons excluded by judicial duty or the law's standards. The general idea is that, upon taking office, judges give up the opportunity to act on some kinds of reasons in the performance of their legal duties – most obviously ad hominem reasons, but also reasons excluded by the law's authoritative standards and moral or policy reasons not warranted by the law as grounds for judicial decision. It will be argued that judges do not recover the opportunity to act legally on excluded or unwarranted reasons even when the law is indeterminate and they have discretion. Rather, they are legally constrained even then to weigh the legal reasons and only the legal reasons.[2] Accordingly, using discretion to recapture forgone opportunities would be bad faith and a breach of judicial duty.

2.2. JUDICIAL DISCRETION

Discretion concerns how judges decide cases when the law proves to be indeterminate in a stubborn way. Discretion then is troubling because two or more outcomes are lawful.

---

2 For elaboration on the problem of weight, see §§ 2.3 and following, 6.4, 7.1, and 7.2. I have no faith that each legal rule has sufficient unstated exceptions to avoid real conflict; compare Michael S. Moore, "Authority, Law, and Razian Reasons," *Southern California Law Review*, 62 (1989): 827–96, at 846–7 (supporting such an understanding of morality), or that there is one master priority rule (like the utilitarian principle) that resolves all conflicts. Compare Jeremy Waldron, "Rights in Conflict," *Ethics*, 99 (1989): 503–19, at 507–9 (criticizing such an understanding in political theory).

Additionally, I assume here that a legal power to overrule common law precedents involves a species of lawmaking that is permitted by the law but is outside the judicial duty to uphold the law, which concerns law application. The distinction between lawmaking and law application is discussed further in §§ 3.4.4, 5.3 and following. Indeed, judges do many things besides uphold the law. Courts also have administrative functions like maintaining records, legislative functions like making rules of court, and policy functions like reviewing petitions for writs of certiorari. Judges also have undertaken managerial functions in civil rights and mass litigation that hardly seem like adjudication at all. See Judith Resnick, "Managerial Judges," *Harvard Law Review*, 96 (1982): 374–448.

Members of the legal community can disagree about an outcome, using all lawyerly skill in good faith, upon full consideration of a case that has materialized. It is too easy, however, to conclude without further thought that any exercise of judicial discretion is unconstrained by the law, as the determinacy condition supposes. That depends in crucial part on exactly what it is that judges have, when they have discretion. The relevant idea of discretion can be clarified when the law is understood in terms of reasons for action.

2.2.1. The force of legal reasons. We should begin with the relationship of the law to practical deliberations and, in particular, the force of legal reasons. For some readers, the following may belabor the obvious, but for others it will be crucial basic background for the arguments that follow. The fundamental background assumption for the good faith thesis is simply that *persons act for various reasons in various circumstances.*[3] Persons are supposed to be agents in the world who have the capacity to deliberate on what to do and to act rationally, irrespective of any inevitable causal chains. The ultimate outcome or result of deliberations is an action, involving such things as physical movements or the utterance of operative language.[4] A judge acts in the requisite sense when issuing a judgment or order. Deliberations involve the identification and consideration of the relevant reasons for action – the pros and cons – whether consciously or not. The circumstances of action are the empirical facts of the particular situation in which action is contemplated, including the immediate factual context, the broader social and historical context, the feelings and beliefs of the actor or others, and

3 Some philosophers would dispute parts of this model, as would be the case for any model. Hard determinists, for example, would dispute the presupposition of free will. Interminable philosophical debates should be set aside within a jurisprudence except insofar as alternative general philosophies have concrete implications for specific jurisprudential problems.
4 See J. L. Austin, *How to Do Things With Words*, 2d ed., ed. J. O. Urmson & Marina Sbisà (Cambridge: Harvard University Press, 1975); John R. Searle, *Speech Acts* (Cambridge: Cambridge University Press, 1969).

the social role in which the actor participates. Facts in the circumstances are candidates for being reasons and, as explained in § 1.4.3, are reasons when coupled with an applicable normative standard.[5] A reason is Janus-faced, with one aspect invoking values and the other invoking plain facts.

The law is supposed to fit into practical deliberations by inserting some kind of reason for action. The matter is highly complicated. For now, let us define rudimentary legal reasons as ordinary facts that are reasons for action for legal purposes, to be considered in legal deliberations, by virtue of the law's standards.[6] For example, the law says that motorists should stop on encountering a red traffic light and go on a green one. To grasp the reason, imagine yourself in the driver's seat when you encounter a traffic signal – not on the curbside observing the correlation between changing traffic lights and traffic in the aggregate. Now, the colored light, together with the relevant legal rule, is a legal reason for you to stop or go as indicated.

Legal reasons can be contrasted with moral and other kinds of reasons that do not depend in any way on the law. A legal reason simply involves plain facts made relevant by a legal standard, a proposition that can be stated with the preface "It is the law that . . . " or the equivalent. A moral reason involves facts made relevant by a moral standard. Other kinds of reasons involve facts made relevant only by the actor's desires or interests. In the traffic situation, you have a moral obligation to drive safely, and you may have desires to get somewhere quickly and to avoid a citation. The legal reason might outweigh or displace some or all other considerations and thereby affect what you do. The traffic laws seek generally to coordinate the conduct of motorists on

5   The model thus assumes that all action is situated in a time and place, and that an abstract and universal norm of action can permit or require different results in different circumstances. Thus, a universal norm may require respect for all persons. Eating another person's body in our culture is a sure violation of this norm. There have been cultures, however, where eating the body of a defeated enemy was a required ritual of respect.

6   See Burton, *Law and Legal Reasoning*, pp. 83, 94–8, 102–7.

the public streets by changing each of their reasons for action. They guide conduct and organize relationships so people can live together in one respect, notwithstanding contrary desires and the potential for collision and harm.

We can summarize the preceding paragraph by saying that the law's standards – whether conceived as commands, rules, principles, policies, examples to be imitated, or all of the above[7] – in a broad sense are normative. The word "normative" sometimes causes unfortunate confusion. The normativity of the law has nothing to do with the social scientist's norm, which refers to the average or typical behavior in a group. That cocaine is commonly used in New York City thus may be "the norm" in the social scientific sense. But that does not mean that using cocaine is lawful or moral there. Moreover, the normativity of the law is distinct from feelings or beliefs about appropriate conduct. That Jones is outraged at Smith for working as an analyst for the CIA and believes she should resign her job is not normally a reason for Smith to resign. She should do so if Jones is correct that the job is immoral or illegal. Jones's feeling or belief is then superfluous, however, because Smith should resign whether or not Jones is angry or believes that she should.

The normativity of the law's standards means simply that the standards are supposed to guide conduct by saying something about what ought to be done, by whom, in some set of circumstances. It does not imply the law's moral soundness or validity, evoking for some misplaced associations with a "brooding omnipresence in the sky"[8] or fears of self-righteousness.[9] The laws of apartheid were evil and also were normative because they claimed to say what people in South Africa should do. We could criticize them cogently for

7 I thus set aside some complex and well-known questions about the nature of the law that judges have a duty to uphold. See Chap. 3, note 26.
8 Southern Pac. Co. v. Jensen, 244 U.S. 205, 218 (1917) (Holmes, J., dissenting).
9 See Charles E. Clark & David M. Trubeck, "The Creative Role of the Judge: Restraint and Freedom in the Common Law Tradition," *Yale Law Journal*, 71 (1961): 255–76, at 270.

providing bad guidance because they were normative in the broad sense. "Normativity" is used in a narrow sense when it is restricted to guidance that is morally sound or valid. Distinguishing between legal and moral reasons is a way of separating these two senses while allowing the law to be held responsible to moral standards.

A way to elaborate is to say that the law has normative content but only inchoate normative force. The distinction is manifest in the abstract form of a general proposition of law, stated as follows for purposes of analysis:

> *It is the law that* when [a factual situation occurs] then [a specified action should be taken].

The content is signified by the unitalicized phrases, which represent some part of the law of the relevant legal system. The content, without more, is merely informative: It only distinguishes a (generic) set of circumstances and links it to the idea of the indicated action. The force of the law, if any, stems in the first instance from the italicized phrase. It presses an actor to take the indicated action in fact when the standard is invoked by the circumstances of action. A proposition of law (as distinct from a statement of it) thus claims to have the power to turn inert facts, like colored lights, into reasons for action. When the requisite facts materialize in the circumstances of action, the law purports to have normative force for persons contemplating action – just because it is the law. Though it may be doubted whether the law actually has such force for all persons to whom it applies, it is reasonably clear that the law has actual force for judges.[10]

Significantly, there are different kinds of normative force. A reason for action can have absolute force because it requires a particular action regardless of other considerations. However, the absolute force ascribed to all valid legal standards by determinate-formalism neglects the other kinds of normative force, resulting in an undue result-orientation in

10   See § 7.3.

American legal theory. A reason can be a consideration to be taken into account and weighed along with other relevant considerations, as in the most common everyday practical deliberations. Moreover, a standard can exclude some kinds of reasons from those on which a person ought to act, as principles of academic freedom ban political considerations from proper tenure decisions and the like.[11] Added to a set of other kinds of reasons, a reason with some force at least will tip the balance of pros and cons in a close case. A standard with force also can tip the balance by excluding other kinds of reasons. The law can be most powerful if it both provides legal reasons for action and excludes most or all other kinds of reasons, as when a traffic law makes a red light a reason for a motorist to stop and excludes from consideration any desire to get somewhere quickly and the driver's independent sense of safety.[12] Legal and other normative standards can guide conduct by changing the relevant reasons for action without determining a particular result.

Now reconsider the ideas of judicial discretion and legal indeterminacy by viewing the law as a provider and excluder of legal reasons that need not have absolute force. Stubborn indeterminacy denies only that the law requires one result in a lawsuit. The foregoing shows, however, that the law's normative function does not require such determinacy of results. The arguments for legal indeterminacy do not deny that the law can admit and exclude reasons for action to be identified and considered in judicial deliberations. The law can constrain the considerations upon which judicial action should be based by defining the set of all (legally) relevant reasons, guiding the judge without dictating a result. Ac-

11 See Joseph Raz, *Practical Reason and Norms* (London: Hutchinson, 1975), pp. 25–8, 35–45; note 22 below.
12 See Joseph Raz, *The Authority of Law* (Oxford: Clarendon Press, 1979), pp. 18, 21–3 (explaining authority as protected reasons, which are reasons for an action and, at the same time, reasons that exclude many other kinds of reasons); Joseph Raz, *The Morality of Freedom* (Oxford: Clarendon Press, 1986), pp. 38–69 (developing the same idea). See also H. L. A. Hart, *Essays on Bentham* (Oxford: Clarendon Press, 1982), pp. 243–68.

cordingly, a judge has discretion in the relevant sense when the legal reasons support incompatible outcomes and no further legal reason requires one result.

2.2.2. Duty and discretion. What does a judge's legal duty require when he or she has discretion? This question would not make sense if judges were constrained by the law only when it determines one result in a lawsuit. When the determinacy condition is accepted, legal duty and discretion cannot coexist. A judge who is under a legal duty has no discretion because only one outcome is lawful, whereas discretion is the situation in which multiple outcomes are lawful. However, judicial duty and discretion can coexist when the law is understood to admit and exclude reasons for action, but not necessarily to determine results. A judge with discretion might be under a legal duty, for example, to decide on the legal reasons and only the legal reasons, if that were possible. A judge's legal duty would serve to structure the legal reasoning in judicial deliberations – the identification and consideration of the legal reasons in a case. Before entertaining this possibility seriously, however, two more commonly advanced alternative understandings of judicial discretion should be considered – the "anything goes" and "extra-legal standards" alternatives. These possibilities will be assessed for their fit with our dispositions to approve or criticize judicial conduct for complying or failing to comply with the judicial duty to uphold the law.

The first alternative supposes that, when a judge has discretion, anything goes. This seems to be the assumption when it is claimed, in legal realist fashion, that judges decide whatever they want to decide when the law is unclear (and it is often or always unclear). A number of similar claims are currently popular. It may be claimed in neopragmatist fashion that judges should decide cases as best they can, taking into account any consideration relevant to deciding the case.[13] Determinate rules may be contrasted with decisions

13 Richard A. Posner, *The Problems of Jurisprudence* (Cambridge: Harvard University Press, 1990), p. 232.

based on the "totality of the circumstances" as if there were no third alternative.[14] A decision maker may be said to have discretion if "he is simply not bound by standards set by the authority in question."[15] Legal indeterminacy consequently may be thought to signify that a judge may decide on the basis of personal or political preferences or interests, or felt identification with a party. This currently popular possibility presents the greatest challenge to the legitimacy of adjudication under law which, by almost all accounts, is undermined when judges decide without justification in law. Fortunately, this possibility is the least intellectually defensible alternative. Of the several reasons that could be given for rejecting it, two suffice for present purposes.[16]

The anything goes alternative gives short shrift to the normativity of the law and the need for judicial action to be justified. Normativity implies only that the law claims to guide action, not that it is morally required that the judge do what the law claims, perhaps improperly, to require. When it is stated that judges with discretion decide on the basis of personal or political preferences or interests, or felt identification with the parties, the statement is best interpreted as a causal or descriptive one about the psychology of judging in some cases. It is a mistake, however, to think that anything goes because the law itself fails to cause a judge to do the legally required thing.[17] Causal reasons concern the factors

14 Antonin Scalia, "The Rule of Law as a Law of Rules," *University of Chicago Law Review*, 56 (1989): 1175–88.

15 Ronald Dworkin, *Taking Rights Seriously* (Cambridge: Harvard University Press, 1977), p. 32.

16 See also Richard A. Wasserstrom, *The Judicial Decision* (Stanford, Calif.: Stanford University Press, 1961), pp. 23–36 (discussing the "irrationalist fallacy" of inferring from the limits of logic that all questions which cannot be settled by appealing to formal logic cannot be settled in any reasonable manner; also distinguishing the process of discovery from that of justification).

17 Some causal reasons bear no relationship to justification. We may be caused to act in some way by misfiring neurons, by operant conditioning, by emotional impulses, or by external threats of harm. Such reasons sometimes are relevant to excuses for doing unjustifiable things, but they do not establish that an act was right or wrong. Other

that, from an observer's standpoint, validly can be believed to be or have been sufficient preconditions for some event to happen. The legal realist slogans may be true as explanations of the causes of some or many decisions and useful as a basis for prediction; at the same time, they may be false *as justifications*. Even the arch-legal realist probably would not argue that a judge with discretion should decide on the basis of such factors. Consider a judge who says, "I did it because I am a political conservative," or "I've got the power and it's your tough luck." I assume that all of us would tell such a judge to get off the bench posthaste because those are not the right kinds of reasons.[18]

Moreover, it may be doubted that judicial duty permits a judge to decide on the basis of personal or political preferences or interests, or felt identification with the parties. A judge might seem to be so permitted if the law runs out of guidance without prohibiting two or more actions in a case. But our common dispositions with respect to judicial duty deny that judges are permitted to act for such reasons.[19] We have seen that the law can have the force of excluding reasons from practical deliberations, as a motorist's desire to get somewhere quickly is excluded from consideration when a red traffic signal is encountered. The judicial duty to uphold the law, in particular, has exclusionary force in that some kinds of reasons are barred from judicial deliberations. This

causal reasons are related to justification. For example, rational people act on their beliefs, including their beliefs about what is right. The belief, however, is not a justification for action since, if it is mistaken, it shows the actor's sincerity but not the correctness of the action. Moreover, emotions and beliefs can be parts of justifying reasons in a way that makes the distinction complex. On the role of character, see §§ 5.4 and following.

18 A judge may give a proper justification for a decision though motivated to reach her result by improper reasons. It makes good sense to say that, if the given legal justification is sound, the decision is legally sound even though improperly motivated. The judge may be criticized personally for acting on the wrong kinds of reasons even while the decision is approved for the reasons given.

19 In a trivial sense each person can act only on his own view of what he should do.

is true if at least one kind of reason is kept out in principle from any justification for a judicial decision. Consider three kinds of reasons. First, there are legal reasons which, as defined above,[20] are plain facts that are reasons for judicial action due to the law's standards. Second, there are moral and policy reasons, important facts by virtue of moral and policy standards respectively. Third, there are personal or ad hominem reasons, those that depend on advantage to self, friends, or groups with which one identifies. By all accounts, action on ad hominem considerations is a violation of judicial duty in principle: Judges have a duty always to act impartially, "without respect to persons."[21] Therefore, the judicial duty to uphold the law excludes some kinds of reasons.[22] Discretion is not a matter of unbridled choice; it is a matter of judgment that may earn respect from members of the legal community and others.

Excluding the ad hominem does not entail that judges can or should strip themselves of all prior experiences in order to decide each case as though they were newborn babies. No one can begin to understand well the law or the facts in any case without drawing pervasively on the accumulated experiences of a lifetime and on a character molded and cultivated over time. Because each judge acts with a different

20 See § 2.2.1.
21 28 U.S.C. § 453 (1982) (oath for federal judges pledges to "administer justice without respect to persons"). See also American Bar Association, *Model Rules of Judicial Conduct*, Canon 3 (1990). "Impartiality" is used here to mean action on reasons other than ad hominem reasons. It is distinct from objectivity or neutrality. See §§ 8.3 and following.
22 This is a key part of what is meant when a legal standard is said to be authoritative. See generally Raz, *Practical Reason and Norms*, pp. 35–48; Raz, *Authority of Law*, pp. 3–27; Raz, *Morality of Freedom*, pp. 23–69; Joseph Raz, "Authority, Law, and Morality," *The Monist*, 68 (1985): 295–322. For philosophical criticism of this approach to authority, see, for example, Moore, "Authority, Law, and Razian Reasons"; Stephen R. Perry, "Second-Order Reasons, Uncertainty and Legal Theory," *Southern California Law Review*, 62 (1989): 913–94; E. Philip Soper, "Legal Theory and the Claim of Authority," *Philosophy and Public Affairs*, 18 (1989): 209–37. For a further defense of the idea, see Raz, "Facing Up: A Reply," *Southern California Law Review*, 62 (1989): 1153–235.

personal history, moreover, each may understand the same case with different emphases; it is important for judges and other members of the legal community to engage in conversation to share insights and correct for blind spots in understanding. There is, nonetheless, a crucial distinction between the knowledge that forms a necessary background for understanding and ad hominem reasons for action. That we think judges *should* share insights and correct for blind spots suggests that their reasons for action are the same in principle in any law case. Exclusion of the ad hominem is necessary to that end. It shows that, as a matter of judicial duty, it is not the case that "anything goes" when a judge has discretion. Judges wield awesome coercive power, controlling important parts of the normative structure of society. The demand that they give legal justifications for their uses of power is an enduring one in American society. The obligation to do so does not vanish when they have discretion.

A second possible standard governing judicial discretion is the extra-legal standards alternative. It supposes that a judge with discretion should reach the best decision on the basis of relevant nonlegal standards, such as those of sound political morality or social policy.[23] By contrast with an anything goes alternative, this one restricts the reasons available in judging to those that could justify a decision, preserving impartiality. By contrast with the good faith thesis, it does not restrict the set of appropriate reasons to those warranted by the law as grounds for judicial decision.

The extra-legal standards alternative is doubtful, however, because the law also excludes moral and policy reasons in many cases even when it is indeterminate. Consider three examples. First, this exclusionary effect is obvious when it comes to a judge's personal conception of the good life: A devout Christian should not exploit vagueness in the First Amendment's Religion Clauses to promote a Christian nation. Second, when a traffic statute imposes a fine for spec-

---

23 This is roughly the position of H. L. A. Hart and Joseph Raz. See Chap. 6, note 25. It also is Ronald Dworkin's main foil. See Dworkin, *Law's Empire*, pp. 108–14.

ified conduct without requiring culpability, we commonly understand that the requirements of effective coordination and individual responsibility have been balanced by non-judicial lawmaking authorities. Whether or not the application of that statute is unclear, a judge qua judge is not permitted to reconsider that balance and to impose a culpability requirement even if it is a good idea. The outcome of the legislative deliberations is authoritative: It excludes from judicial deliberations the arguments that might justify a different law in such situations. Third, consider the case of an ambiguity in the law. Ambiguity is not a pretext for a judge to go outside the law's authority under a license to moralize or dominate. Rather, each prong of an ambiguity with incompatible implications for action, like each of several discrete competing legal standards, has some privileged status because a judge must decide between them. The reasons for making the selection are those that justify the particular law in the first place. The judge's reasons thus may include the considerations of policy or principle that form the background justification for the particular legal standard understood in its legal context. The reasons that oppose a law at the legislative stage, however, in principle are excluded at the law-applying stage.[24]

The exclusion of some moral and policy reasons implies that a judge's duty is to decide on reasons warranted by the conventional law as grounds for judicial decision. Some legal standards provide legal reasons directly by turning ordinary facts into reasons for action: A red traffic light is a legal reason for a motorist to stop, and for a judge to fine a motorist who fails to do so, due only to the traffic laws of the relevant legal system. Other legal standards may warrant reasons based on standards drawn from foreign legal systems, contracts, wills, international law, social policy, and conventional or critical morality. For example, the Eighth Amendment's prohibition on cruel and unusual punishment might warrant moral standards of cruelty as grounds for

24 For elaboration, see § 2.4.

constitutional adjudication under that law. Such reasons are *legal* when the law authorizes a judge to act on them. Accordingly, the idea of a legal reason includes both reasons that are created by the law and independent reasons the law warrants as grounds for judicial action.[25]

The third possible standard governing judicial discretion guides legal deliberations in a case by constraining the considerations that properly enter. When the law is understood as a guide to conduct that admits and excludes reasons for judicial action, the possibility arises that judicial duty requires a judge to act on reasons provided by the law, and not on other reasons, even when exercising discretion. Judges

25 The position taken in the text should not be confused with those in a most important dispute in general jurisprudence. Some, like Joseph Raz, advance the "sources thesis," which holds that all law stems from lawmaking acts identified as such by the legal system's rule of recognition. See Raz, "Authority, Law and Morality," at 311–15. Others, like Jules Coleman, advance the "incorporation thesis," which holds that law may stem from sources or may consist of moral and policy standards incorporated into the law by the rule of recognition. See Jules L. Coleman, "Negative and Positive Positivism," *Journal of Legal Studies*, 11 (1982): 139–64; David Lyons, "Principles, Positivism, and Legal Theory," *Yale Law Journal*, 87 (1977): 415–35; E. Philip Soper, "Legal Theory and the Obligation of a Judge: The Hart/Dworkin Dispute," *Michigan Law Review*, 75 (1977): 473–519. For general jurisprudential purposes, the law is conceived as a system of general propositions unified by a rule of recognition or its counterpart. The issue arises because a warranting proposition might be a part of the law when the proposition thereby warranted is not.

For the purposes of a theory of adjudication, however, the dispute is trivial. Raz, for example, holds that judges should decide on the same grounds that the incorporationists support. He insists only that all of them are not legal in status. Raz would not, I think, deny that a warranting proposition can be a part of the positive law or that a concrete reason for action that is dependent also on a warranted proposition may be a permitted reason for judicial action. The sources thesis seeks only to keep warranting propositions that incorporate morals out of the rule of recognition. From the judge's practical perspective, it is unimportant whether a reason is admitted by virtue of the warranting proposition or the warranted proposition, or whether a warranting proposition is in the rule of recognition itself or, rather, in a rule validated as law by the rule of recognition. It matters whether the judge is to act on a reason based in a warranted proposition, not whether that proposition is part of the law.

would be under a duty to weigh competing legal reasons without relying on reasons not warranted by the law as grounds for judicial decision, even when gauging weight. It is not obvious that it is possible to do this. If it is, such an understanding on its face would fit well with our dispositions to approve and criticize. Demands for fidelity to the law do not evaporate when the law is indeterminate with respect to results. Even when they exercise discretion, judges are criticized for acting on personal or political preferences or interests, felt identification with a party, or moral and policy considerations not warranted by the law as grounds for judicial decision. Both the anything goes and extra-legal standards alternatives fly in the face of this conventional norm. If it were possible for judges to act as required by the third alternative, moreover, it would be easy to see that judges can fulfill their duty to uphold the law even while exercising discretion. Their decisions would be fully in accordance with the law even when they are not dictated by the law. That would be a large advance in our understanding of adjudication.

The good faith thesis relies on the third conception of a judge's legal duty. Of course, more needs to be said to clarify and sustain its plausibility, especially given the central problem of weighing legal reasons without recourse to other kinds of reasons. Weight is a metaphor that has seemed immune to clarification. Indeed, it could be understood as a metaphor for indeterminacy, cycling the analysis back to its starting point. We can, however, try to do better than that.

2.3. WEIGHING REASONS

The problem of judicial discretion is clarified when we understand that it arises only when legal standards have less than absolute force and provide reasons with incompatible implications for action. Clarifying the problem, however, does not illuminate how legal reasons are combined – in particular, how they possibly can be weighed without depending on excluded reasons. It helps to conceive of weighing as a gauging of the relative normative force of the reasons that properly enter judicial deliberations. Two further steps can be taken to enhance understanding. The first concerns what it is that judges weigh – legal standards in the abstract or concrete reasons for action. The second concerns the grounds of weight – the conditions under which claims about weight should be accepted as sound or well supported by reasons.

2.3.1.   What gets weighed? Consider the familiar case of *Riggs v. Palmer.*[26] The New York Court of Appeals held that a named beneficiary under a will, who murdered the testator to prevent him from changing his will, could not inherit property under the will, notwithstanding a statute providing that a person's estate shall pass upon death to those named in a valid written will. There are competing legal arguments for and against the court's holding. To clarify what it is that judges might weigh, the competing arguments can be modeled at three levels of abstraction (though the levels are not strictly distinct in practice).

The three levels reflect the difference between plain facts, concrete reasons for action, and abstract legal standards, such as principles. At the level of plain facts, the competition is particular: The grandson was named as heir in the will but murdered the testator. At the level of reasons for action, general legal standards, including rules, principles, and policies, are combined with plain facts to produce concrete reasons. Thus, against the court's holding: The applicable statute requires the court to recognize the heir named in a valid will, and the grandson was the heir named in the relevant valid will, so the court should recognize the grandson as heir. In favor of the court's holding: Persons should not be allowed to profit by their wrongs, and the grandson would do so if recognized as the heir of a person he murdered, so the grandson should not be recognized as heir. At the level of general legal standards, the competition in *Riggs* seems

26   106 N.Y. 506 (1889).

very abstract and cut off from the facts. The principle of legislative supremacy competes with the principle that no one should profit as intended from his wrongs.

Courts cannot balance the plain facts because the facts are inert, in that they have no justificatory implications for action, apart from a standard of conduct. The values embodied in the standard – its background justification – give the facts normative force with varying intensity in various circumstances. Only then does it make sense to talk about weighing or balancing. Lawyers and judges often speak in a truncated fashion – giving plain facts as reasons – that obscures the role of standards. Implicit standards are accepted by convention and taken for granted in ordinary legal discourse, even if there is disagreement on questions of weight and the justice of conventional legal standards. These conventions make it both possible and desirable for a legal conversation to assume the conventional standards as common ground until someone balks and requests clarification.[27] Such a request commonly asks that an implicit standard be made explicit to complete the argument and expose it to criticism.

Courts normally do not and should not balance abstract legal standards as such when they have discretion in judicial deliberations. That is, they do not decide that one principle prevails over another *whenever* they compete.[28] If standards were being ranked as such in judicial practice, one would expect a stable and comprehensive hierarchy of abstract standards to emerge for each judge or the bench as a whole. But the normative force of standards is felt – they actually guide conduct – only when an occasion for action is present-

27 See Burton, *Law and Legal Reasoning*, pp. 204–14.
28 Judges may balance highly abstract principles to compose mid-level abstractions that, in turn, generate concrete reasons for action. Abstract principles thus may appear to have weight. On analysis, however, the weight turns out to be a property of the set of possible cases that might be governed by the principle. Accordingly, a mid-level principle will seek to distinguish the set of concrete cases in which one principle prevails from the set in which another prevails. Weight remains a property of concrete reasons in possible cases even though judges may generalize to compose a mid-level legal standard.

ed in fact (and perhaps in imagination). Judges or courts that show too much continuing affinity for some abstract standards over others, despite the differences from case to case, are criticized for being ideological, formalistic, and unjudicious. Stable and comprehensive hierarchies of abstract standards generally are not laudable when judges have discretion, though a principle like the principle of legislative supremacy has great force in a democratic system. In constitutional criminal procedure cases, for example, principles of privacy and fair trial commonly compete with principles of public order and deference to law enforcement expertise. Few, however, would praise a court that always found one pair to prevail and decided cases accordingly, regardless of their facts. It is too improbable that the police always or never overstep the bounds. Adjudication is about deciding *cases* according to law, not trumpeting values.[29] Consequently, the weight of the principles should vary in relation to the facts of particular disputes.

Moreover, a practical understanding of adjudication should illuminate that which is distinctive about its central instances. That courts act judicially only in cases is a key distinguishing feature. Divorcing general standards from the circumstances of a case would turn adjudication at best into legislation and at worst into a philosophical or ideological exercise. Though adjudication can be understood from the outside in such terms, the judicial duty takes on a much more concrete character from the judicial standpoint. A trial court's duty normally is to decide whether to grant a specific motion made by counsel, on the record as it has been developed by counsel to that point. Even when using their limited lawmaking power, appellate courts decide primarily whether the trial court erred in such a decision. With few exceptions, courts lack the authority to initiate decision and must respond to a question framed by counsel on the record developed (well or badly) by them. So, distinctive characteristics

29 For a different view, see Owen M. Fiss, "Foreword: The Forms of Justice," *Harvard Law Review*, 93 (1979): 1–58, at 28–44.

of adjudication can be obscured when standards are abstracted from the context of a case before a court.

Judges balance concrete reasons for action in cases, at the mid-level of abstraction combining facts and standards, rather than plain facts or abstract standards. Again, judges may speak in truncated ways, expressing themselves at the plain facts or abstract standards levels rather than the reasons level, which can seem pedantic when spelled out. However, understanding weight as a property of reasons for action has the virtues that the alternatives lack. The factual part of a reason provides the concreteness that distinguishes adjudication from legislation, ideological battle, or moral philosophy. The standards part provides the normative force that is crucial to the intelligibility of weight in the first place. Accordingly, the best understanding is that judges weigh reasons for action under the circumstances of each case.

2.3.2. *The grounds of weight.* The crucial question about weight now can be considered: What are the grounds for the weight of a legal reason? Some writers have suggested that weight is a function of the degree of "institutional support" enjoyed by a legal standard.[30] That is, they suggest, the *frequency* with which a legal standard is exemplified in cases and statutes generates its weight as well as grounding its status as law. The frequency of appeal to a legal standard, however, depends too much on the happenstance of cases thrown up by events for that to be a sound basis for assigning weight. More important, as will be seen, the grounds of weight are not the same as the grounds of law. Nor are they extra-legal considerations, such as personal, political, moral, or policy considerations not warranted by the conventional law as grounds for judicial decision. The best way to describe

---

30 For example, Ronald Dworkin, *Taking Rights Seriously* (Cambridge: Harvard University Press, 1977), p. 40; Rolf E. Sartorius, *Individual Conduct and Social Norms* (Encino, Calif.: Dickinson Pub. Co., 1975), p. 193; Soper, "Legal Theory and the Obligation of a Judge," at 503. See also Melvin A. Eisenberg, *The Nature of the Common Law* (Cambridge: Harvard University Press, 1988).

the grounds of weight is to say that they are "internal to the congeries of reasons in a case."[31] Some explanation will be needed to make that a meaningful idea.

The argument above, rejecting abstract principles as the entities to be weighed, goes a long way toward establishing that the grounds for weighing legal reasons must differ from the grounds of law. Standards of conduct are legal standards by virtue of grounds that stand independently of the facts of any particular case, whether the grounds are fit and justification,[32] the criteria contained in a rule of recognition,[33] or whatever. Legal standards accordingly can be identified and stated in the abstract, as when we say that the law requires residents to pay taxes on in-kind income or that de jure racial discrimination is unlawful, in advance of the materialization of any case and therefore any competition of reasons. An abstract standard has only inchoate normative force and no weight until a case materializes. The standard then can latch onto facts in a context calling for action, admitting and excluding legal reasons from practical deliberations. Accordingly, it would seem that the facts of a case in some way are among the grounds for gauging the weight of legal reasons.

The role of the facts within the grounds for weighing legal reasons can be clarified. To begin, the identification and consideration of legal reasons should be separated for analytical purposes. All of the relevant reasons in a case must be identified before any are assigned a weight. This is because the importance of a legal reason ebbs and flows depending on the congeries of reasons in which it is embedded, even while the law remains unchanged. To illustrate, assume that a

31 This does not endorse the view of law as an "autonomous discipline" or a "self-contained system" because reasons warranted by the law may depend on extensive interdisciplinary inquiry. For criticism of that view, see Richard A. Posner, "The Decline of Law as an Autonomous Discipline: 1962–87," *Harvard Law Review*, 100 (1987): 761–80.
32 See Dworkin, *Law's Empire*, pp. 176–90.
33 See generally H. L. A. Hart, *The Concept of Law* (Oxford: Clarendon Press, 1961), pp. 92–3, 94–6, 97–107; Joseph Raz, *The Concept of a Legal System*, 2d ed. (Oxford: Clarendon Press, 1980), pp. 197–200; Raz, *The Authority of Law*, pp. 90–8.

motor vehicle left the road and damaged a storefront.[34] In a tort action, the fact that the operator had an epileptic seizure at that moment looms large, all else being equal, as a reason to find that the motorist was not negligent. The fact of the seizure seems less weighty, as an exculpatory reason, when it turns out that the motorist did not take antiseizure medication that day. Not having taken antiseizure medication, in turn, is crucial if the motorist had a history of epilepsy and was under doctor's orders to take the medication regularly. It shrinks in significance, however, if the motorist had not had a bout of epilepsy for many years. In the same context, the mere fact that an epileptic was operating a motor vehicle probably is insignificant, but gains salience if the motorist's medical history includes many epileptic seizures even while properly medicated.

Furthermore, the law is spent by the identification of legal reasons and the exclusion of other reasons. All legal considerations to be taken into account enter at the identification step.[35] Reasons are either relevant or irrelevant. Once all relevant reasons have been identified, no new reason can enter as the ground for the weight of any one of them. Irrelevant reasons are irrelevant. Accordingly, the weight of a legal reason must be a function of the other relevant legal reasons together.

The grounds of weight are internal to each case in a way that can be modeled as follows.[36] Suppose a judge has an "action threshold" consisting of the amount of normative force just sufficient to move him or her to act dutifully. This supposition is plausible for two main reasons. First, the judicial duty to settle disputes deliberately constrains a judge to

34 See Hammontree v. Jenner, 20 Cal. App. 3d 528 (1971).
35 See Aleksander Peczenik, *On Law and Reason* (Boston: Kluwer Academic Publishers, 1989), pp. 82–4.
36 What follows is a way of understanding practical deliberations, not a psychological theory. It assumes that "the case" is constituted by the collection of relevant legal reasons, each conceived as a fact in the circumstances made relevant by a legal standard resting on a background justification of principle or policy.

distribute some minimum amount of force over the legal reasons in a case. Judges should not act too casually, which would be the case if the weight of all legal reasons together were insubstantial. Second, the judicial duty to act dispassionately constrains a judge not to distribute more than the minimum amount. Assigning too much weight to the legal reasons in a case would be unjudicious.[37] Thus, deliberate but dispassionate action implies some amount of normative force that is neither too little nor too much.

Accordingly, the weight of each legal reason would be a share of the amount of normative force at the action threshold. In judicial deliberations, one might start by assigning each legal reason an equal share. Each legal reason has equal weight, upon its identification, due solely to its status qua legal. It would be silly, however, simply to count the reasons on each side and let the majority prevail. During the consideration of legal reasons, weight can vary from the starting point due to the play of the background justification for the law invoked by the circumstances. The background justification, however, does not generate a weight simply for the reason it grounds. Rather, each legal reason can justify changing the weight of another reason in the congeries, but only by shifting an increment of additional weight onto itself or giving some up. The weight of one reason ultimately depends on the justifications for the other reasons invoked by the circumstances.

Giving one reason too little weight hence may be checked by the need to give another too much and vice versa. A judge in good faith seeks to give each and every relevant legal reason a proportional share within the frame fixed primarily by the judicial duty to uphold the law.[38] The goal is a

37 By "dispassionate," I do not mean a decision that takes into account only narrowly logical reasoning, but one that takes into account warranted reasons of whatever kind.
38 The frame also is fixed by the background conventions of the practice. A rich web of professional conventions is a condition for the existence of a functioning practice of law and judging. Such conventions consist

ratio of weights in deliberative equilibrium at the action threshold. The judge proceeds by gauging the weight of each legal reason in turn while standing on the ground provided by the other relevant reasons, as one might rebuild a boat plank by plank while at sea[39] – not by a series of deductive inferences resting on an ultimate foundation. The grounds of weight are internal to the case because a congeries of reasons grounds the weight of each reason. Deliberations would continue on this basis, by successive adjustments, until total normative force is distributed at the action threshold, the judge is comfortable stopping, and judicious action ensues. The result will not be arbitrary because it is supported by legal reasons even if a different result also could be so supported.

On this understanding, distributing weight is more like composing a representational painting than like working out a calculus. The problem of weight is qualitative and a matter of proportionality in the ratio of weights among the relevant legal reasons. A classical still life artist can select any size canvas, can decide on any number of objects to depict within that frame, and can paint a pear of any size on that canvas to begin. Having made those choices, however, the painter is constrained to paint an orange within a small range of sizes that do not render the pear and the composition as a whole grotesque. A related image is the Calder mobile, which can achieve balance with any size or number of panels to be hung within the constraints of the formal ratios. The concept of balance at work in the artist's composition evokes the art

of the practices and dispositions of members of the legal community with respect to results. Burton, *Law and Legal Reasoning*, pp. 95–6. As conditions for the existence of law, analytically speaking they are not a part of the law that judges have a duty to uphold: A judge's duty to uphold the law nonetheless includes a duty to respect the conditions for its existence. When reading the example of the epileptic driver above, the reader's dispositions as a member of the legal community guided his or her acceptance or rejection of my suggestions about the relative weight of the various factors in different contexts. See note 1 above; note 55 below.

39 The famous image is from Neurath, "Protocol Sentences," in *Logical Positivism*, ed. Alfred J. Ayer (Glencoe, Ill.: Free Press); pp. 199–201.

of judging. For the judge, however, the counterpart to the objects depicted by an artist are the legal reasons in a case, which should be determined by the law rather than unfettered artistic or political choice.

There are three alternative but less attractive ways of conceiving the grounds of weight. The first employs a mathematical metaphor, but the problem of weight in legal reasoning cannot be quantified. Weight might be conceived on a scale like that used for measuring the length or weight of physical objects. Each reason for action would have a set numerical identity (one, two, three, . . . ∞), and all weights on each side of a dispute could be summed with the greater quantity indicating the winner. But there are no apparent grounds for thus assigning numerical weights.[40] Or weight might be conceived on Libra's scales: One could weigh any two reasons in relation to each other and decide which is the stronger. A rank ordering of all reasons in a case then could be constructed (first, second, third, . . . ∞).[41] The problem here lies in the need to combine the rankings. Or weight might be conceived as the vector of two or more policies or principles.[42] This metaphor supplies no understanding of the grounds of weight and is confusing when there are many relevant legal reasons.

A second alternative urges that the grounds of weight are general considerations of morality or policy chosen by the

40 It is possible that the real or correct weight of every possible legal reason in every possible congeries of legal reasons in principle is fixed in advance of the materialization of a case. See, for example, S. L. Hurley, "Coherence, Hypothetical Cases, and Precedent," *Oxford Journal of Legal Studies*, 10 (1990): 221–51; Michael S. Moore, "A Natural Law Theory of Interpretation," *Southern California Law Review*, 58 (1985): 277–398, at 370–4. Weighing reasons then could be a matter of summing the weights. Even if such real or correct weights existed, it seems fanciful to suppose that they would be accessible in any practicable way to judges engaged in judging cases. The lawful-making characteristics of a judicial decision should all be accessible to judges on the bench.
41 See Dworkin, *Law's Empire*, p. 270 (explaining weight as a ranking).
42 See Duncan Kennedy, "Form and Substance in Private Law Adjudication," *Harvard Law Review*, 889 (1976): 1685–778, at 1712–13.

judge as a matter of discretion, whether or not they form a background justification for the applicable law. Consider, however, a judge who announced that great weight should be attached to the defendant's failure, in the epileptic driver example above, to take prescribed medication because the judge favored a policy of encouraging all people to take their medicine as a matter of good health practice. Such a policy is alien to the law of torts, which does not at present impose strict liability for failing to take good care of one's health. Such a judge should be criticized. Judges have no warrant to treat discretionary cases as pretexts for advancing their preferred social policies outside the applicable law. Moreover, turning to moral and policy considerations does not solve the puzzle of weight. Moral and policy considerations also will generate incompatible implications for action with no privileged tiebreaker.[43] The problem of weight recurs without solution.

The third alternative insists that, because legal, moral, and policy reasons all may generate conflicting reasons, an account of weight must acknowledge a role for personal values, interests, and loyalties. This approach, too, does not solve the problem. No justification for judicial action could flow from a judge's personal values, interests, and loyalties. By all accounts, these ad hominem reasons are excluded by judicial duty when the relevant legal reasons are identified. They remain objectionable when the legal reasons are considered. Moreover, even if we were to admit them, ad hominem reasons also generate conflicting implications for action. Presumably, one should act on the better ones. But what are the grounds for favoring some over others? Turning from legal reasons to moral and policy reasons, and thence to personal values, interests, or loyalties, enters a regress or vicious circle with no end in sight. The regress can be stopped as well with the identification of legal reasons, placing the burden on the law to warrant all appropriate reasons as grounds for judicial decisions.

43   See § 2.2.2.

It is not an alternative to insist a priori that there *must* be objective weights and a result-determining calculus, as though increasingly sophisticated analyses eventually must vindicate determinate-formalism in adjudication. We should resist the temptation to demand a foundation at every step when discretion appears. The very idea of discretion supplants determinate-formalism's ultimate and result-determining foundation with an idea of constrained judgment, exercised pragmatically within a legal framework.[44] Nor is it self-evident that, in the absence of such determinacy, there is something illegitimate about good faith adjudication because it permits "too much" discretion. The question is a practical one requiring a comparison of the available alternatives in light of defensible and practicable criteria. There is no a priori basis for denying that judges may have discretion and, when they do, are under a duty to uphold the law in its exercise. That is, we need an argument if we are to insist that judges fulfill their duty to uphold the law only if the law determines the correct result in a case. Possible arguments for the determinacy condition are considered and rejected in Part II. Anticipating those arguments, we should conceive of the grounds of weight as a ring of relevant reasons impinging on a decision, not a linear regress in search of a result-determining foundation.[45]

Three features of the good faith model deserve emphasis. First, it accounts for the ebb and flow of weight as different constellations of facts are considered in legal reasoning. The dependence of weight on factual context is so salient a feature of the legal experience that this is a strong positive virtue of the good faith thesis. Second, it is a model of judicial discretion because multiple outcomes are lawful.[46] If there

---

44 See §§ 2.4, 6.2.1.
45 For the context of this thought, see §§ 5.3 and following.
46 The discretion contemplated by the good faith thesis thus is stronger than mere judgment, which sense of discretion Dworkin properly dismisses as a trivial concern. See Dworkin, *Taking Rights Seriously*, pp. 32–3. See also Neil MacCormick, *Legal Reasoning and Legal Theory* (Oxford: Clarendon Press, 1978), pp. 246–55.

were five legal reasons and 100 units of normative force, for example, weight could be distributed 20-20-20-20-20, 10-30-10-30-20, and so forth. Indeed, an infinite number of distributions is mathematically possible. It would be far-fetched to claim that there is a single right answer within any practicable frame of reference.[47] Third, however, the set of all possible distributions is constrained. The judge in good faith seeks *not* to jimmy the assignments of weight for excluded reasons. The action threshold should help such a judge to identify mistaken assignments of weight by forcing a review whenever the total gets too large, possibly due to excluded factors, or too small, possibly due to inattention. By requiring that one reason gain weight only at the expense of another, it also effectively requires the proper grounds of weight to remain always dependent on the congeries of reasons. Consequently, different judges can reach different results while all are constrained by the law and in good faith.

2.4. BACKGROUND JUSTIFICATIONS

To elaborate the good faith thesis and to forestall misunderstanding, we now raise and respond to a possible objection akin to that raised by H. L. A. Hart in his famous 1958 debate with Lon Fuller:[48] Can background justifications of legal standards – the principles and policies on which they rest[49] – be admitted to judicial deliberations without reopening all questions relevant to the lawmaking exercise? The objection

47 For a discussion of Ronald Dworkin's right answer thesis, see § 6.4.
48 Lon L. Fuller, "Positivism and Fidelity to Law – A Reply to Professor Hart," *Harvard Law Review*, 71 (1958): 630–72, at 661–9; H. L. A. Hart, "Positivism and the Separation of Law and Morals," *Harvard Law Review*, 71 (1958): 593–629, at 614–15.
49 The background justification does not consist of the motives of legislators who vote for a bill, which commonly include such purposes as serving constituency and contributor interests. Nor does it consist of their hopes, expectations, beliefs, or predictions. Rather, it consists of the arguments that justify the law voted on, such as most arguments that would be given in floor debate without embarrassment. Nor is the background justification identical to legislative intention, both because judge-made laws and administrative rules have background justifications and for reasons mentioned at the end of this section.

continues by posing a dilemma. On the one hand, if the judge does not take into account background justifications, it would seem that legal reasons are cut off from the source of their differing weights. A judge then could not decide as indicated by the good faith thesis. On the other hand, if the judge does take the background justifications into account, it might seem that all legislative considerations can enter the judicial deliberation through the back door. The distinction between the good faith thesis and certain rival theories of adjudication – those claiming that discretion is exercised on the basis of extra-legal factors – would then be lost. Identifying legal reasons based in the conventional law, as a step preliminary to considering their weight, would be rendered largely superfluous.

The good faith thesis does allow that accepted background justifications are cognizable by judges. Such justifications enter judicial deliberations, in both legal interpretation to identify legal reasons and the gauging of weight in their consideration. The alternative, as Frederick Schauer has made clear, is to treat rules as "opaque" to their background justifications and themselves dispositive of legally right results on the basis of facts identified by the rule's literal meaning.[50] That formalistic view of rules is a component of determinate-formalism, which need not be discussed at length.[51]

---

50 Frederick Schauer, "Formalism," *Yale Law Journal*, 97 (1988): 509–48, at 532–5; Frederick Schauer, "Rules and the Rule of Law," *Harvard Journal of Law and Policy*, 14 (1991): 645–94, at 647–51. See also Donald H. Regan, "Authority and Value: Reflections on Raz's *Morality of Freedom*," *Southern California Law Review*, 62 (1988): 995–1095, at 1003–13.

51 Schauer, however, is not a determinate-formalist. He would employ opaque legal rules to govern some disputes within a regime he calls "presumptive positivism." The hallmark of presumptive positivism is the special but limited force assigned to the results reached when playing by the rules formalistically. In his view, these results can be outweighed by strong considerations of general morality or public policy. Schauer, "Rules and the Rule of Law," at 665–91. Schauer's thesis might have some attraction as a descriptive account of some American judicial practices, though it seems to me that background justifications are used regularly in the course of interpreting and applying the rules, not only as countervailing considerations. As a con-

It supposes that the constraint of the law on judges operates semantically and psychologically by making it hard for a judge to write a lawless opinion. It is better, however, to conceive of the constraint of the law as a normative constraint restricting the set of legally relevant reasons for action. This grounds constraint on a judge's undoubted duty to uphold the law, rather than on mercurial judicial scruples. The strength of this constraint may be stronger or weaker in different circumstances depending on the legal culture and the judicial character.[52] There is no conceptual guarantee that it will always be strong enough to assuage fears of judicial abuses of power.

Allowing that accepted background justifications for laws are cognizable by judges does not open the door to general considerations of morality and public policy. Against a backdrop of recent cultural skepticism about values, it might be thought glibly that every value enters when any value enters. Judicial reasoning, however, is intelligible only if we abandon value skepticism in a practical understanding. We can then distinguish among kinds of reasons for action, separating those that enjoy legal status in relation to a particular law from those that do not. Thus, a policy of encouraging people to take their medication is not a part of the background justification for the law of torts, but discouraging wrongs to others surely is. The set of principles and policies on which judges properly act can then be confined in princi-

ceptual and normative matter, however, presumptive positivism seems weak. Conceptually, Schauer is ambivalent as to whether rules provide reasons or determine results, reflecting an omission to distinguish between a rule's determinate content and its determining force. See §§ 6.2 and following. Moreover, the source of a rule's weight for him is not its background justification, and it is unclear. Normatively, his approach excludes from judicial deliberations the background justification for a specific rule, but includes general considerations of morality and public policy. This seems backward, empowering judges unduly in a democratic society like the United States. For further discussion and criticism, see "Symposium on Law and Philosophy," *Harvard Journal of Law & Public Policy*, 14 (1991): 615–852.

52 See §§ 5.4 and following, 8.4.

ple to a subset of all otherwise relevant principles and policies. The background justification for a legal standard should be one or a combination of the following model kinds, which illustrate the distinction between the background justification for a particular law and general considerations of morality and public policy.

First, there are legal standards whose background justifications represent a victory for some moral principles or public policies over others. For example, the First Amendment's guarantee of free speech, by Justice Hugo Black's interpretation, was an absolute ban on restrictions on talking.[53] Justice Black probably would not have denied that there are reasonable arguments for restricting speech because it sometimes harms others and may threaten the national security. For him, however, the Speech Clause was a victory for the arguments against considering those values in particular cases. Its background justification consisted of the arguments supporting the absolute ban; those that would oppose the Speech Clause or support a balancing approach were excluded from his consideration qua judge. A great many legal standards operate like the Speech Clause on this interpretation, though they are not the usual grist for the appellate judge's or legal scholar's mill because they tend to operate unproblematically. The background justification for such legal standards consists of the values or purposes that justify the law – the ones that won. Those that do not justify the legal standard, but argue for a different legal standard, are excluded from judicial deliberations. The source of a legal reason's weight then is the background justification for a legal standard on which a relevant reason depends.

Moreover, there are legal standards whose background justifications represent an accommodation of competing moral or public policy considerations. Consider, for example, a possible legal rule providing that "promises for the sale of goods for more than five thousand dollars are binding

---

53 Tinker v. Des Moines Indep. Community School Dist., 393 U.S. 503, 515 (1969) (Black, J., dissenting).

and enforceable against the promisor only if they are made in writing." The enforceability of promises rests on a cluster of moral and public policy considerations identifiably separate from those on which the writing requirement rests – the morality of promise keeping and its instrumental role in a market economy. The writing requirement, however, rests on policies intended to avoid frauds by insisting on highly reliable evidence that some kinds of promises were in fact made. The background justification of such a legal standard is not a balance of the two sets of considerations. A court does not apply the rule by dispensing with the writing requirement whenever there is other reliable evidence of a promise to sell for more than five thousand dollars and the morality or social value of the particular promise is especially great. Similarly, there is no writing requirement for enforcing promises for the sale of goods for less than five thousand dollars, and the background justification for the writing requirement has no role when interpreting and applying the rule to such contracts. Rather, the five-thousand-dollar ceiling on enforceable oral promises for sales of goods implements a legislative judgment that accommodates the competing considerations in advance. The pair of background justifications coexist within separate spheres demarcated by the legal standard. One might say, alternatively, that one set of background justifications won for contracts above the ceiling while the other won for contracts below the ceiling. The complete set of legislative considerations is not available to judges in a great many particular disputes.

Additionally, there are legal standards whose background justifications represent a hand-off of competing moral or public policy considerations to another decision maker. The obvious example is the legislative charter instructing an administrative agency only to "regulate in the public interest." Even such a broad and inclusive authorization excludes some considerations, notably ad hominem considerations. The hand-off nonetheless is substantially comprehensive because it excludes few significant moral and public policy considerations. A hand-off may, however, be partial, as when child custody disputes are treated under a legal standard awarding custody according to the "best interests of the child." Many competing values are encompassed by such a standard, which often generates competing reasons. The standard also excludes some significant considerations, such as the best interests of the parents or the balance of their custodial and property interests in an equitable divorce decree. The latter are not properly available to judges when gauging weight to apply the "best interests" standard.

A hand-off also may be tilted, as when the legal standard contains adjectival law seeking to assign greater weight to some considerations. Under recent Equal Protection Clause doctrine, for example, laws that burden fundamental rights are unconstitutional unless they serve a compelling state interest. The background justifications for the fundamental right in question and for the challenged law are available to a judge when gauging weight. The relative weight of the two sets of considerations, however, is tilted in advance in favor of judicial protection of the fundamental right. Partial and tilted hand-offs support a distinction between the sets of reasons available in lawmaking and law applying, with the latter a subset of the former due to the exclusion of some general considerations of morals and public policy.

The idea of a background justification involves two areas of deep controversy. First, the background justification discussed here is of a specific legal text or group of holdings – not a general justification that opens the door to all considerations of morality and public policy. The idea that there might be no text is rejected.[54] Second, the idea of a background justification can be understood in four basic ways, with variations on each. The simplest and least plausible interpretation looks to the justification that the specific lawmakers had in mind at the time of the lawmaking. The one associated with the "original understanding" of the Constitution and other legal documents looks to the conven-

---

54 See Stanley E. Fish, *Doing What Comes Naturally* (Durham, N.C.: Duke University Press, 1989); Gary Peller, "The Metaphysics of American Law," *California Law Review*, 73 (1985): 1151–290.

tional understanding of the legal text in the culture at the time of the lawmaking. A third kind of background justification looks to the conventional understanding of the justification for a legal text at the time of the adjudication. A fourth approach looks to what an individual judge can construct as the best interpretation of the legal practice at the time of an adjudication. Each suffers from well-known difficulties, though I continue to prefer a restricted version of the third kind of background justification.[55] For present purposes, it suffices to note that each involves the exclusion of some parts of morals and policy, and each may generate legal reasons to be weighed. That is all that is needed for the good faith thesis to bite.

55 See Burton, *Law and Legal Reasoning*, pp. 83–164. Two objections to my version of legal conventionalism seem most powerful to me. One claims that, even if there is widespread agreement within the legal community on the legally correct outcome in many cases, there will be no consensus in some, including the most important litigated cases. When conventions thus run out, a judge must turn to the fourth kind of background justification. However, the hardest cases should not drive the entirety of a theory of legal reasoning, which is employed by judges and many others both inside and outside the courthouse. Further, there remains in my view a difference between a judge's view of the "best" justification for a legal text, *tout court*, and the judge's view of the "best" justification that will earn the respect of members of the legal community. The latter is constraining by convention. The other objection claims that our conventions themselves may require us to turn to independent general principles of morality or public policy. In that case, the conventions do not constrain the considerations significantly. On this point, it makes a difference whether one conceives of conventions as disciplining rules, salient solutions to coordination problems, or dispositions with respect to the legal result in a particular case. Conventions on the latter view do not refer one to independent (nonconventional) general principles of morality or public policy. See notes 1, 38 above.

Chapter 3

An illustrative case and first objections

3.1. THE JUDICIAL STANDPOINT

Much of the preceding discussion is theoretical in that it concerns how we, as observers of the judicial process, might understand judging, albeit with regard for the judicial standpoint. Typical judges would voice little of it in their opinions or elsewhere. For the most part, judges go about their business on the basis of unarticulated intuitions about the nature of judging. There are no grounds for criticism in that. My goal is not to describe typical judicial beliefs in the American legal culture, which continues to bear the marks of determinate-formalism and legal skepticism in reaction. It is, rather, to elaborate an understanding of how judging in good faith is possible and might be desirable, at a higher level of abstraction and in greater detail than judges have occasion to articulate. A thoughtful and reflective judge should be able to recognize an ideal version of what he or she tries to do from my account, but it is no ground for criticizing the good faith thesis that judges do not explain what they do in similar terms.

It is time, however, to turn from the philosophical outsider's standpoint, take up the judicial standpoint more directly, and get down to cases. There are limits to how effectively any academic writer can do this. The experience of being a judge cannot be fully mimicked or imagined. Possibly important considerations come into view only when one bears the onus of responsibility for resolving the disputes of real people. Nonetheless, it may help in understanding the good faith thesis to reduce the level of abstraction and show how it operates in the context of a specific case and at length. We then will turn to the objections that might be deployed against the good faith thesis.

3.2. *PATTERSON V. MCLEAN CREDIT UNION*[1]

Brenda Patterson was employed as an accounting clerk by the McLean Credit Union from 1972 until 1982. Her duties were mainly filing, although she also served as a backup teller. Patterson testified that she was subjected to racial harassment from the inception of her employment. She apparently was the first black person employed by the credit union and at the outset was informed of her coworkers, all white women: "probably they wouldn't like [her] because they weren't used to working with blacks."[2] Patterson testified that, unlike other clerical workers, she was assigned to dust and sweep the office and that she was singled out for criticism in public. She also testified that she was given an oppressive workload and, when she complained, was given still more work. Patterson said that she was criticized repeatedly for slowness and that her supervisor once commented that "blacks are known to work slower than whites by nature."[3] Other testimony indicated that her supervisor refused to hire other blacks, commenting that "[w]e don't need any more problems around here."[4] Patterson testified that she was never notified of opportunities for promotion and received no training for advancement. Following her layoff and dismissal in 1982, Patterson brought an action claiming,

1 491 U.S. 164 (1989). Parts of the following text are adapted from Burton, "Racial Discrimination in Contract Performance: *Patterson* and A State Law Alternative," *Harvard Civil Rights-Civil Liberties Law Review*, 25 (1990): 431–74 (with permission of the Harvard Civil Rights-Civil Liberties Law Review, © 1990 by the President and Fellows of Harvard College).
2 Brief for Petitioner at 5.
3 Ibid., at 7.
4 Ibid., at 8.

among other things, unlawful racial discrimination on the job under a part of the Civil Rights Act of 1866 now codified at 42 U.S.C. § 1981.

In *Patterson v. McLean Credit Union*,[5] the Supreme Court held that a claim for racial discrimination in the course of contract performance is not actionable under section 1981. For several reasons relevant to the following discussion, the *Patterson* case was something of a cause célèbre. Following oral argument, the Court had requested the parties to brief and argue the additional question whether *Runyon v. Mc-Crary*,[6] decided in 1976, should be overruled.[7] *Runyon* concerned whether section 1981 prohibits private schools from refusing to admit qualified black children solely on the basis of their race. The Court had held that such private discrimination – refusing to enter a contract for racial reasons – was actionable under section 1981 irrespective of state or similar public action. The Court's spontaneous decision to reconsider *Runyon* seemed to signal a new openness to overruling important civil rights decisions. That prospect generated considerable public concern. In the event, however, the Court unanimously affirmed *Runyon*'s holding. A public stir resulted nonetheless because *Patterson* was one of five cases decided the same term that denied claims of discrimination against racial minorities.[8] This resulted in legislation altering the Court's conclusions.[9] The focus of public controversy was on the other cases. The legislation's many sponsors and

5   491 U.S. 164 (1989).
6   427 U.S. 160 (1976).
7   Patterson v. McLean Credit Union, 485 U.S. 617 (1988).
8   Martin v. Wilks, 490 U.S. 755 (1989) (allowing nonparties to challenge judgments or consent decrees even when such nonparties had notice of the prior action); Wards Cove Packing Co. v. Atonio, 490 U.S. 642 (1989) (increasing plaintiff's evidentiary burden in disparate impact cases under Title VII); City of Richmond v. J. A. Croson Co., 488 U.S. 469 (1989) (invalidating minority set-aside program and requiring strict scrutiny for all nonfederal affirmative action programs); Jett v. Dallas Ind. School Dist., 491 U.S. 701 (1989) (denying availability of respondeat superior liability under Section 1981 actions).
9   Civil Rights Act of 1991, § 101, P.L. 102–166, 105 Stat. 6071 (1991).

the Bush Administration agreed from the start that *Patterson* was in error and should be reversed.[10]

For present purposes, the important questions concern the jurisprudence of the case. The facts will be assumed to be as Patterson testified and to establish racial discrimination on the job.[11] It seems safe to suppose further that the injustice of racial discrimination in the performance of a contract is widely accepted. Accordingly, the case is one in which a majority of the Supreme Court concluded that section 1981 provides no legal remedy for an injustice. We will look at the majority and dissenting opinions in turn, criticize them from the standpoint of the good faith thesis, and then describe an alternative opinion illustrating application of the good faith thesis in these circumstances.

3.2.1. The majority opinion. Justice Anthony Kennedy's reasoning for the majority was straightforward. To summarize, at the time of decision, section 1981 provided in relevant part that "[a]ll persons . . . shall have the same right . . . to make and enforce contracts . . . as is enjoyed by white citizens."[12] Justice Kennedy, supported by the conservative justices, found that racial harassment during the *performance* of a contract is neither the *making* nor the *enforcement* of a contract. Therefore, the majority concluded, racial harassment in con-

10 BNA Daily Labor Report, DLR No. 28, Feb. 9, 1990.
11 For testimony contesting Patterson's representation of the employment environment, see Brief for Respondent at 4–7. The trial court ruled that section 1981 did not provide a remedy for racial harassment and dismissed all of Patterson's claims except those pertaining to racial discrimination in promotion and discharge. The jury never considered the evidence of harassment.
12 "All persons within the jurisdiction of the United States shall have the same right in every State and Territory to make and enforce contracts, to sue, be parties, give evidence, and to the full and equal benefit of all laws and proceedings for the security of persons and property as is enjoyed by white citizens, and shall be subject to like punishment, pains, penalties, taxes, licenses, and exactions of every kind, and to no other." 42 U.S.C. § 1981 (1982).

tract performance is not unlawful discrimination under section 1981.

To elaborate, crucial to Justice Kennedy's interpretation of section 1981 is a sharp bifurcation of the statutory reference to "the same right . . . to make and enforce contracts":[13]

> By its plain terms, the relevant provision in § 1981 protects two rights: "the same right . . . to make . . . contracts" and "the same right . . . to . . . enforce contracts." The first of these protections extends only to the formation of a contract, but not to problems that may arise later from the conditions of continuing employment. . . . [T]he right to make contracts does not extend, as a matter of either logic or semantics, to conduct by the employer after the contract relation has been established, including breach of the terms of the contract or imposition of discriminatory working conditions. . . .
>
> The second of these guarantees, "the same right . . . to enforce contracts . . . as is enjoyed by white citizens," embraces protection of a legal process, and of a right of access to legal process, that will address and resolve contract-law claims without regard to race. . . . The right to enforce contracts does not, however, extend beyond conduct by an employer which impairs an employee's ability to enforce through legal process his or her established contract rights.[14]

Applying that bifurcated interpretation of section 1981 to Patterson's claims, Justice Kennedy found that the matter on appeal did not involve either a refusal to make a contract or an impairment of her ability to enforce established contract rights. Consequently, Patterson's federal remedy for racial discrimination on the job would stem solely from Title VII of the Civil Rights Act of 1964, which was more limited at the time.[15]

13 Ibid.
14 491 U.S. at 176–8.
15 42 U.S.C.§§ 2000e-2000e-17 (1982). Unlike Title VII at the time, section 1981 applied to nonemployment contracts, allowed compensatory damages, applied to employers with fewer than fifteen employees, had a longer statute of limitations, and allowed punitive damage awards in some cases.

The majority opinion is remarkable for its simplistic reasoning, evoking a text-oriented determinate-formalist jurisprudence that even the Rehnquist Court does not manifest in most of its work. In all likelihood, several justices in the majority did consider the intent of section 1981 when it was enacted in 1866. Justice Byron White, who joined the majority in *Patterson*, had dissented in *Runyon v. McCrary* on the ground that the original intent of the statute did not encompass discrimination by private actors (like contract parties); rather, it was intended to remove then-existing discrimination against the former slaves in state law, including barriers to access to the courts to protect contract rights.[16] Several members of the majority in *Runyon* had agreed with Justice White's interpretation of the history. They applied section 1981 to private discrimination to avoid incoherence resulting from what they regarded as a mistaken precedent from 1968.[17] Following *Runyon*, similar reasoning might have led the majority to affirm *Runyon* as an embedded mistake, but to refuse to extend it into the performance stage of a contract. They might have thought it imprudent to say so: Public suspicions that the Court was retreating markedly on civil rights would have been seriously aggravated had the application of these civil rights laws to private discrimination been called a "mistake." In any event, later precedents aside, the historical line of reasoning provides stronger support for the result in *Patterson* than Justice Kennedy's slim argument.

Accordingly, there would seem to be two arguments supporting the Court's decision in *Patterson*. One is textual, relying on the literal meaning of the statutory terms. The other looks to one interpretation of the original intention of the statute's authors. Thus reconstructed, the majority position represents a jurisprudence of text and original intention advocated by prominent conservative thinkers, including, in

16 See Runyon v. McCrary, 427 U.S. at 202 (1976) (White, J., dissenting).
17 The precedent was Jones v. Alfred H. Mayer Co., 392 U.S. 409 (1968) (interpreting 42 U.S.C. § 1982).

their jurisprudential writings, Justice Antonin Scalia and former Judge Robert H. Bork.[18]

3.2.2. The dissenting opinion. Justice Brennan's dissenting opinion accepted the majority's bifurcation of section 1981 into a protection against racial discrimination in contract formation and a separate protection against such discrimination in contract enforcement. To support Patterson's claim under section 1981, he consequently was forced to argue that racial harassment on the job is discrimination in the *making* of a contract.

Following a spirited defense of the correctness of *Runyon*, Justice Brennan concluded accordingly that section 1981 prohibits racial harassment on the job when such postformation conduct "demonstrates that the contract was not really made on equal terms at all."[19] He continued:

> The question in a case in which an employee makes a § 1981 claim alleging racial harassment should be whether the acts constituting harassment were sufficiently severe or pervasive as effectively to belie any claim that the contract was entered into in a racially neutral manner. Where a black employee demonstrates that she has worked in conditions substantially different from those enjoyed by similarly situated white employees, and can show the necessary racial animus, a jury may infer that the black employee has not been afforded the same right to make an employment contract as white employees.[20]

Two arguments were given in support of this conclusion. The first looked to the legislative history of section 1981. Justice Brennan found that section 1981 was originally intended in part to reach employment practices by which

18 Robert H. Bork, *The Tempting of America* (New York: Free Press, 1990); Antonin Scalia, "The Rule of Law as a Law of Rules," *University of Chicago Law Review,* 56 (1989): 1175–88.
19 491 U.S. at 207.
20 Ibid., at 208.

former slaves were employed in the South only on terms approximating their former slavery.[21] Accordingly, he inferred, its authors must have intended it to reach postformation conduct. The second argument was more conceptual: Under the majority view, section 1981 prohibits contracts entered into on racially discriminatory express terms; for example, an employer cannot lawfully require a black employee's assent to contract terms permitting racial discrimination on the job. Justice Brennan saw "no relevant distinction between that case and one in which the employer's different contractual expectations are unspoken, but become clear during the course of employment."[22]

Justice Brennan is correct if he meant that there is no moral distinction between one case in which an employer requires a black employee's assent to racially discriminatory contract terms, thereby discriminating in the making of a contract, and another case in which the discriminatory intention is revealed later. He might err, however, in claiming that there is no "relevant" distinction and that a jury therefore might infer from serious discrimination in contract performance that the contract was not made on equal terms at all. The omission of any express reference to contract performance in the statutory text itself could make the distinction legally relevant, with the consequence of leaving the law vulnerable to moral criticism. Moreover, an employer might change his mind between formation and performance, thereby breaking the validity of any inference back to a discriminatory intent at formation. Justice Kennedy reasonably rejected Justice Brennan's argument on the ground that a "plaintiff's ability to plead that the racial harassment is 'severe or pervasive' should not allow him to bootstrap . . . into a claim under section 1981 that the employer refused to offer the petitioner the 'same right to . . . make' a contract."[23]

Even to a sympathetic interpreter, Justice Brennan's opinion seems to start with the unstated assumption that the law

21 Ibid., at 193–6.
22 Ibid., at 208.
23 Ibid., at 184.

in principle envisions a racially just society and that statutes should be interpreted to achieve that end, through manipulation and artifice if necessary. Racial harassment in contract performance surely is unjust. Struggling to bring racial discrimination in contract performance within the concept of contract formation therefore would be tempting. The Court majority, by contrast, does not assume that the law envisions a racially just society in all respects, justifying the manipulation of statutes to reach results indicated by that vision. Rather, it assumes that the statutory civil rights laws should be understood as a representation of Congress's vision of a racially just society only in some respects – namely, those enumerated in specific legislation. Racial discrimination in contract performance is not among the enumerated protections in section 1981. Therefore, the majority concluded, any remedies for such discrimination are left to other statutes, state law, and private conscience even when racial injustice results.[24] The majority and dissenting opinions thus suggest two fundamentally different approaches to judging, which in brief may be called a jurisprudence of text and a jurisprudence of principle.

To many, the difference between these two prominent jurisprudences of judging is a deep and unbridgeable gap between two different activities, both of which happen to be called judging. To model them, a jurisprudence of text conceives of the law strictly as promulgated by human beings. On this view, the text, the meanings of the text in ordinary language, and the intentions of the authors of the text, are all that there is to consult. A jurisprudence of principle, by contrast, conceives of the law as general principles of justice

24 Ibid., at 188 ("our role is limited to interpreting what Congress may do and has done. The statute before us, which is only part of Congress' extensive civil rights legislation, does not cover the acts of discrimination alleged here"). See also Patterson v. McLean Credit Union, 485 U.S. 617, 619 (1988) (ordering rehearing on question of whether *Runyon v. McCrary* should be overruled) ("the claim of any litigant for the application of a rule to its case should not be influenced by the Court's view of the worthiness of the litigant in terms of extralegal criteria").

implicit or imperfectly manifested in rules and cases crafted by human beings. On this view, the judge is to do justice in each case, paying lip service to the rules as prudent to avoid losing public respect for the Court. There might be little common ground from which to carry on an intelligent discussion between these two jurisprudences, each of which claims to identify the law as something else altogether. Accordingly, Justice Kennedy presumably thinks that Justice Brennan is plain wrong to treat the principle of racial justice as a part of the law, while Brennan thinks that Kennedy is similarly wrong to deny the legal status of that principle. Disagreement on the proper application of section 1981 in *Patterson* results. The disagreement on the statutory question thus slides into jurisprudential disagreement, about which the justices have little to say to one another. Polarization occurs when the justices retreat from the common ground to their jurisprudential bunkers.

3.2.3. Results or reasons? From the standpoint of the good faith thesis, two features of the jurisprudences of text and principle, represented by the opinions in *Patterson*, merit attention. First and foremost, both opinions treat legal standards as providers of determinate results. The majority opinion moves in its reasoning from the statutory text directly to the result in the case. In straight syllogistic form, it focuses on the omission of any express reference in section 1981 to the performance of a contract and therefore refuses to draw the conclusion that racial discrimination in contract performance is actionable under that statute. Justice Brennan similarly moves from a general principle of racial justice directly to the result, adding a doubtful link to the statutory text as a formality or an afterthought. Neither jurisprudence allows room for a legal standard – whether statutory text or implicit principle – to generate a reason instead of a necessary result.

The second interesting feature is that the opinions seem to claim a kind of jurisprudential exclusivity, as though the standards each identifies as the law were the *only* kind of legal standards. Justice Kennedy paid homage to the principle of racial justice rhetorically, but did not even hint that it might generate any reasons for judicial action to be weighed in judicial deliberations.[25] Justice Brennan's situation is different. He could not have granted that the statutory text supported the majority while claiming that it was outweighed by the principle of racial justice. Due to principles of legislative supremacy, his job was to interpret that statutory text, not to supplant it. Crucially, he did not seem aware of any good argument from the text. So he gave a bad one, trying to cram contract performance into formation.

Determinacy of results and jurisprudential exclusivity work together to produce an appearance of recalcitrant disagreement. The judge in any event must reach one and only one result because only one action is possible at the outcome of a judicial deliberation. Determinacy of results, however, requires each genuine and applicable legal standard to dictate the result. When two standards indicate incompatible results, therefore, exclusivity requires one of them to be denied any legal effect. Consequently, judges in disagreement must deny all validity to the competing arguments of their colleagues. Recalcitrant disagreement follows because they then have nothing in common to talk about. Onlookers might think that the law itself is plagued by stubborn indeterminacy and political combat.

Whether in the mind of the judge or the interpreter, however, determinacy of results and jurisprudential exclusivity are consequences of accepting the determinacy condition – the presupposition that judges deciding controversies can fulfill their duty to uphold the law only when the law determines one correct result in a lawsuit and they reach that result. By rejecting the determinacy condition, the good faith thesis offers a way to a depolarized jurisprudence of judging. The good faith thesis would not move from a legal standard directly to the result, as Kennedy moves from statutory text to result and Brennan moves from principle to

25 Ibid. ("The law now reflects society's consensus that discrimination based on the color of one's skin is a profound wrong of tragic dimension").

result. Rather, the statutory text, implicit legal principles, and all other relevant legal standards *first would generate reasons*, all of which must be identified before any are assigned a weight. Results would be based on the weight of the reasons at a next step. The good faith thesis consequently allows all relevant legal standards to keep their legal status even when they do not control the result in a case.[26]

Inserting a role for legal reasons between the legal standards and the result allows for an entirely different kind of disagreement. Judges can acknowledge the existence and relevance of all the legal reasons while they disagree on questions of weight and the outcome. Thus, even within the jurisprudence of text, it might be that the original intent and the ordinary meaning of the text support different results. There is no need to adopt a rigid hierarchy between the two interpretative modes or to omit reference to one without explanation as though it did not even generate a reason. It is more plausible to suppose that each generates a reason for one result, but that the reasons must be weighed before reaching a result. More important, there is no need for the justices to align themselves with one or the other jurisprudence of judging, denying the validity of reasons generated within the other approach. Justice Kennedy could acknowledge the relevance and force of Justice Brennan's historical argument while finding that the weight of that argument is

26 The good faith thesis thus takes a partial position on the content of the law that judges have a duty to uphold. The jurisprudence of text denies that principles, unless expressed in the document, are a part of the law. The good faith thesis rejects this view. The constitutional text and history contain no evidence of a constitutional power for Congress to raise an air force, but the principle of national security implicit in the power to raise an army and navy, U.S. Const. Art. I, § 8, surely suffices to sustain that congressional power. Further, adherents of the jurisprudence of text commonly rely on principles of federalism and separation of powers; they should be hard-pressed to deny that implicit principles are a part of the law. The important debate is about which implicit principles are law, not whether implicit principles as such can be law. See David Lyons, "Substance, Process, and the Outcome in Constitutional Theory," *Cornell Law Review*, 72 (1987): 745–64, at 746–8.

weaker than the combination of Justice White's history and the ordinary meaning of the text. Justice Brennan could acknowledge the relevance and force of Justice Kennedy's textual argument while attaching greater weight to the principle of racial justice (if the necessary implications of a constitutional statute are not disregarded). Disagreement would be on questions of weight and results, not on the identity of the law. The common ground, in which collegial discussion can be held and respect for differences earned, thereby would be secured jurisprudentially.

3.3.   AN ALTERNATIVE OPINION

The principal ramifications of the good faith thesis can be made concrete and explicit by describing an alternative opinion on the facts of *Patterson* and the law in force when it was decided. In operation, the good faith thesis allows text, history, principle, and precedent to be integrated into a single mode of adjudication that accommodates disagreement. It is not necessary for a judge to prove the negative by denying every argument for a conclusion contrary to the one reached in the event. That seems necessary only when discretion to weigh relevant reasons is thought to be lawless and impermissible. A judge, however, may acknowledge and take into account conflicting reasons and weigh them in good faith.[27] Consequently, the range of relevant reasons may expand beyond that considered in either opinion.

The starting point should be the statute. The Court has both legal and moral duties to uphold the law.[28] In this case, 42 U.S.C. § 1981 is the law invoked by Patterson in her complaint. It provides in relevant part that "[a]ll persons . . . shall have the same right . . . to make and enforce contracts . . . as is enjoyed by white citizens." This rule designates a class – all persons – and attaches a legal consequence to membership in that class – shall have the same right to

27 See Part II.
28 See § 7.3.

make and enforce contracts. It is settled law that racial discrimination within the prohibition of section 1981 entitles the victim to compensatory and possibly punitive damages.[29] The question in this case is whether Brenda Patterson was denied equality in the right to make and enforce contracts because she is black. Deciding this question requires interpretation of the key phrase in section 1981, which mandates equality of contract between the races.

At least six legal reasons support or deny Patterson's claim under section 1981. First, the ordinary meaning of the key phrase suggests that Patterson was not denied equality of contract. As Justice Kennedy might argue, the process of contracting is divided into formation, performance, and enforcement stages. Patterson claims that she was a victim of racial discrimination in the performance stage of her employment contract. The statute does not refer to the performance stage, however. Therefore, the statutory language yields no obvious reason for concluding that Patterson should receive compensation under this statute. The identification of legal reasons, however, does not stop with the ordinary meaning. Only if the law must dictate the result must we confine our search for reasons to the most obvious one. Because we conclude only that section 1981 by its ordinary meaning generates no reason to grant Patterson's claim, we can go on to identify other legal reasons to be considered in legal deliberations.

Second, the legal meaning of the key phrase might suggest that Patterson was denied equality of contract. Section 1981's reference to the "right . . . to make and enforce contracts" is ambiguous. It might refer to two separate rights, or to one unified right amounting to the legal power of contract. If it refers to two separate rights, then rights of performance as such drop out of the protection of section 1981, as all nine justices of the Supreme Court supposed. If it refers to one legal power of contract, however, that power might encom-

---

29 Charles A. Sullivan, Michael J. Zimmer, & Richard F. Richards, *Employment Discrimination*, 2d ed., vol. 2 (Boston: Little, Brown & Co., 1988), § 15.1.

pass the performance stage along with formation and enforcement in an integrated whole. The credit union's discrimination against Patterson while she was on the job would then be a reason for it to compensate her under section 1981.

The legal meaning of the phrase should be determined according to the law of contracts, which constitutes the right in question. Section 1981 does not establish an independent statutory right to make and enforce contracts. No one interprets that statute to support a claim upon which relief may be granted for breach of contract. Section 1981 therefore must refer to a right that exists in the law of contracts. Moreover, section 1981 does not establish an independent federal contract right for persons of color. It requires that all persons have the same right "as is enjoyed by white citizens." The contractual rights of white citizens are not established by the statute. The rights of whites and persons of color would not be the same if only the latter rights originated in a federal statute. Additionally, the statute's dependence on the law of contracts is evidenced by the power of state courts and legislatures to change the right to make and enforce contracts, maybe even including its abolition, on a racially nondiscriminatory basis. Section 1981 does not freeze the rights of persons of color due to the supremacy of federal statutes while the rights of others can be changed because they are based in state law.[30]

According to the law of contracts, the power of contract

---

30 A related question is whether the relevant law of contracts is that prevailing in 1866, the time of statutory enactment, or that prevailing now. Two arguments establish that the relevant one is the contemporary understanding of what it means in law to make and enforce contracts. First, it would be absurd to interpret section 1981 to guarantee nonwhites the same rights that white citizens had in 1866 when white citizens now have different rights. Second, section 1981 should be interpreted in a way that coordinates the statute with the law that actually governs the relevant transactions and relations as a practical matter. Accordingly, the contemporary law of contracts should determine whether the language of section 1981 comprehends separate rights to make and enforce contracts or, rather, a single power of contract encompassing formation, performance, and enforcement.

encompasses rights of performance within an integrated concept of contract. Forming a contract creates obligations of performance for later. The world envisioned by the contract must be represented in its terms, and the parties must commit themselves each to do his or her part to bring that world into being by acting according to its terms in the future. A contract at its inception looks forward to its performance and enforcement. Performing a contract, in turn, depends centrally on formation. Performance occurs when a party in fact does his or her part to bring the world then envisioned into being. Enforcing a contract looks backward to both formation and performance. The primary judicial remedies for breach of contract depend on a comparison of the contract as formed with the contract as performed.[31] The contract will not be enforced at all if the world envisioned at formation does not fix the obligation to perform it later. Nor will the contract be enforced unless harm due to nonperformance is the measure of the remedy. A contract is enforced when compensation is measured by the difference in value to the injured party between the possible world envisioned by the contract at formation and the actual world as it happens during performance. The performance stage of a contract cannot be excised from the "right . . . to make and enforce contracts" within a coherent understanding of the modern law of contracts. Accordingly, the legal meaning of the key phrase refers to a unified legal power of contract and generates a reason supporting Patterson's claim.[32]

The third and fourth reasons stem from the legislative history of section 1981, in which we again find two interpretations, one of which supports Patterson's claim. On one interpretation (third), the authors of section 1981 were concerned only to invalidate state laws and state action, such

31 For instance, the standard measure of damages for breach of warranty in a contract for the sale of goods is the difference in value between the goods as promised and as delivered. U.C.C. § 2-714.
32 For elaboration, see Burton, "Racial Discrimination in Contract Performance," at 455–58; Steven J. Burton & Eric G. Andersen, "The World of a Contract," *Iowa Law Review*, 75 (1990): 861–76.

as the Black Codes adopted in the Reconstruction South, that discriminated against former slaves.[33] Patterson, however, claimed that a private employer discriminated against her. *Runyon v. McCrary* applied section 1981 to private discrimination in the making of a contract, but it might be treated as an embedded mistake that should not be extended to the performance stage. So this interpretation of the history supplies a reason to deny her claim. On the other interpretation (fourth), following Justice Brennan, there is some evidence that the authors of section 1981 also sought to reach employment practices by which former slaves were employed in the South only on terms approximating their former slavery.[34] This would encompass postformation conduct by a private actor, like the alleged discrimination against Patterson by the credit union. Each of these interpretations generates a legal reason for deciding *Patterson* one way or the other. There is no "contradiction" between these two interpretations of the history any more than among all of the relevant reasons; a choice between them is compulsory only if each must dictate the result.

Fifth, *Runyon* is a precedent that generates a further reason for upholding Patterson's claim under the principle of equal treatment under law. It would be anomalous to hold that a private school must admit persons of all races without racial discrimination, but may require blacks to sit in the back of the classroom without any federal remedy for that discrimination.[35] Similarly, we should not hold that an employer violates section 1981 by refusing to hire someone on racial grounds, but may fire an employee on racial grounds the next day without liability under that law.[36]

---

33 See Runyon v. McCrary, 427 U.S. at 202 (1976) (White, J., dissenting).
34 Patterson v. McLean Credit Union, 491 U.S. at 193–6 (Brennan, J., dissenting).
35 Address by Laurence H. Tribe, U.S. Law Week Constitutional Law Conference (Sept. 8–9, 1989), reprinted in 58 U.S.L.W. 2200, 2201 (1989).
36 Contra, Taggart v. Jefferson County Child Support Enforcement Unit, 935 F. 2d 947 (8th Cir. 1991) (en banc) (making eight circuits holding

Sixth, as Justice Kennedy wrote, "The law now reflects society's consensus that discrimination based on the color of one's skin is a profound wrong of tragic dimension."[37] Particular instances of this general principle include the Civil War Amendments to the Constitution, the Civil Rights Acts of 1866 and 1964, the Voting Rights Act of 1965, and numerous other statutes. The principle of racial justice that ties these laws together has been used by the Court in numerous cases since *Brown v. Board of Education*[38] to provide legal redress for that wrong, including cases reinvigorating section 1981[39] and related statutes.[40] It is conventionally accepted as law by members of the legal community and others. The principle of racial justice, too, provides a reason for upholding Patterson's claim of racial discrimination. Racial justice is not only a general principle of political morality, which generates moral reasons for action. Reasons stemming from the concurring legal principle are warranted as grounds for judicial decision by convention, though results indicated by this principle should not be contradicted by the implications of a clear (and constitutional) statutory text. The principle of racial justice generates a legal reason supporting Patterson's claim because it is well embedded in the authoritative legal materials and is consistent with the legal meaning of the key statutory phrase, interpreted in accordance with the law of contracts.

We have identified six legal reasons generated respectively from six abstract legal standards – the ordinary meaning of the key statutory phrase, the legal meaning of that phrase, each of two interpretations based in the legislative history, the principle of equal treatment, and the principle of racial justice. There is no need for a theory of interpretation to arrange these legal reasons in a stable and comprehensive

that a claim of discharge on the basis of race is postformation conduct outside scope of section 1981 after *Patterson*).
37 491 U.S., at 188.
38 347 U.S. 483 (1954).
39 Runyon v. McCrary, 427 U.S. 160 (1976).
40 Jones v. Alfred Mayer Co., 392 U.S. 409 (1968) (interpreting 42 U.S.C. § 1982).

hierarchy of authorities based on the jurisprudential status of the generating abstract standards. Only if the law must dictate the result must we create such a hierarchy to avoid concluding that the law is "contradictory" because it requires incompatible judicial actions. We may do so in part, as when the principle of legislative supremacy in a democratic government implies that the principle of racial justice cannot support a result contradicted by the implications of a clear (and constitutional) statute. Weight otherwise is a property of the concrete legal reasons in a case, not of abstract legal standards.[41] Moreover, the weight of each legal reason varies depending on the congeries of reasons in which it is located.[42] Consequently, having identified the legal reasons in *Patterson*, and found two plausible interpretations of the legislated text, we should weigh all six in legal deliberations.

Each of the six legal reasons, upon its identification, has an equal share of the total weight at the action threshold. On consideration, however, they are not thus unweighted. Consider first the fact that the discriminatory action by the McLean Credit Union was private action, which might be outside the prohibition of section 1981 following one interpretation based in the legislative history. This would be a much stronger reason if *Runyon* did not impose section 1981 liability when a private employer refuses to hire someone on racial grounds. Its force when an employer engages in racial harassment on the job, even if not dispositive, blunts the force of Justice White's interpretation based in the legislative history on the same facts. The *Runyon* reason takes on that increment of weight. Moreover, the anomaly of requiring nondiscriminatory hiring while permitting discriminatory employment practices thereafter is repulsive, in light of both the principle of racial justice and the contract law meaning of the key statutory phrase. The reasons generated by those two legal standards also should get more than their initial weights at the expense of the reason generated by Justice

41   See § 2.3.1.
42   See § 2.3.2.

THE GOOD FAITH THESIS

White's history. It could be argued, to the contrary, that *Runyon* was mistaken due to the legislative history and should not carry the full force of precedent. On this basis, someone else might hesitate to extend section 1981 to prohibit racial discrimination in the performance of a contract. I do not understand the principle of equal treatment to allow a precedent to be undercut based only on reasons that were available to the deciding court.[43] If someone else has a different and defensible understanding of precedent in statutory cases, he or she can assign the weights differently without entering the forbidden realm of judging in bad faith. I would think them mistaken nonetheless.

The fact that the alleged racial discrimination occurred in the performance stage of a contract, which is not expressly mentioned in the statutory text, might retain its initial weight. It can be argued, however, that this reason should lose some weight to the contract law meaning, which emphasizes the unity of the legal power of contract. A statute whose obvious purpose is to guarantee equality of contract should not be interpreted to split the power of contract up unnecessarily, producing avoidable inequality of contract in practice. The power to make contracts on a racially nondiscriminatory basis is pointless when breach and discharge are allowed on a racially prejudiced basis. The power to enforce contracts, moreover, is hollow if limited to the right to file a lawsuit while race-based breach is left unremedied. The right to make and enforce contracts better serves its accepted background justification if it is interpreted as a single integrated legal power, not two separate rights bifurcated to exclude performance. Section 1981 would then envision a world in which persons of all races have the same legal power of contract, which also comports well with the conventional principle of racial justice.

The weight of each legal reason in *Patterson* thus depends on the other reasons in the case. The problem of weight can

43 Patterson v. McLean Credit Union, 491 U.S. 164, 172–5 (requiring "special justification" for any departure from the doctrine of stare decisis). See § 3.4.4.

be approached in two steps. Having identified the legal reasons, each can be assigned an equal share of the total at the action threshold due to their legal status. The ratio of weights then can be adjusted as the ensemble of background justifications indicate in the circumstances, taking weight from one reason to enhance another while maintaining a constant sum. Additional adjustments can be made as needed until a concrete judgment emerges. The law does not dictate a result in advance because the full congeries of reasons is too variable and unforeseeable. Judges consequently must sift the combinations and permutations of legal reasons after the case materializes in litigation. They cannot then *prove* that the judgment, and no other, is legally required. We cannot give a determinate calculus for discretionary judgment. Nonetheless, the judicial duty to uphold the law can be fulfilled when a judge has discretion by making that judgment which, in the judge's good faith opinion, is supported by the stronger legal reasons.

Recalcitrant jurisprudential or political disagreement need not lie beneath the disagreement in *Patterson*, as so many contemporary legal theorists suppose. To be sure, my disagreement with both the majority and the dissent is jurisprudential. I think they are mistaken to rely on one standard or two consistent legal standards to the exclusion of other relevant law like the law of contracts. But disagreement on the legal result surely is possible in a way that places all positions in good faith – by dispensing with any need to dismiss as legally invalid the standards relied on by another. We can agree on all the relevant legal reasons at the same time we disagree on the result due to disagreement on matters of weight. Once the ensemble of relevant legal reasons is expanded, there is every reason to expect that some judges would come to a different conclusion.

3.4. FIRST OBJECTIONS

The good faith thesis offers a coherent and, at first sight, attractive alternative to the politicized jurisprudence that results from a hidden obeisance to the determinacy condition. However, the now-apparent undesirability of the determinacy condition does not show it to be unsound conceptually or indefensible normatively. The next three chapters will explore at length the grounds for accepting the determinacy condition, which poses the major objection to the good faith thesis. First, however, we will raise and respond to four less threatening objections, the responses to which further clarify the good faith thesis and head off possible misunderstandings.

3.4.1. *Meanings of "good faith."* Some might think that the good faith thesis provides a very weak constraint on judicial conduct because good faith is all that is required. This would confuse two related meanings of "good faith." The thesis takes its name from a legal obligation very often imposed in American law on a person who enjoys a discretionary legal power. Sometimes, good faith requires only that a person exercise discretion honestly or sincerely – with a kind heart and an empty head, as the saying goes.[44] This is the normal meaning of the term in commercial law, such as the law of good faith purchase. Bad faith occurs, on this meaning, when a person uses discretion dishonestly or maliciously.[45] This requirement alone would be a weak constraint on judicial conduct. In other contexts, however, good faith requires a person with discretion to act on the right kinds of reasons.

---

44 Professor Soper in his theory of law uses good faith in the sense of honesty. See E. Philip Soper, *A Theory of Law* (Cambridge: Harvard University Press, 1984), pp. 79, 80, 119–22 (1984). See also H. L. A. Hart, *Essays on Bentham* (Oxford: Clarendon Press, 1983), pp. 155–61 (judges need not believe or pretend to believe that legal obligations are moral obligations for citizens); Joseph Raz, *The Authority of Law* (Oxford: Clarendon Press, 1979), p. 155 (judge must either believe or pretend to believe that the law imposes moral obligations). These uses of good faith go to a judge's honest belief in the morality of a decision, not its conformity to the law.

45 U.C.C. § 1-201(19). Some recent developments in the law of torts seem to equate bad faith with malicious conduct or intentional harms to pecuniary interests. See, for example, Seaman's Direct Buying Service, Inc. v. Standard Oil Co. of Calif., 36 Cal. 3d 752 (1984).

Bad faith in the second sense is an abuse of discretion of a particular kind. By using the latter of these meanings, the good faith thesis permits a discussion of judicial duty without implying that bad faith must involve personal dishonesty, dissembling, or depravity. Good faith in the latter sense requires judges to uphold the law, not only to believe sincerely that they are doing so.

To clarify, consider by analogy familiar parts of the law governing persons who enjoy discretion under a legal duty. For example, a contract for the sale of goods might confer discretion in performance on one of the parties, as when a buyer promises to take the goods and pay a fixed price only if personally satisfied with their quality. The buyer by agreement in such a case enjoys discretion to judge the quality of the goods but is committed to pay the agreed price if the goods are satisfactory to him or her. The buyer forgoes the opportunity to substitute a buy on the market for the contract for the sole reason that the price falls before performance. In principle, a buyer can get out of the deal legitimately by claiming dissatisfaction based on the qualities of the goods. A buyer breaches the contract by acting in bad faith when dissatisfaction is feigned as a pretext to take advantage of a fallen market price. More generally, any contract can be breached when discretion in performance is used to recapture the opportunity to act on a reason forgone on formation of the contract.[46]

Similarly, government officials may enjoy discretion within the bounds of the law and must exercise it in good faith. For example, a criminal prosecutor has great discretion to decide which criminal cases to pursue. That discretion is fully respected by the law as long as decisions are taken on appropriate grounds of policy or principle. A prosecutor can decline to prosecute cases involving the simple possession of marijuana while allocating prosecutorial resources to cases of

46 For example, Greer Properties, Inc. v. LaSalle National Bank, 874 F.2d 457 (7th Cir. 1989); Steven J. Burton, "Breach of Contract and the Common Law Duty to Perform in Good Faith," *Harvard Law Review*, 94 (1980): 369–403.

sale and distribution or to violent crimes. Prosecutors may differ on how to pursue the goals of public order within available resources, in which the weight of deterrence, retributive, and other legitimate considerations properly can be different for different prosecutors. But a prosecutor cannot properly decide to prosecute a case because he or she received a bribe, or because the defendant is Afro-American, or to gain political advantage with his partisan sponsors, even with full disclosure. Some such instances of bad faith are unlawful; others are only unethical. In either case, the bad faith prosecutor uses his discretion to act on an improper reason – one excluded by his duty to enforce the law.

The good faith thesis claims that judges are under a legal duty in all cases to exercise discretion on the basis of reasons provided by the law, and not on reasons excluded by judicial duty or the law's standards. Upon taking office, judges give up the opportunity to act on some kinds of reasons in the performance of the duties of their office – most obviously ad hominem reasons, but also reasons excluded by the law's authoritative standards and moral or policy reasons not warranted by the law as grounds for judicial decision. Using judicial discretion to recapture such forgone opportunities is bad faith and a breach of judicial duty. Thus, judicial duty requires judges to weigh the relevant legal reasons in good faith even when the outcome is underdetermined by the law.

Judicial discretion of course need not be coextensive with the discretion of a contracting party, a criminal prosecutor, or any other legal actor. The concept of discretion implies that a person acts under some kind of constraint. The scope of discretion depends on the reasons excluded by the relevant duty and the standards it activates. A contracting party, for example, might enjoy discretion in performance and exercise that discretion in good faith by acting for some but not other reasons of advantage to self. A judge, by contrast, thereby would violate the principle of impartiality. A criminal prosecutor might properly act on reasons of resource scarcity to decline a prosecutorial opportunity. A judge, however, might not properly act on such reasons to decline to try a criminal defendant. In general, it seems likely that the reasons excluded by judicial duty and the law's standards constrain judges more than other actors. When judges weigh legal reasons in good faith – without recapturing the forgone opportunity to act on excluded reasons even in assigning weight to a legal reason – they are constrained by the law even when they have discretion.

3.4.2. Opportunism. Neither the law nor judicial duty can guarantee that judges in fact will act in good faith. A judge acting in bad faith may lack the will to engage in the kind of legal reasoning outlined by the good faith thesis. The law can do nothing to prevent such bad faith on the part of judges with faulty characters. The possibility of bad faith by conscious lying is a feature of all possible versions of judicial duty; this possibility cannot distinguish good from bad practical understandings. It might be thought, however, that the good faith thesis is especially inviting to opportunistic behavior by judges with guile. The thesis might have inadequate bite because there are so many legal reasons that can be conjured up in cases that come before judges; the six identified in the alternative opinion in *Patterson* might be contracted or expanded to suit a judge's hidden agenda instrumentally. The ability to manipulate the list of legal reasons, and thereby to counterfeit the weights, it might be claimed, leaves a judge effectively unconstrained with respect to the result in the case.

A judge conceivably might approach the law as a bull-headed lawyer would approach a contract he wants to break. Such a judge might be dissuaded from advancing his or her own agenda only by the kind of determinacy of results required by determinate-formalism, if then. Even a modicum of sensitivity to the diversity of ways in which facts can combine themselves, however, counsels a rejection of such simpleminded formalism, especially as a definition of what it means for the law to constrain judges.[47] Rather than throw-

47 See §§ 5.3 and following.

ing the gates open to unbridled judicial license, the alternative is to develop an ethic of good judging requiring judges in the first place not to take up a bullheaded attitude toward the law.

Judges acting within the scope of their office are not in the same situation as a private citizen or a lawyer with a client.[48] They do not act under a default rule that might leave them free to do whatever they want to do in the absence of a determinate legal directive to act otherwise. The default rule for them is a duty to uphold the law in all cases; demands for lawful conduct do not evaporate when a judge has discretion. For a judge who takes that duty seriously, the constellation of facts in the case constrains deliberations by invoking a limited set of legal reasons. In a tough case, they will be numerous and competing. It may be better nonetheless for judges to take into account all the relevant legal considerations than artificially to exclude all but one or two for the sake of determinacy. It remains fruitless to try constraining a judge who, anyway, is in bad faith. The law should not turn its back on any of the reasons that should be considered in order best to do justice under the law.

3.4.3. *Particularism and balancing.* It might be objected that the good faith thesis calls for decision of each particular case on its own facts in a way that seems incompatible with the Rule of Law. Basic standards of legality and practical reasoning require that a justification be generalizable.[49] That is, variable outcomes of the kind allowed by the good faith thesis might be thought incompatible with the idea of legally justified action. In legal terms, this objection might question whether the good faith thesis conforms to such requirements as that rules be applied consistently, that like cases be decided alike, or that the law be interpreted as a matter of integrity, all of which are versions of the generalizability requirement.

48 See § 4.4.2.
49 See § 8.3.

Crucially, however, the requirement that a justification be generalizable can latch onto either reasons or results. In most philosophical discussions, the distinction is unimportant because each reason is isolated for consideration in the abstract on the assumption that it requires a result, all else being equal. In actual adjudication, however, all else never is equal. The distinction takes on significance.

The good faith thesis accepts a requirement of generalizability over legal standards and legal reasons – the identification of legal reasons in any case. It is crucial that the judge act on legal reasons each of which, if a reason in one case, would be a reason in any case containing the relevant facts. However, for two now familiar reasons, legality can be maintained in their identification while weight varies in their consideration. The force of the applicable law is to provide a reason to be considered along with other legal reasons, and the weight of a legal reason varies with the congeries of reasons in which it is located. Consequently, justification is maintained in the practical sense that the result must be supported by good and adequate legal reasons. We might follow the mature Karl Llewellyn by insisting that a judge have a *disposition* to generalize the ratio of weights and the result in a case.[50] This highlights the fact that a particular judicial action should be generalizable at the time it is taken. It would seem incompatible with the purposeful pragmatism of adjudication, however, to require a judge to follow weightings set in advance of a case or to establish weightings for cases that have not yet materialized. The identical congeries of reasons is unlikely to recur. Even a small change in the facts can have a large effect on weight.

A related objection might claim that the good faith thesis endorses "balancing" as distinct from "categorization," as the terms are sometimes used in U.S. constitutional theory.

---

50 Karl N. Llewellyn, *The Common Law Tradition: Deciding Appeals* (Boston: Little, Brown & Co., 1961), pp. 217–19 ("To be . . . lawful exercise of discretion . . . , the action . . . must be undertaken with a feeling, explicit or implicit, of willingness, or readiness, to do the like again, if, as, and when a like case may arise").

It may be said that approaching adjudication as an exercise in categorization surely could be judging in good faith. In *Tinker v. Des Moines Independent Community School District*,[51] for example, the Supreme Court held that a high school student who wore a black arm band to a public school in 1965 to protest the Vietnam War could not be suspended from school for that reason. This protest was held to be "symbolic speech" within the protection of the First Amendment. Justice Hugo Black dissented in a familiar way, maintaining that wearing the black arm band was not within the Speech Clause.[52] For him, talking was within the freedom of speech; other expression was outside that category, regardless of any balance of reasons. One can disagree with Justice Black's conclusion and method, but it is hard to believe he was judging in bad faith.

The problem with this objection lies in a certain analytical imprecision in the contrast drawn between categorization and balancing. Indeed, unless determinate-formalism is embraced as the only sound theory of adjudication, categorization and balancing are not analytically distinct modes of adjudication. Judicial categorization of a case surely depends on reasons. A need to balance the reasons can be avoided only if the law in question limits the relevant reasons to one or makes one reason overriding regardless (determinate-formalism). As soon as the law admits that there may be two coequal reasons for a categorization, the possibility of conflict arises and the need for balancing is presented. The outcome of the balancing of reasons will be a categorization, as the majority in *Tinker* considered the relevant reasons and concluded that wearing the arm band was within the freedom of speech. The theoretical contrast in fact concerns the aspects of legal reasoning to be made salient to the judge or in the opinion, which may be important rhetorically. But a rhetorical objection does not challenge the good faith thesis on its own terms, which are conceptual and normative.

51   393 U.S. 503 (1969).
52   393 U.S. at 515.

3.4.4 Judicial lawmaking. Judges can be bound to uphold the law only if there is binding law they have a duty to apply. It may be objected that a distinction between lawmaking and law applying is not maintainable. Judges may have the power to make the law, explicitly by overruling or surreptitiously by interpretation. Consequently, it may seem that judges are not in fact bound by the law because they themselves can change it in any case. The problem is most acute in the controversial cases decided by the Supreme Court and the highest courts of the states. In these cases, it might be thought, the judges have more room for choice than that contemplated by the good faith thesis.

The good faith thesis does not deny that judges sometimes make law. The judges of a highest state court doubtless have an important legal power to make and revise the common law, as well as to supervise the lower courts for error. Cases like those shifting from products liability only for negligence to strict liability can have large consequences in the economy.[53] The Supreme Court's power to make constitutional law, by contrast, is hotly contested at least with respect to its scope. No doubt law is being made when the Supreme Court announces, for example, that a confession may not be admitted in evidence in a criminal proceeding unless the police issued a Miranda warning in a timely fashion, following closely the language of the Supreme Court's opinion.[54] The explosive growth of statutory law since the New Deal raises interesting and difficult questions about judicial lawmaking when the legislature has spoken constitutionally though not recently.[55] Especially when statutes are broad and vague, like the Sherman Antitrust Act,[56] a distinction between statutory interpretation and lawmaking is blurred. Statutes like Article 2 of the Uniform Commercial Code were probably

---

53 For example, Greenman v. Yuba Power Prod., 59 Cal. 2d 57 (1963).
54 Miranda v. Arizona, 384 U.S. 436 (1966).
55 See Guido Calabresi, *A Common Law for the Age of Statutes* (Cambridge: Harvard University Press, 1982).
56 15 U.S.C. § 1 et seq.

intended to wipe the slate clean of ossified law and to start a process of accretive judicial lawmaking anew.[57]

There is no need here to take positions on controversial questions about the scope of the judicial lawmaking powers. The common law power is sufficiently settled to serve as the vehicle for discussion. To the extent they exist, constitutional and statutory lawmaking powers might be understood by analogy to the common law power with adjustments as needed. This tack leaves open many important and interesting questions. The scope of the Supreme Court's constitutional power, for example, is contested as a matter of constitutional law and theory. The good faith thesis takes no stand on this question, though it might have implications for the terms in which the constitutional debates should be carried out. In particular, the thesis suggests that the determinacy condition may have played an inapt role with untoward consequences in many of the discussions, much as it crimps the deliberations in *Patterson*. The thesis suggests further that the discussions might be more fruitful if they were recast with resolute regard toward reasons for action. It is not among the present ambitions of the good faith thesis, however, to propose solutions to the longstanding problems of constitutional law and theory or to trace out its ramifications in other specific areas of the law.

The problem with the objection to distinguishing lawmaking and law application is twofold. First, it seems that, for many, the law is whatever determines the result in a case. For example, the Sherman Antitrust Act's prohibition on "unreasonable restraints of trade" does not, without more, sufficiently indicate the result in any case. A court supplies the "something more" and, mainly on that basis, reaches a decision. By giving the determinacy condition undue weight, the something more may be considered the relevant law. It would be difficult or pointless indeed to dis-

57 Richard Danzig, "A Comment on the Jurisprudence of the Uniform Commercial Code," *Stanford Law Review*, 27 (1975): 621–35; Zipporah Batshaw Wiseman, "The Limits of Vision: Karl Llewellyn and the Merchant Rules," *Harvard Law Review*, 100 (1987): 465–545, at 495–503.

tinguish between the making and application of law if the law consists of whatever determines the result in a case. But that is a poor way to go about conceiving the law. One counterexample should suffice to reject it: A court might hold that equal athletic facilities for men and women in universities are not required by an antidiscrimination law because, it says, women do not enjoy sports as much as men do. The belief that women do not like sports determines the result at least as much as anything does. That belief is not the law, however, because it does not, without more, guide conduct. Rather, it is a (stereotyped) factual generalization of the kind Kenneth Culp Davis called a "legislative fact."[58] Accordingly, we should reject the premise that treats as "law" whatever determines the result in a case.

The second problem with the objection lies in the oversimple way of referring to the making, interpretation, and application of law. Without a clear idea of what each of these terms encompasses conceptually, it would not be surprising for them to seem so intertwined that a clear distinction cannot be sustained. This is the thrust of the objection. As throughout this book, we should draw the needed distinctions in terms of reasons for action or, more specifically on this occasion, sets of reasons. The different terms can then bear intelligible distinctions even if individual cases in actual practice remain puzzling. It will then be seen that the imaginary critic's point lacks force.

Law interpretation and lawmaking both stand in contrast to the pure case of law application. Let us stipulate that, in pure law application, a legal standard provides a reason for someone to perform a specified act in specified circumstances and there are no competing reasons pertaining to that act. There may be few cases of pure law application that reach the appellate courts and deserve significant judicial energy, if there are any. There are a great many in the lower courts, which also matter in a practical understanding of

58 Kenneth C. Davis, *Administrative Law and Government* (St. Paul, Minn.: West Pub. Co., 1960), pp. 283–9.

adjudication. In lawmaking, whether by courts pursuant to a legitimate legal power or by legislatures, all reasons of political morality are available for the deliberation.[59] In law interpretation, by contrast, only the reasons that won in a prior lawmaking – the background justification for the specific law – are available. As argued above,[60] the background justification serves as the source for the differing weights of competing legal reasons. Accordingly, the difference between lawmaking, interpretation, and application lies in the difference between the sets of reasons available in the deliberation. Reasons of political morality that cut against the lawmaking proposal fall out of interpretive and applicative deliberations governed by that law. Those reasons reenter proper judicial deliberations when the court exercises its lawmaking power.

On this basis, there is a distinction to be drawn in principle between adjudicatory activities in which the court is applying the law, interpreting the law, and making the law. Moreover, a court might consciously shift from one activity to another by admitting or rejecting the sets of reasons as indicated above. Most important, a court consequently may require a justification for moving from the applicative and interpretive activities most characteristic of its agenda to lawmaking activities that are less common. The present objection can be seen to go astray in light of the need for such a justification.

The judicial lawmaking power is exercised at common law most dramatically by overruling. The overruling possibility is not incompatible with judging under the law.[61] Overruling is not permitted just because the judges in a later court would weigh differently the reasons available to the earlier court. Very few courts have the power to overrule prece-

---

59 Lawmaking by administrative agencies is another matter. Authorizing legislation may exclude some reasons while leaving a subset of conflicting reasons for agency consideration.
60 See §§ 2.4, 5.3.4.
61 Accord, Duncan Kennedy, "Freedom and Constraint in Adjudication: A Critical Phenomenology," *Journal of Legal Education*, 36 (1987): 518–62, at 537–8; Joseph Raz, "Facing Up: A Reply," *Southern California Law Review*, 62 (1989): 1153–1235, at 1172–3.

dents. Even for them, it is not a matter of simple regret or mistake, as though the mere fact of a change in the composition of a court would justify overruling. Rather, there must be a *new and adequate reason* after the lawmaking for a court to be justified in asking the overruling question as a threshold matter.[62] The new reason may be a change in the legal context so the precedent now works at cross purposes to related laws. It may be a change in the social and historical circumstances, such that the background justification no longer sustains the law in operation as it once did. Less clearly, it may be a new argument that was unavailable in the legal culture to the court that decided the precedent, as the contract law argument in *Patterson* was apparently unavailable to the Supreme Court. An appellate court may be justified in asking the overruling question only when an adequate new reason exists. When a court is justified in asking the overruling question, then, all the original reasons both for and against the precedential law properly enter the deliberations. Without an adequate new reason, however, the original reasons against the precedential law are excluded from judicial deliberations.

The judicial lawmaking power in common law cases is also exercised by accretive lawmaking. This occurs, for example, when a court adds an exception to a general common law rule. This is not interpretation because the legal standard, prior to the engrafting of an exception, may clearly govern a case that must be decided differently by lower courts after the exception. Interpretation concerns the meaning of a rule, not its text or syntax. Again, however, a court is not justified in adding an exception only because the judges in a later case would weigh differently the reasons available to the earlier court. It should ask the exception question only when there is a new and adequate reason to do so – one that was unavailable to the lawmaking court. The new reasons can be any of those appropriate to an overruling exercise, but the

---

62 For example, Arizona v. Rumsey, 467 U.S. 203, 212 (1984) ("any departure from the doctrine of *stare decisis* demands special justification").

rule may continue to be justified in the precedent in which it was announced. It may be that the case was unforeseen by the court deciding the precedent, and a distinction can be articulated. In asking the exception question, the court allows all reasons of general political morality to reenter for the limited purpose. There is nothing illicit in doing so if the court has the power to make common law and is justified in asking the exception question.

Consequently, a court may have the power to make the law by which it then is bound. It may not, however, legitimately exercise that power in any and all cases without special justification. Rather, the court must have a good reason, independent of the reasons for and against making new law, for embarking on the exercise of its lawmaking power. When it has such a good reason, it is justified in making the law and then applying it consistently with the requirements of generalization. This does not defeat the good faith thesis. Most courts by far have no lawmaking power, and most cases do not involve good reasons to embark on lawmaking. There are important cases when there are such reasons, and in which courts should make law, taking into account all good reasons of political morality. In all others, however, judges are meaningfully bound by their duty to uphold the law to act only on reasons warranted by the existing law as grounds for judicial decisions.

This chapter completes the main development of the good faith thesis. It remains to defend this thesis against the important possible objections to it. Most important, the determinacy condition holds that judges can fulfill their duty to uphold the law only by reaching the one right answer required by the law. Some theorists accept or postulate the determinacy condition and assert that it cannot be satisfied, leading to various forms of legal skepticism. Others presuppose it, insisting that it can be satisfied because the law necessarily requires determinate right answers. In either case, the good faith thesis fails if the determinacy condition prevails. Part II contains crucial arguments that the determinacy condition is unsound. Because the determinacy condition is so central to contemporary debates in legal theory, these arguments suggest that much contemporary legal theory is misdirected.

Part II

The permissible discretion thesis

Chapter 4

Science and skepticism

4.1. PERMISSIBLE DISCRETION

The primary objection to the good faith thesis asserts that the idea of a legal constraint on discretion is conceptually confused. The general objection claims that judges can fulfill their duty to uphold law only when the law determines one correct result in a lawsuit and the judge reaches that result. If this were so, it would follow that judges cannot fulfill their duty to uphold the law when the law is indeterminate. Judicial discretion as currently practiced would be impermissible, and the good faith thesis would be pointless. The objection asserts the determinacy condition, which currently underlies and shapes a large part of the debate over legal indeterminacy, judicial discretion, and the legitimacy of adjudication. In those debates, the determinacy condition generally is taken for granted, not defended.

The next three chapters will advance the permissible discretion thesis, which contradicts the determinacy condition. This thesis holds that judges can fulfill their duty to uphold the law by exercising discretion in good faith. If so, judicial discretion exercised in good faith would be compatible with legitimate adjudication in a constitutional democracy (though other conditions would remain to be satisfied). The next three chapters will argue that the determinacy condition is unsound by considering a range of plausible arguments for it. Rejecting the most plausible arguments cannot prove that the determinacy condition is false because all possible grounds are not thereby eliminated. The arguments here, however, should throw the burden onto others to defend the determinacy condition explicitly. Pending the development of new and better arguments, my argument against the determinacy condition, together with those supporting the good faith thesis, should suffice to sustain the permissible discretion thesis.

In contesting the determinacy condition, I do not wish to deny either that the law in practice determines one correct legal outcome in many cases or that this is often desirable. The question here is whether determinacy of results is necessary *whenever* judges are bound by the law. If it were, judges would be free of legal duties in every case where the law is indeterminate with respect to results. The alternative explanation of determinate cases is that they are governed by legal standards which, contingently, provide judges with either one legal reason while excluding all other considerations, legal reasons that all cut the same way, or legal reasons with predominant weight favoring one result according to the prevailing professional conventions. The determinacy condition fails as a conceptual objection to the good faith thesis if determinate cases are contingent phenomena.[1] Moreover, if determinacy is contingent, we could insist on it only when it is more important than countervailing considerations, not because it is necessary for all legitimate adjudication. Further debate would focus normatively on the content of particular laws as they operate in various circumstances.

4.2. EPISTEMIC DETERMINACY

The determinacy condition might be supposed to stem, first, from a general epistemic doctrine that is central to the dominant intellectual traditions in twentieth-century Anglo-American philosophies of science – logical empiricism and

---

1 The determinacy condition might be resurrected as a *normative* objection to the good faith thesis. This would require a critic to argue that determinacy of results is essential to good law or good judging, rather than to law or judging as such, and thus to advocate determinate-formalism.

its cousin, empirical pragmatism. These philosophies sought to reduce that which exists to that which could be known by verifiable methods of inquiry. In light of the vast influence of these philosophies, it is plausible to hypothesize that a kindred reductionist epistemology underlies parts of twentieth-century legal theory. The determinacy condition would be a rough counterpart to the verifiability requirement in logical empiricism and empirical pragmatism. As the philosophies of science reduced what there is to what can be known verifiably, so the content of judicial duty might require that judges act only on laws that require results which in principle can be identified verifiably by logical or empirical means. That would be an epistemic version of the determinacy condition.

I will argue, however, that a reductionist epistemology does not ground a valid determinacy condition within a practical understanding of law and judging. Scientific and practical knowledge are fundamentally different.[2] An abstract epistemic determinacy condition is appropriate, if at all, for scientific pursuits by observers outside the practice in question.[3] Practical knowledge, by contrast, is adapted to the purposes for which it is pursued by actors within the practice. For a judge, practical knowledge concerns the best of the available alternative legal actions under a concrete set of circumstances in which the judge must act on the available reasons, whether or not they satisfy external epistemic standards. The theorist of judging avoids disconnecting from the activity of judging only by maintaining a vigilant sensitivity

2 An alternative and more common approach argues that modern science does not satisfy the logical positivist or any similar epistemology requiring determinacy. See generally Thomas S. Kuhn, *The Structure of Scientific Revolutions*, 2d ed. (Chicago: University of Chicago Press, 1971); Richard J. Bernstein, *Beyond Objectivism and Relativism* (Philadelphia: University of Pennsylvania Press, 1988). What will not work for science, it is argued, surely will not work for law.

3 I take no position here on the important philosophical debates about verificationism in a general epistemology or on the role of verificationism in a philosophy of science. The point is only that, even if verificationism is valid for some purposes, it is not valid as a condition of practical knowledge.

to the law as it appears to judges in practical terms. When this sensitivity is maintained, a reductionist epistemology does not support the determinacy condition for either the judge or the theorist of judging.

The logical empiricist and empirical pragmatist epistemologies sought, each in its own way, to dismiss all statements not reducible to statements that can be verified or at least falsified. For logical empiricists, a statement could be true, if at all, only by virtue of the logic of its concepts or by experiment. For many pragmatists, a statement could be true only if it would not produce disappointing empirical results when acted on.[4] Both schools were deeply skeptical about the meaningfulness of claims not reducible to hard analytic or observable stuff. When this epistemology is accepted, all normative statements, including legal and moral statements, fall into meaninglessness. Because this epistemology has been so widely accepted, a skeptical attitude toward normative inquiry has pervaded intellectual activities throughout most of the twentieth century and continues to have considerable influence.

A similarly reductionist epistemology was introduced to legal theory by Holmes who, writing in the late nineteenth century, brilliantly anticipated later developments. His framework implicitly confined all possible legal knowledge to the logical and the empirical when he proclaimed that "[t]he life of the law has not been logic: it has been experience."[5] He reduced the law to observable judicial behaviors when he confined it to "prophecies of what the courts will do in fact, and nothing more pretentious."[6] He anticipated the banishment of all normative statements when he sought to substitute a scientific foundation for talk of "rights" and "duties" because they were "empty words."[7] For Holmes,

4 I here emphasize Jamesian pragmatism over the Peircian varieties.
5 Oliver Wendell Holmes, *The Common Law*, ed. Mark D. Howe (Boston: Little, Brown & Co., 1963), p. 5.
6 Oliver Wendell Holmes, "The Path of the Law," in *Collected Legal Papers* (New York: Harcourt, Brace and Howe, 1920): 167–202, at 173.
7 Holmes, "Law in Science and Science in Law," in *Collected Legal Papers*:

talk of rights was an obscure way to talk of predictions that "the public force will be brought to bear on those who do things said to contravene it – just as we talk of the force of gravitation accounting for the conduct of bodies in space."[8] Similarly, talk of duties involved "nothing but a prediction that if a man does or omits certain things he will be made to suffer in this or that way by judgment of the court."[9] Thus, for Holmes, all meaningful propositions of law could be confirmed by empirical means.

These sweeping banishments might seem to remove any normative concept of law or judicial duty, and therefore the determinacy condition, from Holmes's jurisprudence. A thoroughgoing verificationism would do so. Normative ideas remained, however, despite the subtle incoherence. Consider Holmes's famous statement of judicial duty after he was on the bench: "I hope and believe that I am not influenced by my opinion that [the Sherman Act] is a foolish law. I have little doubt that the country likes it and I always say, as you know, that if my fellow citizens want to go to Hell I will help them. It's my job."[10] This understanding of judicial duty suited Holmes's normative vision of law: "The first requirement of a sound body of law is, that it should correspond with the actual feelings and demands of the community, whether right or wrong."[11] These ideas reduce the suspect normative element to a bare minimum. Judicial duty, in particular, would require reaching results indicated by empirically knowable beliefs about the desires of people in the aggregate. A version of the determinacy condition thus ap-

210–43, at 229; Holmes, "The Path of the Law," at 171 ("The law talks about rights, and duties, and malice, and intent, and negligence, and so forth, and nothing is easier . . . in legal reasoning, than to take these words in their moral sense, at some stage of the argument, and so to drop into fallacy").

8   Holmes, "Natural Law," in *Collected Legal Papers*: 310–16, at 313.
9   Holmes, "The Path of the Law," at 169.
10 Letter to Harold Laski of March 4, 1920, in *Holmes-Laski Letters: The Correspondence of Mr. Justice Holmes and Harold J. Laski, 1916–1935*, vol. 1, ed. Mark D. Howe (Cambridge: Harvard University Press, 1953), pp. 248–9.
11 Holmes, *The Common Law*, p. 36.

pears to have been grounded on the epistemic considerations that otherwise pervaded Holmes's legal theory.

Major strands of legal realism followed Holmes and par-
ticipated in the Zeitgeist by defining law as the observable
regularities in judicial or other official behavior and supplanting doctrinal analysis with social scientific methods of
study.[12] These strands complemented the skeptical strands
of legal realism, which also followed Holmes by debunking
legal rules and principles, substituting psychological, an-
thropological, political-scientific, and sociological understandings.[13] The legal realists' attraction to social scientific
methods and skepticism about normative rules and principles was not historically accidental. Throughout the Anglo-
American intellectual world, the disciplines were insisting
on scientific determinacy by conforming their methods to the
reductionist epistemology.

In recent years, the legacy of logical empiricist social scientific legal studies has been carried most prominently by those
engaged in the economic analysis of the law. One of the great
pioneers was Richard A. Posner,[14] whose economics project
is the apotheosis of the Holmesian project begun a century
earlier. His views illustrate the contemporary influence of
the Holmesian legacy. Posner started by advancing the idea
of economic efficiency as the hidden logic of the common law
of negligence.[15] That study took the classical form of a social

12 See Edward A. Purcell, *The Crisis of American Democratic Theory* (Lex-
    ington: University Press of Kentucky, 1973), pp. 74–94; Robert S.
    Summers, *Instrumentalism and American Legal Theory* (Ithaca, N.Y.:
    Cornell University Press, 1982); John Henry Schlegel, "American
    Legal Realism and Empirical Social Science: From the Yale Experi-
    ence," *Buffalo Law Review*, 28 (1979): 459–586.
13 For example, Jerome Frank, *Law and the Modern Mind* (New York:
    Brentano's, 1930); Karl N. Llewellyn & E. Hoebel, *The Cheyenne Way*
    (Norman, Okla.: University of Oklahoma Press, 1941); Myres S. Mac-
    Dougal & Harold D. Lasswell, "Legal Education and Public Policy:
    Professional Training in the Public Interest," *Yale Law Journal*, 52
    (1943): 203–95.
14 The other was Guido Calabresi. See § 4.4.2.
15 Richard A. Posner, "A Theory of Negligence," *Journal of Legal Studies*,
    1 (1972): 29–96. See also William M. Landes & Richard A. Posner, *The*

scientific study concerned with the regularities in judicial behavior. It put forward the efficiency hypothesis, which claimed in effect that judges find negligence when a party's act does not maximize the aggregate economic values at stake. Posner's study treated the case law as the data with which this hypothesis could be falsified. He claimed that the data supported his view that economic efficiency was the best prediction of judicial behavior. Posner broadened the thesis to advance economic efficiency as the hidden logic of the common law more generally, also depending on positive economic analysis to defend predictive claims.[16]

Effective criticism focused on Posner's claim that the efficiency hypothesis – as a claim about the law – could be sustained by positive economic analysis alone. In response, Posner turned his attention to a normative argument supporting a version of efficiency (wealth maximization) as the principle that should guide judges at least in common law cases.[17] Holmes had urged that the law should operate to satisfy the desires of individuals, whatever they may be. Posner argued normatively that maximizing wealth was the best way to do this.[18] After his appointment to the United States Court of Appeals for the Seventh Circuit, however, Posner realized that he needed a jurisprudential theory to allow a judge to pursue a social vision that places such great value on economic wealth maximization.[19] Accordingly, his recent writings in jurisprudence manifest a deep skepticism

Economic Structure of Tort Law (Cambridge: Harvard University Press, 1987), p. 8.

16 Richard A. Posner, *Economic Analysis of Law,* 3d ed. (Boston: Little, Brown & Co., 1986; first edition, 1972).

17 Richard A. Posner, "Utilitarianism, Economics, and Legal Theory," *Journal of Legal Studies,* 8 (1979): 103–40.

18 See, for example, Richard A. Posner, *The Economics of Justice* (Cambridge: Harvard University Press, 1981); Richard A. Posner, "Wealth Maximization and Judicial Decision-Making," *International Review of Law and Economics,* 4 (1984): 131–5.

19 For his most recent statement, see Richard A. Posner, *The Problems of Jurisprudence* (Cambridge: Harvard University Press, 1990), pp. 353–92.

about the conventional law,[20] which continues to talk of rights and duties in the way Holmes thought empty.

Posner's argument for legal skepticism, and therefore for the freedom of a judge from the constraints of conventional law, depends squarely on a determinacy condition grounded in the reductionist epistemology. The argument starts with Posner's definition of "exact inquiry." In his view, following the classic logical empiricist line, exact inquiry is composed of two scientific methods used to acquire beliefs.[21] One method is logical deduction. It is used in law, according to Posner, to answer easy questions. It has been of little interest to him because such questions are not often litigated.[22] The other method is empirical observation. It involves systematic empirical inquiry through experimentation leading to verification or, at least, falsification.[23] Posner laments that neither scientific method plays a significant role in judicial reasoning. Therefore, "[l]egal reasoning is not a branch of exact inquiry . . . although continued progress in the economic analysis of law may compel a modification of this conclusion eventually."[24]

Two kinds of skepticism flow from this conclusion. First, Posner advances a familiar epistemic skepticism evocative of legal realism: Many legal questions are indeterminate by the methods of judicial reasoning; answers to these questions turn on the policy judgments, political preferences, and ethical values of the judges.[25] Second, Posner advances a perhaps misnamed "ontological skepticism": Law does not exist

20 See ibid.; Richard A. Posner, "The Jurisprudence of Skepticism," *Michigan Law Review*, 86 (1988): 827–91. Parts of the following passage are adapted from Steven J. Burton, "Judge Posner's Jurisprudence of Skepticism," *Michigan Law Review*, 87 (1987): 710–23 (with permission of the *Michigan Law Review*).

21 Posner, *The Problems of Jurisprudence*, pp. 38, 74.

22 Ibid., pp. 56–7; Posner, "The Jurisprudence of Skepticism," at 832. There are well-known objections to grounding a sweeping legal skepticism on examination only of cases that are litigated or, worse, litigated to the highest appellate courts.

23 Posner, *The Problems of Jurisprudence*, pp. 61–70.

24 Posner, "The Jurisprudence of Skepticism," at 858–9.

25 Posner, *The Problems of Jurisprudence*, pp. 37–100.

because it is not an observable entity; it is not a thing or set of concepts that guides judges or anyone else.[26] Law, rather, is simply the name of the activity of judges.[27] Attempts to discern the observable regularities in judicial behavior, like the behavior of rats or comets, are all we can discuss.[28]

These two skepticisms depend directly on Posner's logical empiricist conception of exact inquiry. Posner's epistemic skepticism follows from the unavailability of scientific experiments or calculations verifying or falsifying the truth of legal claims. His ontological skepticism is a special case of his general doubt about the existence of entities that cannot be known in that way. His jurisprudence thus reduces the law to judicial behavior as seen by a scientific observer. He imposes a scientific determinacy condition on the law and, on that basis, reaches skeptical conclusions from a scientific observer's standpoint.[29]

Posner's stance creates a problem from the judicial standpoint. Notwithstanding his sweeping skepticisms, Judge Posner wants to affirm that most judicial decisions are reasonable. Recognizing that the methods of exact inquiry are rarely usable by judges deciding cases, Posner shifts from the standpoint of an observer to that of an actor. He then asserts that judicial reasoning is mainly a branch of what he calls "practical reason."[30] He defines the practical judicial method as an agglomeration of "the methods by which people who are not credulous form beliefs about matters that cannot be verified by logic or exact observation."[31] In his

26 Ibid., pp. 161–246.
27 Ibid., p. 225.
28 Ibid., pp. 220–8. In this respect, Posner's approach is rooted in a major strand of the legal realist tradition. See, for example, Walter W. Cook, "Scientific Method and the Law," *American Bar Association Journal*, 13 (1927): 303–9.
29 Richard A. Posner, *The Federal Courts: Crisis and Reform* (Cambridge: Harvard University Press, 1985), p. 203 (decisions involving value judgments "are by definition not scientific, and therefore not readily falsifiable or verifiable either, and as a consequence not always profitably discussable").
30 Posner, *The Problems of Jurisprudence*, pp. 71-3.
31 Ibid., pp. 71–2.

view, "[i]t is a grab bag that includes anecdote, introspection, imagination, common sense, empathy, imputation of motives, speaker's authority, metaphor, analogy, precedent, custom, memory, 'experience,' intuition, and induction."[32] Judges resort to this grab bag when, as is often the case, the reliable methods of exact inquiry are not adequate. Posner assures us that practical reason can answer legal questions sufficiently well to avoid willful or arbitrary judicial decisions of an objectionable sort.[33]

Rejecting a scientifically based skepticism about the law is not surprising for a sitting judge, who is neither an academic or scientific observer nor a practicing lawyer seeking to predict the outcome of judicial deliberations. This case is interesting, however, in light of this judge's previously exclusive commitment, when an academic observer, to logical empiricist methods in the positive economic analysis of the law. In a recent essay, Posner acknowledged his formerly strict logical empiricism and, at the same time, abandoned it.[34] Now he assures us that there are good answers to many ethical and legal questions independent of the verifiability or falsifiability of those answers by scientific means.[35] He claims that, by contrast with the methods of exact inquiry, including economic analysis, practical reason comprises "our principal set of tools for answering questions large and small."[36] These are important revisions to a formerly rigorous scientific web of beliefs about law.

It is highly suggestive that Richard Posner, when on the bench, could not maintain his former epistemic commitments. The judicial standpoint, by contrast with the academic or scientific, might make a major difference in how the law appears. If so, we could hardly claim to understand the law or judging without taking into account the practical stand-

32 Ibid., p. 73.
33 Ibid., pp. 77–123.
34 Posner, "The Jurisprudence of Skepticism," at 839, 866, 888–9, 890.
35 Posner, *The Problems of Jurisprudence*, pp. 71–116.
36 Ibid., p. 73.

point of a judge. Acknowledging the judicial standpoint, however, has far greater implications than those outlined by Judge Posner, who continues to be hampered by a "thin and unsatisfactory epistemology."[37] Despite his rejection of logical empiricist criteria for successful judging, Posner's skepticisms about law and judicial reasoning continue to depend on the rejected criteria. As will be seen, however, the scientific epistemology is not relevant to law and judicial practice in a way that grounds this version of the determinacy condition.

4.3. THE THEORETICAL AND THE PRACTICAL

Different intellectual discourses, or "language games,"[38] can be distinguished in five respects: They proceed from different standpoints, in different vocabularies, with reference to different entities, guided by different ground rules, and under different criteria for success. Consider, for example, the familiar distinction between "analytic" discourses, like mathematics, and "synthetic" discourses, like the empirical sciences. Ordinary mathematics proceeds in terms of number, equality, proof, transitivity, infinity, recursion, and the like, reflecting the entities, relationships, and modes of existence recognized within the mathematical world. This discourse in principle requires rigorous warrants for making inferences at every step, and a successful proof must be replicable by any competent mathematician at any time or place. Empirical sciences, by contrast, use a language of hypothesis, data, measurement, probability, statistical significance, and the like, in part reflecting their interest in a different set of entities in different kinds of relationships and with different modes of existence. The rules of this discourse require

---

37 Paul M. Bator, "The Judicial Universe of Judge Richard Posner," *University of Chicago Law Review*, 52 (1985): 1146–66, at 1161.
38 See generally G. Ryle, *The Concept of Mind* (London: Hutchinson, 1949); Ludwig Wittgenstein, *Philosophical Investigations*, trans. G. E. M. Anscombe (Oxford: B. Blackwell, 1958).

experimentation and are far more concerned with excluding the prejudices of the inquirer. The conceptual difference between the two discourses explains why it is obviously a mistake to criticize a mathematical claim for lacking empirical support.

The difference between analytic and synthetic discourses (hereafter called "theoretical discourses") is taken for granted in a culture like ours, which has been heavily influenced by logical empiricism. In philosophical circles, however, logical empiricism is generally ridiculed despite (or because of) its continuing influence in the wider culture. It failed as a philosophy of science.[39] More important for present purposes, it failed to confine all legitimate discourse to the logical and the empirical. As it is silly to criticize a mathematical claim for lacking empirical support, so it is a mistake to order a person forthwith to obey the law of gravity. The explanation for the latter mistake is that there is a third kind of discourse – one for practical matters, notably morals, politics, and law. We are not only analysts and observers who form beliefs. We also are intentional actors with the capacity to reason about what we should do. A practical discourse, accordingly, uses the language of rights, duties, principles, responsibilities, and excuses, with which reference is made basically to reasons for action. The ground rules require normative argument, not proof or experimentation. Valid claims to practical knowledge must satisfy criteria appropriate to a discourse directed to action in real-world circumstances, not criteria imported from discourses directed to the passive formation of general beliefs. Accordingly, practical knowledge looks for the best of the available alternative actions in concrete circumstances, not verifiable generalities.

H. L. A. Hart did much to break the philosophy of law (though not most American legal theory) out of the reduc-

---

39 See, for example, Herbert Feigl, "New Reflections on Empiricism," in *New Readings in Philosophical Analysis*, eds. Herbert Feigl, Wilfrid Sellars, & Keith Lehrer (New York: Appleton-Century-Crofts, 1972): 1–12, at 12.

tionist stranglehold and to relegitimate a practical discourse. His legal positivism is often confused with logical positivism (also called logical empiricism). In fact, he unambiguously rejected that philosophy:

> According to [the Oxford ordinary language] conception of philosophy it had been a blinding error of much philosophy in the past, and most recently and notably of the Logical Positivism of the pre-war years, to assume that there are only a few forms of discourse (empirical 'fact-stating' discourse or statements of definitional or logically necessary truths) which are meaningful, and to dismiss as meaningless or as mere expressions of feeling all other uses of language which, as in the case of some metaphysical statements or moral judgments, could not be shown to be disguised or complex forms of the few favoured types of discourse.[40]

Crucial to Hart's effort was his insistence that law be understood with (nonexclusive) regard for the internal or practical standpoint of the persons whose actions are guided by it.[41]

Recall Hart's famous treatment of legal obligation.[42] He set up the gunman situation in which A orders B to hand over

40 H. L. A. Hart, "Introduction," in *Essays in Jurisprudence and Philosophy*, ed. H. L. A. Hart (Oxford: Clarendon Press, 1983): 1–18, at 2–3.
41 H. L. A. Hart, *The Concept of Law* (Oxford: Clarendon Press, 1961), pp. 55–6, 86–8, 96, 99–100; H. L. A. Hart, "Scandinavian Realism," in *Essays in Jurisprudence and Philosophy*: 161–9, at 166–7. In this respect, Hart's philosophy has been widely influential. See, for example, Ronald M. Dworkin, *Law's Empire* (Cambridge: Harvard University Press, Belknap Press, 1986), pp. 11–14, 13–15, 101–4; John Finnis, *Natural Law and Natural Rights* (Oxford: Clarendon Press, 1980), pp. 3, 234–7; Joseph Raz, *The Authority of Law* (Oxford: Clarendon Press, 1979), pp 155–7. See also Lon L. Fuller, *The Law in Quest of Itself* (Chicago: The Foundation Press, 1940), p. 3; Philippe Nonet, "In the Matter of *Green v. Recht*," *California Law Review*, 75 (1987): 363–77, at 374. For a different understanding of the internal, see Ernest J. Weinrib, "Legal Formalism: On the Immanent Rationality of Law," *Yale Law Journal*, 97 (1987): 949–1016, at 952 (internality involving a coherence and mutual dependence of legal ideas).
42 Hart, *The Concept of Law*, pp. 79–88. See also Hans Kelsen, "The Pure Theory of Law," *Law Quarterly Review*, 50 (1934): 474–98, at 477–9.

B's money and threatens to shoot him if he does not comply. Hart suggested that we would misdescribe that situation in saying that B had an obligation; rather, we would say that B was obliged to hand over his money. The latter, Hart suggested, is a descriptive psychological statement about the beliefs and motives that cause an action to be done. It might be relevant to an observer's prediction of B's behavior and, "writ large," might help support generalizations about the regularities of behavior in a social group. But, Hart argued, the statement that someone had an obligation to do something is of a different type. Statements of obligation, Hart insisted, presuppose the existence of rules that provide standards of conduct, deviations from which are met with insistent and strong social criticism.[43] The normative vocabulary of the law, especially "right" and "duty," is used to draw attention to the rules, which are regarded *by those who accept them* as justificatory reasons for conforming their conduct and for criticizing deviations by others. Legal rules do not, by his account, explain, predict, or describe anything. They prescribe lawful conduct.

Consequently, Hart argued, Austin's view of laws as commands habitually obeyed, Holmes's view of laws as predictions of what courts will do, and legal realist views of laws as observable regularities in aggregate official behavior, were all deficient. They missed what could be grasped only with sensitivity to the actor's standpoint: "[The] external point of view, which limits itself to the observable regularities of behaviour, cannot reproduce . . . the way in which the rules function as rules in the lives of those who normally are the majority of society."[44] One of the most remarkable facts

43 On social rules, see Hart, *The Concept of Law*, pp. 54–60.
44 Hart, *The Concept of Law*, p. 88. See also Richard A. Wasserstrom, *The Judicial Decision* (Stanford, Calif: Stanford University Press, 1961), p. 181 n. 36 ("definitions of 'law' phrased in terms of 'what the courts will do' or 'what the courts have done' will not prove very useful to a judge who is asking himself what law applies, or ought to apply, to a given case").
Hart later endorsed Joseph Raz's suggestion that an external observer can make "detached normative statements." H. L. A. Hart,

about much recent American legal theory is its failure either to contest this powerful argument of Hart's or to recognize its implications for understanding the law and judging. The popular economic analysis of the law, for example, operates mainly on behaviorist assumptions when observing aggregate behavior; critical legal studies scholars endorse versions of legal skepticism from their standpoint as the radical outsider. My best guess as to the reason for this persistent error centers on the continuing influence of an epistemic determinacy condition stemming from Holmes, the legal realists, and reductionist epistemologies in the philosophy of science – even when the radical outsider uses it only in an "internal critique."[45] The best evidence, though it could be a coincidence, is that their reductionism excludes appreciation of the actor's standpoint and the normativity of the law.[46] Hart's expansionism relegitimates both.

Essays on Bentham (Oxford: Clarendon Press, 1962), pp. 153–5; Joseph Raz, *Practical Reason and Norms* (London: Hutchinson, 1975), pp. 175–7; Raz, *The Authority of Law,* pp. 132–59. Such statements are to be understood as we understand the Christian who says to his Orthodox Jewish friend, who is about to eat some pork with fried rice: "You ought not to eat that." This is a fully normative statement in that it guides conduct. The Christian, however, speaks from the standpoint of one who accepts the laws of Kosher without thereby endorsing those laws as right or good. Similarly, we can say that the law in South Africa required blacks to use separate public facilities without thereby approving any part of apartheid. The detached normative statement permits a legal theorist, teacher, or practitioner to say "what the law is" and treat the law as a normative matter – a guide to conduct – without thereby confusing the law as it is with the law as it ought to be, and without endorsing it as right or good. The statements of law in this book generally are detached normative statements.

45 See §§ 5.1 and following.
46 Posner's main response to my previous criticism – that he had unwisely ignored Hart's primary lesson – is to admit with obvious reluctance that the judge is an actor who must offer good reasons for judicial action, but to claim that he is unable to find content in the literature spawned by Hart's insight. For him, what would count as "content" would involve "exploring the resources for decision making that people use when they are in a hurry, or lack the skills or resources for patient, disinterested mathematical or scientific research, or are dealing with a question not amenable to logical or scientific inquiry." Posner, *The Problems of Jurisprudence,* p. 72. His

An actor's capacity for practical reason is unfamiliar in a culture that has not taken it seriously for many decades.[47] This can have unfortunate consequences for legal theory. Judge Posner's jurisprudence, for example, dismisses the prescriptivity of the law because he holds it to requirements of exact inquiry, as though the law stood wholly aloof from the world, like mathematics, or described empirical facts with which its representations could be falsified, like positivist sociology. He tries to reconceive the law as a set of empirically knowable propositions:

> [Judges] do not act in accordance with something called "law" – they just act as best they can. They decide the case, and as a by-product throw out clues to how they might decide the next case. The law is the set of hypotheses that lawyers and lower-court judges propose concerning the regularities in the higher courts' behavior.[48]

This descriptive concept of law leaves judges to do the best they can to muddle through, using their own social visions, if any.[49] But the relevant social vision is represented prescriptively by the legal standards which constitute the law that judges have a duty to uphold. The traffic laws, for example, represent a complex set of coordinated actions that ought to be taken by motorists in response to various colored lights and signs with various shapes. To a remarkably large extent, motorists are guided by the law to take those actions and

idea of practical reason is introduced as a response to the need for this *descriptive* inquiry, which he does not think will do a very good job at providing justifications for judicial decisions. This flight from the prescriptive to the descriptive only repeats the error alleged in the prior criticism. See Burton, "Judge Posner's Jurisprudence of Skepticism."

47 See Mark V. Tushnet, *Red, White, and Blue: A Critical Analysis of Constitutional Law* (Cambridge: Harvard University Press, 1988), p. 161 ("The idea of a faculty of practical reason is, if not entirely foreign to us, at least far enough removed from our way of thinking to require some effort to understand").

48 Posner, *The Problems of Jurisprudence*, p. 225.

49 Posner, "The Jurisprudence of Skepticism," at 849–57, 863.

thus to actualize the traffic laws.[50] Conventional legal standards seem meaningless when they are taken to describe an empirical reality knowable by Posner's methods of exact inquiry, but the appearance of meaninglessness results from a discredited epistemology – a philosophical mistake.

The observer's epistemology can infect adjudication as well as legal theory. Consider the Peyote Case before the U.S. Supreme Court.[51] The U.S. Constitution precludes states from prohibiting the free exercise of religion. The Supreme Court, in an opinion by Justice Antonin Scalia, held that a state may prohibit the *act of ingesting peyote* even when it is a part of a religious ritual of the Native American Church, if the prohibition is not aimed at acts performed only within a religious context.[52] The effect of Justice Scalia's characterization of the act is to obviate any need to inquire into the reasons, intentions, or meaning accompanying the physical act of ingesting the drug in various contexts. This excludes the significance of the act, confining judicial inquiry to the physical behavior as seen by a Holmesian observer. Justice Harry A. Blackmun's dissenting opinion, by contrast, sought to understand the peyote ritual as it is understood by its practitioners. He characterized the relevant act as an *act of worship.*[53] The act in question can be accurately described either as an act of ingesting a drug or as an act of worship. It is both. Justice Scalia's exclusive choice of the behavioral mode reflects his objectivist epistemic commitments. But it is right there – in the choice of a behaviorist characterization of the act – that the values sought to be protected by the Free Exercise Clause are excluded. All religious worship is internal to a person or a practice. Consequently, as Hart sug-

---

50 Other laws, like those prohibiting the sale or use of cocaine, represent a part of the normative organization of society but are notoriously ineffective. The empirical world is brought into conformity with such laws, if at all, when legal sanctions are imposed on violators as the alternative to compliance represented by the law.

51 Employment Division, Department of Human Resources of Oregon v. Smith, 494 U.S. 872 (1990).

52 Ibid., at 1599–602.

53 Ibid., at 1615, 1622.

gested, it is invisible to the behaviorist observer. By contrast, Justice Blackmun sought a practical understanding of the religious ritual. This approaches the act with regard for the standpoint of the actor, allowing its judicial treatment to be sensitive to the constitutional values at stake, whatever the outcome.

The abstract distinction between practical and theoretical discourses is ancient and fundamental, with important ramifications.[54] Most significantly for our purposes, the meanings of "determinacy" and "constraint" shift significantly when we think within a practical discourse. On the theoretical side, "determinacy" and "constraint" both refer to the idea that events are caused or determined by prior specific conditions.[55] When the use is theoretical, it might make sense to call for verifiable predictions in the Holmesian manner. On the practical side, however, "determinacy" means that the law contains a single correct answer to a legal question. "Constraint," by contrast, means only that the law restricts the reasons on which judges act within their duty. That is, judges are constrained by the law when the legal reasons available within good faith deliberations are a subset of all otherwise relevant reasons for action. The determinacy condition must be well grounded, if at all, as a practical matter and by contrast with constraint. The epistemic requirements of sound scientific theorizing cannot provide the ground needed to challenge the good faith thesis on this point.

4.4. THE ROLE OF SOCIAL SCIENCE

In practice both theoretical and practical elements are combined in any endeavor. The distinction is conceptual and should aid clear thinking by helping to disentangle what-is-

---

54 See, for example, Aristotle, "Nicomachean Ethics," in *The Basic Works of Aristotle*, ed. Richard McKeon (New York: Random House, 1941): 927–1112 (at 1138b35–1139b18); Immanuel Kant, *Critique of Practical Reason*, trans. Lewis W. Beck (Indianapolis: Bobbs-Merrill, 1956).
55 For further discussion, see §§ 5.3.2, 5.3.4.

a-reason-for-what. For example, a scientist who forms a true but private belief that a massive nuclear explosion is possible should have appropriate reasons for the belief. The reasons for belief will involve primarily theories and facts within the domain of nuclear physics. By contrast, ethical obligations are attracted by the acts of building a device or detonating it. Such acts should be justified by appropriate reasons for action, which would involve moral principles. Theoretical beliefs enter practical deliberations when relevant under a normative principle. To stay with the obvious, if weapons of mass destruction ought not to be built or detonated, theory is crucial to assess whether nuclear weapons are weapons of mass destruction. Social scientific and other theories have a similar place within judicial deliberations under the law. Such theories are misused, however, when deployed to support jurisprudential skepticism about the conventional law.

4.4.1. *Law and society.* Perhaps no jurisprudential slogan has been more influential in the United States than Holmes's definition of the law as "prophecies of what the courts will do."[56] The definition tolerates both logical empiricist and pragmatist interpretations,[57] both of which foster an epistemic determinacy condition in the pursuit of predictability. On the logical empiricist interpretation, law is reduced to theoretical propositions describing regularities in judicial practice that might be verified experimentally by observing the behavior of judges. On the pragmatist interpretation, law is reduced to the predictable consequences of action to help the actor pursue his or her goals more effectively, whatever they may be. Holmes's definition was addressed to an au-

---

56 Note 6 above and accompanying text.
57 See, for example, Catharine Wells Hantzis, "Legal Innovation Within the Wider Intellectual Tradition: The Pragmatism of Oliver Wendell Holmes, Jr.," *Northwestern University Law Review*, 82 (1988): 541–95; Robert W. Gordon, "Holmes' *Common Law* as Legal and Social Science," *Hofstra Law Review*, 10 (1982): 719–46; Thomas C. Grey, "Holmes and Legal Pragmatism," *Stanford Law Review*, 41 (1989): 787–870.

dience of lawyers, who were advised to counsel clients solely on the basis of the lawyer's predictions of the judicial consequences, if any, of client action. Jurisprudentially, however, the same definition leads to a denial that law has any existence except in its observable regularities or consequences in society.

To illustrate, Stewart Macaulay's work follows the Holmesian program when it sets social scientific theories about contract practices against conventional rules of contract law. He does this both to challenge the latter's status as law and to generate skeptical jurisprudential conclusions. Macaulay's pioneering studies make a valuable contribution when they suggest that contract law plays a largely marginal role in contracting practices: It is good to know that contract parties do not usually plan transactions in detail or insist on their legal rights when deals sour, preferring for the most part to settle disputes cooperatively when they arise.[58]

On the basis of these studies, however, Macaulay argues that "contract law is not now and never was a descriptively accurate reflection of the institution in operation."[59] Consequently, he asserts more generally,

---

58 See Stewart Macaulay, *Law and the Balance of Power: The Automobile Manufacturers and Their Dealers* (New York: Russell Sage Foundation, 1966); Stewart Macaulay, "Non-Contractual Relations in Business: A Preliminary Study," *American Sociological Review*, 28 (1963): 55–67; Stewart Macaulay, "Private Legislation and the Duty to Read – Business by IBM Machine, the Law of Contracts and Credit Cards," *Vanderbilt Law Review*, 19 (1966): 1051–121. See also Ian R. MacNeil, *The New Social Contract* (New Haven, Conn.: Yale University Press, 1980).

59 Stewart Macaulay, "An Empirical View of Contract," *Wisconsin Law Review* (1985): 465–82, at 466. See also Stewart Macaulay, "Elegant Models, Empirical Pictures, and the Complexities of Contract," *Law & Society Review*, 11 (1977): 507–28. In this respect, Macaulay follows Karl N. Llewellyn, "Some Realism About Realism – Responding to Dean Pound," *Harvard Law Review*, 44 (1931): 1222–64, at 1237 (legal realists shared a "[d]istrust of traditional legal rules and concepts insofar as they purport to *describe* what either courts or people are actually doing"); Cook, "Scientific Method and the Law," at 308 (legal rules and principles describe past behavior of judges).

Much of law operates under the Wizard of Oz principle of jurisprudence – you will recall that the Great Oz was a magnificent and wonderful wizard until Dorothy's dog knocked over the screen so all could see that the Wizard was a charlatan.[60]

Macaulay here draws sweeping skeptical jurisprudential conclusions from his empirical investigations. He does not, however, make it clear from what jurisprudential premise it follows that such skepticism is in order due to the marginality of the law's effects in practice.

There are two ways to fill in the missing premise. One, loosely associating views like Macaulay's with the logical empiricist strand in the Holmesian tradition, supposes that legal rules should describe the general run of behavior in the society. From Macaulay's empirical findings on the marginality of contract law, it would follow that contract law is engaged in false wizardry. It is highly implausible, however, to suppose that legal doctrine purports to describe the general run of contract or other legal practices. As argued above,[61] the law does not describe social practices; rather, it prescribes appropriate conduct. The law envisions a world in which no one sells or possesses hard drugs. The sale and possession of hard drugs is widespread, but these facts do not show that such conduct is lawful. Rather, it shows that the drug law is ineffective.[62] The law cannot be reduced to the observable regularities in behavior without ejecting its normativity on

60 Macaulay, "An Empirical View of Contract," at 478.
61 See § 4.3. Moreover, Macaulay's studies may show only that parties with great frequency elect not to pursue their legal rights.
62 The existence of a *legal system* may depend in part on some degree of effectiveness in its operation. Hart, *The Concept of Law*, pp. 109–14; Joseph Raz, *The Concept of a Legal System*, 2d ed. (Oxford: Clarendon Press, 1980), pp. 103–8. As the Stalinist leaders of Eastern Europe found out in 1989, a legal system obeyed by no one is an ideology. A particular law, however, is in force when it is part of a legal system that is in force. Particular laws thus can be laws even while they are individually ineffective. For a different view, see Lawrence M. Friedman, *The Legal System: A Social Scientific Perspective* (New York: Russell Sage Foundation, 1975), pp. 1–24.

discredited epistemic grounds. Consequently, no quick move is available from the empirical results to the conclusion that law is false wizardry, as though the law must be empirically verifiable.

The second way to make jurisprudential sense of a claim like Macaulay's is to invoke an empirical-pragmatic determinacy condition, following the second strand of the Holmesian tradition. This occurs when it is argued that the "law cannot be defined other than by the difference it makes in society, and empirical inquiry is necessary to determine what that is."[63] The empirical-pragmatic approach is akin to the logical empiricist approach in its reduction of law to empirical facts on epistemic grounds, leaving the normativity of the law out of account. Much of what is said above counsels a rejection of empirical pragmatism in a theory of adjudication. It is different from logical empiricism, however, in that it shifts attention from descriptions of observable behavioral regularities to the empirical consequences of human action.

Empirical pragmatism makes the most sense when a goal is fixed in advance and strategies are needed to pursue that goal effectively. An individual pursues goals, based in his or her own desires, and often wants to know which actions will aid in the pursuit of those goals. Pragmatism counsels the individual to hold only those beliefs that, when acted on, advance the desired project. To be sure, reliable predictions, though factual, can lead to reasons for action when conjoined with individual desires. It often makes sense for a lawyer to adopt a pragmatic attitude in the Holmesian fashion. The primary general norm governing the lawyer's conduct requires loyalty to the client. Accordingly, the desires of the client supply the goals guiding a lawyer's actions on the client's behalf.

A judge, however, should not act on his or her own desires and has no client whose desires fix the goals. Empirical pragmatism consequently has no normative compo-

---

63 David M. Trubeck, "Where the Action Is: Critical Legal Studies and Empiricism," *Stanford Law Review*, 36 (1984): 575–622, at 581.

nent for judges. At the most practical level, it supplies no criteria, apart from someone's desires, for distinguishing relevant from irrelevant facts in a case. It thus lacks an essential part of a successful practical understanding of law and adjudication. Moreover, the empirical-pragmatist determinacy condition lacks any serious bite in constraining judges from abuses of power. Rather, like the other versions of a determinacy condition based in a reductionist and scientific epistemology, it generates legal skepticism by destroying the tradition without building something new and better. It seeks to free judges to do whatever they want to do; if successful in achieving general adherence by judges, it would amount to a self-fulfilling prophecy for legal skepticism. It should not gain such adherence, however, because it rests on a mistaken quick move to legal skepticism. A legal rule does not describe regularities of behavior in society, nor does it exist only insofar as it is demonstrably effective in controlling aggregate behavioral patterns.

4.4.2. The client writ large. The need for desires to fix the goals for a legal pragmatist has further implications for legal theory. Given the practitioner orientation of the common professional training, it is easy for a judge or legal scholar, not having a client, to look for a functional equivalent to a client's desires for the normative element needed to generate reasons for action. Holmes, in his few theoretical comments on what judges should do, treated satisfaction of the aggregate wants and desires of the community, whatever they may be, as the appropriate touchstone.[64] Perhaps that thought developed over the decades into sophisticated, normative versions of law and economics.

Guido Calabresi, for example, premised his landmark study of accident law on satisfying social "desires" that can be revealed only by "careful empirical research."[65] He then

---

64 See § 4.2.
65 For example, Guido Calabresi, *The Costs of Accidents* (New Haven, Conn.: Yale University Press, 1970), p. 15. In this respect, Calabresi,

proposed a framework for developing strategies to pursue an optimal mix of those satisfactions, evoking an image of the legal theorist as lawyer for the society as a whole. Within the Holmesian tradition, there are two reasons for finding such an approach attractive. One: by focusing on empirically knowable aggregate desires, whether expressed in the market, by voting, or through social scientific research, the basis for the law's normativity seems to be reduced to hard, knowable stuff in a manner compatible with the reductionist epistemology considered above. The other reason is that one thereby avoids any need to take responsibility for making normative judgments oneself. Rather, the judge or legal scholar can remain detached, like a lawyer, while serving the interests of a client writ large – the market, the electorate, or other aggregate expressions of wants and desires.

Premising public policy on the satisfaction of community desires in this way may be fine when making law within the permitted range, at least in the legislative arena as Calabresi intended. The reasons for thus framing public policy, however, are not the epistemically driven reductionist and responsibility-avoiding reasons rooted in the Holmesian tradition. The good reasons stem, rather, from principles of political morality, including principles of democracy and conceptions of the good. These principles, like principles of the right, can supply reasons for action for legislators and other lawmakers. They require, however, full normative consideration. They should not be adopted only because they satisfy a hidden epistemic standard.

Others, however, would treat all adjudication as an exercise in consequentially satisfying aggregate popular desires, especially those expressed economically. This is objectionable as an implicit theory of adjudication when it is based on external epistemic standards. Such standards do not dis-

too, follows an important strand of the legal realist tradition. See, for example, Cook, "Scientific Method and the Law," at 308 ("the worth or value of a given rule of law can be determined only . . . by ascertaining . . . whether it promotes or retards the attainment of desired ends").

tinguish among different laws or elements of laws; rather, they regard all legal concepts as empty of meaning insofar as they purport to establish rights and duties. The Holmesian approach has the curious result of understanding all legal standards to generate the same question, despite the differences in their texts. Calabresi, for example, argues that civil liability should be placed on the cheapest cost avoider, the party in the best position to do the cost-benefit analysis and act on it.[66] Legal rules draw distinctions between tort and contract and, within tort, between requirements of intentional conduct, negligence, causation, and harm. Under Calabresi's approach, however, these doctrines collapse into the same question.[67] Accordingly, whether Garcia caused harm to Williams in a tavern by punching him in the nose may be thought to require consideration of whether Garcia, Williams, the bartender, the tavern owner, the other customers, the tavern owner's insurer, the bartender's possible insurer, or just about anyone else was the cheapest cost avoider. Whether Garcia intended to punch Williams requires the same analysis, and whether the tavern had a contractual obligation to protect Williams again turns on the same considerations.[68] Despite this caricature, it is easy to see the economic analysis of law at work in its characteristic fashion, treating the legal rules and other standards as meaningless in their own terms – as mere pretexts for engaging in at-large policy analysis.

66 Guido Calabresi & Jon T. Hirschoff, "Toward a Test for Strict Liability in Torts," *Yale Law Journal*, 81 (1972): 1055–85, at 1060.
67 See Guido Calabresi, "Concerning Cause and the Law of Torts: An Essay for Harry Kalven, Jr.," *University of Chicago Law Review*, 43 (1975): 69–108, at 100–8. It might be argued that such uses of economic analysis are meant to be normative even when a case is used as the vehicle for evaluating the law. If so, however, it would be entirely unnecessary to frame a question in doctrinal terms of intentional conduct, causation, or harm and then to answer the question on economic grounds. Since conventional doctrinal terms are often used to frame questions and to state conclusions, it seems that economic grounds are being offered to those who are bound to work within those terms.
68 I thank Jules Coleman for the example.

131

When the reductionist epistemology is jettisoned, however, it can be seen that the law may require a judge to take an action that does not, on balance, satisfy the greater desires. For one thing, the background justification for a law might exclude such consequential considerations. Thus, the Eighth Amendment's prohibition on cruel and unusual punishments prohibits torture, as do international human rights covenants, because it is wrong. It excludes case-by-case balancing of the public policy benefits of torturing a prisoner against the suffering experienced from the torture. For another thing, a legal standard may seek to satisfy aggregate desires as a rule. That is, it may succeed only if it is applied in each case without exception when it is over-inclusive. The reductionist epistemology does not permit such a law to be interpreted and applied by judges effectively to achieve its goal, even when the law is produced by democratic processes.

4.4.3. *Social science in judging.* The foregoing criticisms of certain recent uses of social science in legal theory should not be understood to express hostility to social science. It is important for many purposes to develop better empirically based theories of the role of law in society. Such theories are academically valuable because they advance understanding for its own sake, all the better when the limits of external understandings are made clear. Moreover, such studies can have important implications for law reform. Many laws are based on general background empirical beliefs in addition to the more explicit normative premises. The law might fail to realize its purposes in the social and business context in which it operates because those empirical assumptions turn out to be false or misleading. Empirical studies can establish the need for law reform based on more realistic premises. Similarly, empirical studies can highlight the unseen costs of existing laws, identify the need for new laws, and help in the development of better legal strategies.[69] Additionally, em-

69 See, for example, Teresa A. Sullivan, Elizabeth Warren, & Jay Law-

pirical studies and narratives can correct for stereotypical background beliefs that can distort understanding of the facts in cases. The critical points are only that empirical approaches to law, driven by a mistaken determinacy condition, do not sustain any quick moves to skeptical jurisprudential conclusions about the conventional law.

The framework of reasoning offered by the good faith thesis helps to clarify the place of social scientific and other findings of fact in judicial deliberations. Like any plain fact, each social scientific finding is, without more, inert, having no force in practical deliberations. It takes on normative force, and becomes a legal reason for action, when it is coupled with a prescriptive standard that gives it that significance. The descriptive aspect of a legal reason might thus depend on scientific support, but the necessary prescriptive aspect does not (unless it is equated with someone's desires, which equation itself requires a normative basis). Judges and legal scholars should not, for epistemic reasons, neglect the prescriptive aspect. Social science should not be used to avoid normative argument, deliberation, judgment, responsibility, and accountability.

Consider a social scientific study that concludes the imposition of death as a penalty for murder is more likely for a criminal defendant if his victim was white.[70] That study may have significance for many purposes; it suggests, for one thing, that death penalty practices manifest a disturbing background cultural disposition to value white lives more highly than black lives. It is a different question, however, whether the scientific finding is a reason for concluding that the death penalty is cruel and unusual punishment within the meaning of the Eighth Amendment to the U.S. Constitution. The Supreme Court has held that the death penalty is unconstitutional if it is imposed in a way that discriminates

rence Westbrook, *As We Forgive Our Debtors: Bankruptcy and Consumer Credit in America* (New York: Oxford University Press, 1989).

70   See David C. Baldus, Charles A. Pulaski, & George Woodworth, *Equal Justice and the Death Penalty* (Boston: Northeastern University Press, 1990).

on the basis of the race of the defendant.[71] It also has held, however, that it is not unconstitutional if it discriminates due to the race of the victim, even assuming the validity of a study finding such discrimination in Georgia.[72] One can quarrel with the Court's normative judgment. *That* should be a major focus of argument. Whichever way one leans on that question, however, the Court was correct in considering the validity of the study a separate question from its legal significance. Moreover, the social scientific findings pertaining to the race of the victim are, for the time being, legally irrelevant in death penalty litigation under the federal Constitution. The corpus of law, as interpreted by the Supreme Court, includes no prescriptive standard that makes the race of the victim a legal reason in that context.

In adjudication, social science may supply facts that are legal reasons by virtue of the law's standards. Social science itself does not indicate what a judge or anyone else should do, and it is not so obvious where justice lies that explicit normative argument is superfluous. The point may seem banal to some, but it is neglected often enough to justify making it again.

71 Furman v. Georgia, 408 U.S. 238 (1972).
72 McClesky v. Kemp, 481 U.S. 279 (1987).

Chapter 5

Critical claims

5.1. POLITICAL DETERMINACY

There are two ways of attempting to ground the determinacy condition from a critical and political standpoint, outside the practice of law and judging. One, developed by members of the critical legal studies movement, holds the law up to the claims it is said to make for itself. That is, the law is criticized for failing to deliver on its own pretense though the critic thinks the pretense unfounded. General determinacy of results, it is urged, is one of those claims. Prevailing practices are said to show this claim to be a pretense with harmful implications for our understanding of law, hampering social change. The second seeks to derive the determinacy condition from accepted principles of political morality, notably Rule of Law values said to be implicit in traditional democratic political theory. Neither of these political claims, however, adequately grounds the determinacy condition in a way that threatens the good faith thesis. The reasons for this conclusion help to clarify what it means for a judge to be constrained by the law.

5.2. INTERNAL CLAIMS OF THE LAW

Legal indeterminacy claims advanced by adherents of critical legal studies might start with the claims the law makes for itself and question whether the law lives up to its own advertising. To agglomerate several versions of this "internal cri-

135

tique,"[1] the argument is that (1) the law, as conventionally understood at the present time, claims that the outcomes of judicial decisions are generally determined by legal rules.[2] But, according to one version (2A), legal rules are either so many that they conflict or so few that they are over- and under-inclusive, in either case requiring judges to exercise a hidden discretion.[3] According to another version (2B), law-makers are animated by such a hodgepodge of conflicting impulses that the corpus of law is incoherent, again requiring judges to make fresh choices in adjudication.[4] A third version (2C) holds that every legal problem triggers our deep impulses for needing and simultaneously fearing others, producing a fundamental contradiction that permeates the law and generates pervasive and stubborn indeterminacy.[5] Consequently, the argument goes, (3) the law cannot live up to the pretense of its own claims to determinacy.

Most scholarly debate has focused on the three specific

1   Professor Joseph Singer has given the clearest statement of the status of the indeterminacy thesis as internal critique:

>   Two points must be made at the outset about the character of the claim that law is indeterminate. First, it is an empirical claim about existing legal theories and arguments. . . . Second, it is an internal critique. This is a critique from within, a critique that uses the premises of traditional legal theory against itself.

Joseph W. Singer, "The Player and the Cards: Nihilism and Legal Theory," *Yale Law Journal*, 94 (1984): 1–70, at 10. The technique was pioneered in Roberto M. Unger, *Knowledge and Politics* (New York: Free Press, 1975).

2   For example, Singer, "The Player and the Cards," at 12 ("Determinacy is necessary to the ideology of the rule of law, for both theorists and judges. It is the only way judges can appear to apply the law rather than make it.").

3   Duncan Kennedy, "Form and Substance in Private Law Adjudication," *Harvard Law Review*, 89 (1976): 1685–778.

4   Roberto M. Unger, *The Critical Legal Studies Movement* (Cambridge: Harvard University Press, 1986), p. 9.

5   Duncan Kennedy, "The Structure of Blackstone's Commentaries," *Buffalo Law Review*, 28 (1979): 209–382, at 211–12. See also Mark G. Kelman, *A Guide to Critical Legal Studies* (Cambridge: Harvard University Press, 1987), pp. 15–113.

arguments for indeterminacy (2A–C), which do not bear on the grounds for accepting the determinacy condition.[6] We need not review these extensive debates because the good faith thesis accepts that the law may be stubbornly indeterminate in a significant way. For present purposes, the focus is on the assertion (1) that the law at present claims that the outcomes of judicial decisions are generally determined by legal rules. If this were so, the determinacy condition might be internally grounded. Accepting stubborn indeterminacy in the law would then imply the internal incoherence of judging under law within a constitutional democracy. The internal critique does not get off the ground, however, if (1) is false because the law does not in fact claim to achieve determinate results across the board. Two questions require attention to assess the critical postulate. First, what does it mean for "the law" to make a claim? Second, is the requisite determinacy claim in fact made?

It is only in part an empirical question whether the law *claims* that it produces determinate results. The first step toward an answer is conceptual: Who is entitled to make claims on the law's behalf? The critics might think that their indeterminacy claims get off the ground by working from the claims of "liberal legalism" without endorsing them. To defend the determinacy condition, they often look to intellectual defenders of liberalism who write about the role of law in a liberal society. In his internal critique, for example, Joseph Singer mainly cites philosophers and academic lawyers such as John Rawls, Ronald Dworkin, Bruce Ackerman, and the like.[7] David Trubeck traces the liberal idea of a legal order to Max Weber.[8] Others look to Langdell or Bentham.[9]

6 For discussion of an important critical work involving adjudication directly, see §§ 5.4 and following.
7 Singer, "The Player and the Cards," at 10–14.
8 David M. Trubeck, "Where the Action Is: Critical Legal Theory and Empiricism," *Stanford Law Review*, 36 (1984): 575–622, at 577–8.
9 See Gerald J. Postema, *Bentham and the Common Law Tradition* (Oxford: Clarendon Press, 1986); Thomas C. Grey, "Langdell's Orthodoxy,"

This threatens to turn the debate into a self-conscious one about academic theorizing, not about the law. For the purposes of a critique internal to the law, the proposition that the law claims to be determinate is not supported by citing the reformist aspirations of a philosopher like Bentham, the theories of a sociologist like Weber, or the casebooks of a teacher like Langdell. No professor speaks for the law. No reformist or academic theory constitutes the law's claims.[10]

If it makes sense to talk about the claims of the law at all, the determinacy claim must be made by the law through its own official spokesmen. Judges and other public officials might make such claims in the course of practice. As Joseph Raz put it when arguing that the law claims to possess legitimate authority: "The claims the law makes for itself are evident from the language it adopts and from the opinions expressed by its spokesmen."[11] Judges do speak to citizens affected by the law from the bench and in their opinions. These expressions can be parsed for evidence of a determinacy claim.

The second step toward an answer is empirical: Do judges and other officials in practice claim that their actions are determined by the law without intervening discretion? The language of the law and judicial opinions contain evidence in support of affirmative and negative answers. For the affirmative, it might be suggested that laws commonly use mandatory language and that judges write of their decisions as "compelled" or "required." A judge may say there is "no choice" when in fact an argument can be developed for a

---

University of Pittsburgh Law Review, 45 (1983): 1–53. Less vulnerable to this criticism is Duncan Kennedy's study of Blackstone, whose influence on the law was sufficiently direct and substantial to sustain the role assigned to him. Kennedy, "The Structure of Blackstone's Commentaries." For criticism of Kennedy, see Alan Watson, "Comment: The Structure of Blackstone's Commentaries," Yale Law Journal, 97 (1988): 795–821.

10 On the claims of liberalism, see §§ 5.3 and following.
11 Joseph Raz, "Authority, Law and Morality," The Monist, 68 (1985): 295–322, at 300. See also Joseph Raz, The Authority of Law (Oxford: Clarendon Press, 1979), pp. 28–33.

different decision. These uses of language sound like a claim of determinacy. For the negative, however, the reply is, first, that such language is ambiguous. Legal duties are mandatory in a normative sense because the action supported by the stronger reasons is compelled. Given the disrepute of determinate-formalism, even a grudgingly charitable interpretation would require that these language uses do not implicate general determinacy of results. Moreover, the institutionalized language of judicial practice is strong evidence that the law does not claim to dictate results. Judges write "opinions" and issue "judgments," both terms highlighting tolerance for legal indeterminacy. A great many rules of appellate practice refer to a trial court's "discretion" on many matters. Indeed, among all legal officials, the prevalence of officially acknowledged discretion is great, and much of it is intentionally conferred on officials by the law. The balance of evidence seems not to support the determinacy condition on these grounds, but no firm conclusion would be well grounded. As with most such things, the truth probably is that judges and other legal officials disagree if they have thought about it.

The inconclusiveness of the empirical evidence should not be surprising, especially to members of the critical legal studies movement. Truly, "the law" cannot be said to make the determinacy claim without making the very reification error its critics commonly complain of.[12] A principal mission in much of the recent critical literature has been to deny that law is an objective entity with one essence or with a timeless and inevitable shape. Rather, it is seen as a contingent, multifaceted practice that can be molded to many purposes. For example, Roberto Unger grounded his indeterminacy claim in the improbability of many minds with many convictions converging to make laws with sufficient completeness and coherence to produce determinate results.[13] Paul A. Brest argued powerfully, in opposition to constitutional in-

12 Peter Gabel, "Reification in Legal Reasoning," *Research in Law & Sociology*, 3 (1980): 25–51.
13 Unger, *The Critical Legal Studies Movement*.

terpretivists who advanced original intent theories, that there was in fact a multiplicity of original intents at different levels of abstraction, leaving the Constitution open to a wide range of interpretations.[14] Robert Gordon suggested that one mark of critical legal histories is the inclination to take each event "as situated not on a single developmental path but on multiple trajectories of possibility."[15] It is therefore surprising that some critical indeterminacy arguments seem to rest on a premise asserting that the law as practiced judicially at present makes one univocal claim to general determinacy of results. When this is rejected, even as internal critique, this part of the critical indeterminacy debate simply evaporates. The determinacy condition is not well grounded in the claims, if any, that the law makes for itself.

5.3. INTERNAL CLAIMS OF LIBERALISM

A further possible way to ground the determinacy condition – and the most important one – looks to the ideology of political liberalism within which the law is supposed to operate at present.[16] Unlike a critique internal to the law, this approach begins by describing the features a legal system should possess if it is to govern legitimately according to liberal theory, whether or not one endorses the theory. In a constitutional democracy, the demand for legitimacy requires that judicial decisions be justifiable uses of the power of the state.[17] The question is: *By what right* does the indi-

---

14 Paul A. Brest, "The Misconceived Quest for the Original Understanding," *Boston University Law Review*, 60 (1980): 204–38, at 234. See also Mark V. Tushnet, *Red, White, and Blue: A Critical Analysis of Constitutional Law* (Cambridge: Harvard University Press, 1988).

15 Robert W. Gordon, "Critical Legal Histories," *Stanford Law Review*, 36 (1984): 57–125, at 112.

16 For these purposes, "liberal" should be understood to encompass almost everyone in the political mainstream in the United States. It stands in contrast to totalitarian, socialist, or communitarian political systems, not in contrast to "conservative."

17 See Steven J. Burton, *An Introduction to Law and Legal Reasoning* (Boston: Little, Brown, 1985), pp. 165–216; R. Kent Greenawalt,

Critical claims

vidual sitting behind the bench use official power to take another person's property, liberty, or life? The law, by prescribing the permissible uses of governmental power, is supposed to protect the liberty of citizens from arbitrary or abusive governmental action. Judges review the legality of official actions by others and wield official power themselves. Consequently, the political legitimacy of a judge's action depends crucially on its accordance with the law.[18] This ensemble of values is expressed by the liberal ideal of a Rule of Law.[19]

5.3.1. The rule of law. The determinacy condition often is thought to hold a key place in the Rule of Law, requiring that "[r]ule must be by law and not discretion."[20] Given the wide-

"How Law Can Be Determinate," *UCLA Law Review*, 38 (1990): 1–86, at 2–3; Ken Kress, "Legal Indeterminacy," *California Law Review*, 77 (1989): 283–337, at 285.

18   The concept of legitimacy is distinct from the social-theoretic concept of legitimation – perceived legitimacy – as well as from de facto authority. Legitimacy is a normative concept which signals that a government's use of coercion is justified. It includes the idea of legitimate authority, implying that citizens are under a moral obligation to obey the law, whether or not they believe they have this obligation. Legitimation, by contrast, is relevant mainly in explanatory, predictive, or descriptive inquiries within a theory about the law. It signals that citizens generally believe, perhaps mistakenly, that the law has legitimate authority. On legitimation theory, see Alan Hyde, "The Concept of Legitimation in The Sociology of Law," *Wisconsin Law Review* (1983): 379–426. De facto authority concerns only the effective power of the rulers to rule.

19   See John Rawls, *A Theory of Justice* (Cambridge: Harvard University Press, Belknap Press, 1972), p. 235. For a sample of recent accounts of the Rule of Law, see Andrew Altman, *Critical Legal Studies: A Liberal Critique* (Princeton, N.J.: Princeton University Press, 1990), pp. 9–13, 22–7; Ronald Dworkin, *A Matter of Principle* (Cambridge: Harvard University Press, 1985), pp. 9–32; Lon L. Fuller, *The Morality of Law*, 2d ed. (New Haven: Yale University Press, 1969), pp. 33–94; Michael S. Moore, "A Natural Law Theory of Interpretation," *Southern California Law Review*, 58 (1985): 277–398, at 313–18; Margaret Jane Radin, "Reconsidering the Rule of Law," *Boston University Law Review*, 69 (1989): 781–819; Joseph Raz, *The Authority of Law* (Oxford: Clarendon Press, 1987), pp. 210–32; *The Rule of Law: Ideal or Ideology?*, eds. Allan C. Hutchinson & Patrick Monahan (Toronto: Carswell, 1987).

20   Allan C. Hutchinson and Patrick Monahan, "Democracy and the Rule of Law," in *Rule of Law: Ideal or Ideology*: 97–119, at 101.

spread presence of discretion in existing adjudicatory practices, the determinacy condition consequently can be used as a strong reason for restricting their scope.[21] Friedrich von Hayek, for example, claims that the Rule of Law "means that government in all its actions is bound by rules fixed and announced beforehand – rules which make it possible to foresee with fair certainty how the authority will use its coercive powers in given circumstances."[22] Former Attorney General Edwin Meese III argued that the constitutional Founders supported a "government of laws and not of men,"[23] and expected "the judges . . . to resist any political effort to depart from the literal provisions of the Constitution."[24] Justice Antonin Scalia believes that "[p]redictability . . . is a needful characteristic of any law worthy of the name."[25]

Such claims are advanced most often by those who disapprove of the creation of new rights (the right to privacy, for example) by courts.[26] These political or substantive goals, however, do not provide grounds for requiring determinacy of results as a matter of legal theory. That would give priority to the political over the intellectual.[27] The better rationale for this version of the determinacy condition is the value of liber-

---

21   The determinacy condition affords a ready-made argument for conservatives who disapprove of the recent history of expansive adjudication by the U.S. Supreme Court. See, for example, Robert H. Bork, *The Tempting of America* (New York: Free Press, 1990), pp. 140–1. From a more moderate perspective, Professor John Hart Ely implicitly uses a strong determinacy condition as his standard of criticism when rejecting "fundamental value" theories of constitutional adjudication. See John Hart Ely, *Democracy and Distrust* (Cambridge: Harvard University Press, 1980), pp. 43–73.

22   Friedrich von Hayek, *The Road to Serfdom* (Chicago: University of Chicago Press, 1944), p. 54. Note, however, that even von Hayek calls only for "fair certainty."

23   Edwin Meese, "The Supreme Court of the United States: Bulwark of a Limited Constitution," *South Texas Law Review*, 27 (1986): 455–66.

24   Ibid., at 456.

25   Antonin Scalia, "The Rule of Law as a Law of Rules," *University of Chicago Law Review*, 56 (1989): 1175–88, at 1179.

26   For example, Bork, *The Tempting of America*, pp. 110–26.

27   See §§ 1.4 and following.

ty, understood solely as the absence of external restraint. For many conservatives, a rule of determinate law is attractive in theory because it is thought to enhance (negative) liberty by letting everyone know when the public force may fall on them. Individuals can adjust their conduct accordingly, relying on the state to leave them unencumbered in all other respects. This virtue of determinate law, however, is not a constant property of all laws. It may be most important, for example, when transactions are planned and people both know the law and rely on it, as in many real property transactions. It may be unimportant when advance planning is not a realistic part of the picture, as in many tort or discrimination contexts. The good faith thesis allows for determinate laws when determinacy is more important than the countervailing considerations. Liberty should count in the balance when designing laws, but liberty is not a political value that dominates all others in all circumstances.[28] Hence it is not a sufficient ground to make determinacy of results a necessary condition for fulfillment of the judicial duty to uphold the law.

When it is given such a central role, determinacy of results is an inviting target for radical criticism of the legal tradition. Sustaining the claim that the law is generally indeterminate would seem to require that the scope of legitimate adjudication be restricted to the vanishing point or, alternatively, that it be opened up to previously unacceptable possibilities. Duncan Kennedy once drew a close connection between the consent of the governed and the determinacy of the law in his characterization and critique of a popular version of the liberal theory of justice

> which asserts that justice consists in the impartial application of rules deriving their legitimacy from the prior consent of those subject to them. . . . [A] distinction between rule making and rule applying cannot be made to legitimate the coer-

---

28 See Isaiah Berlin, *Four Essays on Liberty* (Oxford: Oxford University Press, 1968).

cive power of judges. . . . [L]iberal thought has been unsuccessful in the attempt to use a theory of [determinate] rules to transfer the postulated legitimacy of decision based on consent to the judicial administrators of a body of legal rules.[29]

Critical indeterminacy claims seek to establish that legal conclusions can find no adequate grounding in the authoritative legal materials and that law applying blends into lawmaking, allowing political and ideological struggle within the law. The law, as conventionally understood, would thus be deprived of its privileged position in public debate. The field on any occasion, including adjudication, would be opened to unbridled politics, legitimating efforts at radical change.

The determinacy condition, however, is not as central to the Rule of Law as the conservatives or the critics might wish. Some mainstream theorists have supported the determinacy condition, but many have not. They agree, however, that the Rule of Law rules out arbitrariness of a politically objectionable sort.[30] To see why determinacy of results is not required to avoid objectionable arbitrariness, we should distinguish three kinds of relationships that might obtain between legal standards and the results in cases. Critical claims about determinacy are often ambiguous about whether they deny a causal relationship, a deductive relationship, or a relationship of authorization. I will argue that the determinacy condition is not central to the Rule of Law because a causal or deductive relationship is not required. The authorization relationship, which limits a judge's legitimate reasons for action, constrains judges sufficiently to satisfy the

29 Duncan Kennedy, "Legal Formality," *Journal of Legal Studies*, 2 (1973): 351–98, at 351, 354.
30 Dicey made nonarbitrariness central to the idea of a "rule of law." Albert Venn Dicey, *Introduction to the Study of the Law of the Constitution*, 8th ed. (London: Macmillan, 1915), p. 198 (the Rule of Law means "the absolute supremacy or predominance of regular law as opposed to the influence of arbitrary power, and excludes the existence of arbitrariness, or prerogative, or even of wide discretionary authority on the part of the government"). See also John Locke, "Of the Extent of the Legislative Power," in *The Second Treatise of Government* (Indianapolis, Ind.: Bobbs-Merrill, 1952), pp. 75–81.

requirements of democratic political theory. The good faith thesis fits within that conception of the Rule of Law requiring only the constraint of a chain of authorization.

5.3.2. Causal chains. One way to make sense of the claim that indeterminacy implies arbitrariness is by analogy to an external causal theory. "Constraint" and "determinacy" might be metaphors for a causal connection between the law and judicial outcomes.[31] If so, the law would supposedly constrain or determine judicial behavior, if at all, as laws of nature determine the behavior of billiard balls. This might make it possible to explain and understand the genesis of the judicial decision, as well as to predict the future course of adjudication. The indeterminacy of the law's official standards in that light is like a gap in the causal chain that defeats the power of those standards to affect the behavior of judges. Failure of the law to cause a judge to reach a particular result would leave only two alternatives: Either there are other, nonlegal causes for the result or, failing an adequate causal explanation, the result must be arbitrary. The result would be unconstrained and arbitrary even if there were good nonlegal causal explanations because nothing except the law satisfies the Rule of Law's requirements.

The opening passage in Holmes's *The Common Law,* quoted at the beginning of Chapter 1, invited a shift from the study of legal doctrine to studies of the genesis of the law.[32] Accepting Holmes's invitation, many legal realists sought, as outside observers of the judicial process, to explain the psychological, social, and political causes of judicial decisions in

31 See § 4.3.
32 As Wasserstrom put it:

> The dictum that "general propositions do not decide concrete cases" and the assertion that "the life of the law has not been logic: it has been experience," have been taken to signify that rules of law were not the means by which courts decided particular cases.

> Richard A. Wasserstrom, *The Judicial Decision* (Stanford, Calif.: Stanford University Press, 1961), p. 16.

order better to predict what judges will do in cases.[33]
Causal metaphors also underlie the work of leading critical
scholars who adhere to the indeterminacy thesis, though
they have little interest in prediction. Summarizing critical
indeterminacy claims, sociologist David Trubeck argues that
critical legal studies "look at the operations of the law from
the outside, asking what causes the law to develop as it does
and what impact the law has."[34] Historian Robert Gordon
also characterizes the claim in causal terms:

> The same body of law, in the same context, can always lead to
> contrary results because the law is indeterminate at its core, in
> its inception, not just in its applications. [Critics] . . . don't
> mean . . . that there are never any predictable *causal relations*
> between legal forms and anything else. . . . [T]here are plenty
> of short- and medium-run stable regularities in social life, in-
> cluding regularities in the interpretation and application, in
> given contexts, of legal rules. . . . The Critical claim of inde-
> terminacy is simply that none of these regularities are *neces-
> sary consequences* of a given regime of rules.[35]

The connections from democratic consent to lawmaking to
law applying to the social consequences of the law perhaps
could be understood theoretically through the metaphor of a
causal chain.

Indeterminacy implies arbitrariness, however, only if we
accept both that the causal metaphor is the relevant one and

33 For example, Felix Cohen, "Transcendental Nonsense and the Functional Approach," *Columbia Law Review*, 35 (1935): 809–49, at 849
("legal criticism is empty without objective description of the causes
and consequences of legal decisions").
34 Trubeck, "Critical Legal Theory and Empiricism," at 587.
35 Robert W. Gordon, "Critical Legal Histories," *Stanford Law Review*, 36
(1984): 57–125, at 114, 125 (some emphasis added). See also Kelman,
A Guide to Critical Legal Studies, pp. 245–6 (explaining legal indeterminacy as indeterminacy of the claimed genesis of laws from social
conditions); Unger, *The Critical Legal Studies Movement*, p. 9 (incoherence of law results from the many conflicts of interests and
vision that lawmaking involves); Kennedy, "The Structure of Blackstone's Commentaries," at 210–13 (laws result from and reflect contradictory feelings involving needs for others and fear of them).

that causal determination and randomness exhaust the possibilities. The causal metaphor should be rejected for many reasons.[36] Most important, causal explanatory theory can be pursued only by observers from outside judicial practice, which is the vantage point for critical legal studies. As indicated above,[37] external observers are prone to miss how the law functions normatively in the lives of participants in judicial practice. Moreover, they are prone to conflate problems of legal indeterminacy – whether multiple outcomes are "lawful" in a normative sense – with the classic problems of free will and (causal) determinism. Judges do not understand themselves to be explaining the psychological, social, or political causes of their own decisions, to be predicting what they themselves will do, or to be describable scientifically like rats. From the practical standpoint, we seem unable to conceive of our own actions as wholly determined causally, though, as observers, we sometimes see the actions of others as obeying scientific laws. From a normative standpoint, moreover, we seem unable to dispense with a concept – whether we call it "free will" or not – that demarcates the kinds of acts for which people are responsible.

Judges understand themselves as, among other things, free agents who are duty bound to uphold the law by taking legally justified official acts.[38] Judicial critics fault judges soundly for failing in that endeavor or for undertaking and continuing it in an unjust legal regime. The claims of judges and of judicial critics are intelligible only if we assume that judges are responsible for the decisions they take.[39] Accordingly, a practical understanding of adjudication focuses in

36 See also § 2.2.2.
37 See § 4.3.
38 Herein lies a possible explanation for why judges generally have not responded to the legal realists' call for them to disclose the "real grounds" for their decisions. The legal realists thought the "real grounds" are causally explanatory reasons, whereas the judges might reasonably think the "real grounds" are justificatory reasons of just the sort they routinely give.
39 External descriptive and causal theories can supplement a practical understanding with an additional kind of understanding. Neither alone completes the picture.

147

the first instance on the content of judicial duty, involving what judges ought to do. The legitimacy of the law and adjudication, in turn, is understood to depend on critical standards of judging that also say what judges and other legal actors ought to do, whether or not they agree.

A determinacy condition for fulfilling the judicial duty to uphold the law cannot be grounded in the requirements of causal explanatory theories. These theories say nothing about the guiding norms of judicial duty. Intellectual clarity requires the conclusions of causal and other external theories to be carefully qualified by the limitations implicit in the kind of theoretical inquiry that produced them.[40] To say that the law, without more, does not sufficiently *cause* judges to reach their particular decisions is unobjectionable (and unremarkable). Nothing follows, however, to establish the sort of arbitrariness that cannot be tolerated by the Rule of Law. Causal determination and randomness do not exhaust the possibilities because judges are not like turtles that respond to external stimuli without pause for thought. Judges are, or in jurisprudence are presupposed to be, responsible agents with rational capacity even when bound by the law. The implication of arbitrariness from causal indeterminacy is fallacious because it is absurd to believe either that we are never responsible for our acts or that all responsible action is either arbitrary or involuntary.

5.3.3. Deductive chains. The second way to understand the nonarbitrariness requirement of the Rule of Law conceives the tie between the law and judicial decisions as a chain of deductive logic, supplemented only by straightforward findings of fact. Von Hayek claims that judicial decisions "must be deducible from the rules of law and from those circumstances to which the law refers and which can be known to the parties concerned."[41] In an early work that inspired

---

40   The same is true for internal theories or practical understandings.
41   Friedrich von Hayek, *The Constitution of Liberty* (Chicago: University of Chicago Press, 1960), pp. 213–14. See also Richard A. Posner, *The Problems of Jurisprudence* (Cambridge: Harvard University Press, 1990), p. 43.

much of the critical literature, Kennedy similarly defined decision according to rule in the typical case as "the application of *per se* rules, that is, decision by the selection of one (or a very few) easily identifiable aspects of the situation, and the justification of the decision uniquely by appeal to the presence or absence of that element."[42] Such rules "identify small groups of easily determined factual aspects of situations as the triggers for the mechanical application of official sanctions."[43] In several works, Kennedy argued that more open-ended legal standards also are generally available to justify contrary results. The decision to use rules or standards cannot be determined by the rules.[44] So judging is open to an indefinite range of political arguments and actions. He effectively asserted that the Rule of Law is an illusion because its requirement of deductive determinacy is illusory.[45]

Does judicial duty in a constitutional democracy require a deductive determinacy condition? We are in trouble if it does because repeated critiques of determinate-formalism over this century have devastated any lingering beliefs that a jurisprudence requiring only deductive chains and univocal findings of fact is practicable.[46] It is questionable, however, whether anyone of much repute ever defended the idea of deductive chains in the strong form used as a foil by critics.[47]

42 Kennedy, "Legal Formality," at 355.
43 Ibid., at 356 n. 11.
44 Ibid.; Kennedy, "Form and Substance."
45 See also David Kairys, "Legal Reasoning," in *The Politics of Law*, ed. David Kairys (New York: Pantheon Books, 1982): 11–17, at 11; Singer, "The Player and the Cards"; Joseph W. Singer, "The Legal Rights Debate in Analytical Jurisprudence from Bentham to Hohfield," *Wisconsin Law Review* (1982): 975–1059, at 1015; Mark V. Tushnet, "Following the Rules Laid Down: A Critique of Interpretivism and Neutral Principles," *Harvard Law Review*, 96 (1983): 781–827.
46 The original is Roscoe Pound, "Mechanical Jurisprudence," *Columbia Law Review*, 8 (1908): 605–23.
47 One obscure writer did say that "[e]very judicial act resulting in a judgment consists of a pure deduction." John M. Zane, "German Legal Philosophy," *Michigan Law Review*, 16 (1916): 288–375, at 338. A common citation is to Justice Roberts's famous description of the Supreme Court's job in constitutional litigation:

As Ronald Dworkin nicely put it, "So far [critics] have had little luck in caging and exhibiting mechanical jurisprudents (all specimens captured – even Blackstone and Joseph Beale – have had to be released after careful reading of their texts.)"[48] Judicial opinions in which it is claimed that a conclusion is "required by" an argument do not imply that all that is involved is the plugging of clear facts into deductive chains of legal rules. The stronger reasons for action normatively *require* action accordingly by a judge who is in good faith. In the identification of legal reasons, logic plays its limited roles – to transfer the truth value of the premises to a conclusion and to preserve consistency. Logic does not affirm the truth of the premises or, therefore, the conclusion.[49] It is necessary to legal reasoning, but in itself is of trivial importance. Accordingly, the idea that a democratic conception of the Rule of Law requires a deductive determinacy condition is doubtful on its face because unintelligent.

There are two further arguments as to why the Rule of Law should not be understood to require deductive chains. One argument, focusing on the demand for legitimacy, was developed by Ken Kress.[50] He believes that "[i]ndeterminacy matters because legitimacy matters" and that legitimacy implies that citizens have a prima facie moral obligation to obey

> When an act of Congress is appropriately challenged in the courts as not conforming to the constitutional mandate the judicial branch of the government has only one duty, – to lay the article of the Constitution which is invoked beside the statute which is challenged and to decide whether the latter squares with the former.
>
> United States v. Butler, 297 U.S. 1, 62 (1936). The squaring metaphor is ambiguous. A full reading of the opinion provides a context that does not support a deductive interpretation. See also Wasserstrom, *The Judicial Decision*, pp. 12–38.

48 Ronald Dworkin, *Taking Rights Seriously* (Cambridge: Harvard University Press, 1977), pp. 15–16.
49 What matters is the identification and formulation of the premises, which cannot be understood as the conclusions from other deductive chains without entering an infinite regress.
50 Kress, "Legal Indeterminacy." See also Burton, *Law and Legal Reasoning*, pp. 165–214.

the law.[51] He challenged the assumptions, however, that consent legitimates the legal system and that "the *only* way judicial decisions could be legitimate is if they rigidly follow ('strictly interpret or construe') statutory or constitutional provisions, themselves legitimated by consent."[52] Leading scholars in political philosophy recently exploded the idea that consent legitimates the legal system, arguing that there are a number of grounds for legitimacy, no one of which legitimates existing legal practices in toto.[53] Accordingly, there may be no general, prima facie moral obligation to obey the law just because it is law or democratically made law. Rather, there may be particular obligations for some people to obey all law, or for all people to obey some laws, due to a mix of the grounds for political obligation – consent, tacit consent, legitimate authority, fair play, the duty to uphold just institutions, fraternity, and utility.

In other words, legitimacy attaches to particular kinds of laws in relation to particular groups of persons in various circumstances, not to legal systems or practices as such (or to "liberal legalism"). Professor Kress reviewed the grounds of legitimacy and found that, "For nearly every such alleged ground, with only occasional exceptions, either (1) the ground fails to generate a true moral obligation to obey, or if it does obligate, then (2) it obligates even when the law is indeterminate."[54] For example, surely everyone does not give an informed, deliberate, and voluntary consent to obey all the laws of their government, just because they are the

---

51 Kress, "Legal Indeterminacy," at 285. See also Burton, *Law and Legal Reasoning*, pp. 199–214; note 18 above.

52 Kress, "Legal Indeterminacy," at 288 (emphasis in original). The second of these assumptions interprets determinacy as a deductive chain.

53 See, for example, R. Kent Greenawalt, *Conflicts Between Law and Morals* (New York: Oxford University Press, 1987), pp. 47–203; Joseph Raz, *The Morality of Freedom* (Oxford: Clarendon Press, 1986), pp. 70–105; A. John Simmons, *Moral Principles and Political Obligations* (Princeton, N.J.: Princeton University Press, 1979); M. B. E. Smith, "Is There a Prima Facie Obligation to Obey the Law?," *Yale Law Journal*, 82 (1973): 950–76.

54 Kress, "Legal Indeterminacy," at 290.

151

laws. Some, like naturalized citizens, do. For those who do, the question is whether they consent to obey only those laws that are determinate with respect to results. It may be that they consent to obey the government as an institution, indeterminacy and all. Kress concluded that "indeterminacy appears to have limited relevance to legitimacy because only infrequently does any valid ground of obligation require determinacy to succeed."[55] His arguments establish that a general determinacy condition lacks any grounding in the requirements for political obligation in a constitutional democracy.

The other part of the argument for denying that the Rule of Law requires deductive determinacy presents a different and better way of understanding its requirements. It is not that deductive determinacy is the conclusion we should reach unless there is a better understanding of determinacy. The present point is to deny that determinacy of results is a necessary condition for judges to fulfill their duty to uphold the law and for the outcome of adjudication to be legitimate. The Rule of Law, however, is an important normative standard for evaluating a legal system. Some understanding of the conceptual tie between the law and judicial outcomes is needed to render the Rule of Law intelligible. Because of the incompleteness of deductive chains, some critics would have us abandon the Rule of Law together with the constraints on legal reasoning it imposes. The availability of an alternative and intelligible understanding would intervene to defeat this claimed political consequence of the critique of determinate-formalism. The alternative offers an affirmative case for the permissible discretion thesis in support of the good faith thesis.

5.3.4. Authorization chains. The relationship between legal standards and the results in cases should be understood as an authorization chain, which is more like a chain of command than like the chains that control a wild beast. This kind

55 Ibid., at 295.

of chain begins with the broad set of all possible reasons for action, divided into all kinds. The broad set will include good reasons and bad ones, selfish reasons and generous ones, deontological reasons and consequentialist ones, and so on. It narrows at the first legal stage, where the lawmaker is authorized to act only on a subset of all possible reasons, as provided by a theory of legislation. In a democracy like the United States, one legislator might interpret the lawmaker's duty to require action on what is good for his or her constituents while another understands it to require his or her own best judgment about what is good for the whole country, inviting the constituents to express any serious disapproval at the ballot box. Both, however, acknowledge that their legitimate reasons for action are limited, for instance, by excluding reasons of personal financial gain.

At the next stage, lawmaking can be understood as a further exclusion of reasons, leaving a narrower subset of reasons on which a law-interpreting and -applying official legitimately acts. Consider a products liability statute abolishing strict liability for defective products that cause harm and reinstituting a traditional regime of negligence. The justifications for strict liability and fault-based law have been balanced by the lawmaking authorities. Whether or not the application of that statute is indeterminate, a judge qua judge is not permitted to reconsider that balance and to impose a strict liability requirement for the same reasons considered by the lawmakers. The outcome of the legislative deliberations is authoritative for the judge: It excludes from judicial deliberations the reasons that might justify strict liability for defective products that cause harm; at the same time, the background justification for negligence liability remains available to the judge engaged in interpretation and the weighing of reasons. Accordingly, looking at each step down an authorization chain, the set of all possible reasons is progressively restricted as the law demarcates the next official's legal reasons for action and excludes other reasons. Looking up the authorization chain, the set of legitimate reasons for action progressively expands for each official.

153

The Rule of Law in a constitutional democracy should be understood to require official action in accordance with the law, understood as a provider of legal reasons for action within a complex authorization chain.[56] Justice Scalia contrasts the Rule of Law as a deductive chain with the anything goes interpretation of discretion.[57] The contrast raises an antimajoritarian specter; judges with unbridled discretion are not constrained by any popular consensus reflected in democratically made laws and are not usually accountable to the electorate in any effective way. When exercised in good faith within an authorization chain, however, discretion does not so offend democracy. Democratically founded laws may demarcate the reasons that count in a proper judicial decision. As general laws, understood as practical guidance, they do not purport to fix the weight of all legal reasons in a case and therefore to determine results. Rather, general laws admit and exclude generic reasons, leaving the job of judging cases to judges. When the Rule of Law is so understood, there is no requirement of either causal or deductive determinacy, nor is there tolerance for judicial arbitrariness or abuse of power. At the judge's end of the chain, there well may be reasons supporting two incompatible actions. Either action, however, is in an important sense nonarbitrary just because it is supported by legal reasons. Indeed, the difficulty of judicial decision in hard cases arises precisely because incompatible actions are amply supported by legal reasons. The legitimacy of adjudication within a legal system is a matter of respect for a judge's reasons for action, not agreement with the results.[58]

It might be objected that the choice between incompatible actions must be arbitrary, opening the door to opportunism,

---

56 I do not wish to imply that the chain flows from some "basic norm" along one dimension from the citizenry to the judge. More likely, the chain would form a complex web of authorizations along the lines suggested in Joseph Raz, *The Concept of a Legal System*, 2d ed. (Oxford: Clarendon Press, 1980), pp. 93–167.
57 Scalia, "The Rule of Law as a Law of Rules."
58 See § 2.1.

domination, and conflict over the basic terms of social life, and defeating implementation of a Rule of Law. The choice might be thought arbitrary because, in cases of stubborn indeterminacy, it cannot be based on a further reason. At some point, however, the requesting of further reasons must come to a stop.[59] The judge must take responsibility for acting pragmatically within the framework of law, risking criticism for error. The result is hardly a picture of randomness. Judicial discretion is cabined within deliberations structured and guided by the law, which admits and excludes the reasons for a judicial decision and requires those reasons to be weighed in good faith. "Arbitrariness" is a word, like any other, with meanings that vary with the context. The authorization chain may tolerate "arbitrariness" by contrast with the certainty sought in theoretical inquiries into the causal laws of nature or chains of logical inference. It does not tolerate "arbitrariness" by contrast with action for good and sufficient reasons, as relevant in a practical understanding of adjudication.

The idea of an authorization chain, within the larger good faith thesis, rules out opportunism as a matter of judicial duty. The crucial focus in this respect is on the reasons excluded from judicial deliberations, rather than the reasons on which a judge is authorized by the law to act. Recall that opportunism is a violation of judicial duty whereby a judge recaptures the forgone opportunity to act on reasons excluded from lawful judicial deliberations.[60] It is a synonym for bad faith within the good faith thesis. The identity of excluded reasons varies from law to law, and between different kinds of courts. No compendium of excluded reasons can be composed without developing a negative picture of the entirety of the law in a legal system. Ad hominem reasons, however, are always excluded. Clear instances of opportunism occur, accordingly, when a judge acts for reasons

59 See § 2.3.2. A philosopher can go on to request further reasons ad infinitum. Whether even the philosopher should do so is debatable. See, for example, Dworkin, *A Matter of Principle*, pp. 171-7.
60 See § 3.4.2.

155

of advantage to self, friends, or groups with which he or she identifies. The most important legal debates concern the identity of other excluded and included reasons – debates that are about the law judges have a duty to uphold, not the judicial duty to uphold the law.

The idea of an authorization chain also rules out domination, which should be considered in two forms. Generically, domination is the unjustifiable use of power over another person. In the case of judges, it cannot be equated with action for reasons excluded from judicial purview because the law might or might not be morally permissible. When the law is morally permissible, the judge who upholds it is not dominating anyone. Only the judge who acts opportunistically, using the law as a pretext for acting on excluded reasons, may be dominating and would be in bad faith. The judge who dutifully applies a morally impermissible law, however, would be dominating a citizen even while fulfilling his or her legal duty. The good faith thesis does not protect against domination due to morally impermissible laws. It is a theory of adjudication under the law that does not suppose either that the law is always just or that the legal duty of judges is to apply only just laws.[61] The good faith thesis leaves it entirely open to critics of the law to argue that the law is wrong, in particular respects or in general. It doubts that such a point can be made soundly by advancing indeterminacy claims and the like.

The constraint of an authorization chain in principle distinguishes adjudication under the law from open-ended conflict over the basic terms of social life.[62] The idea of an authorization chain supports the good faith thesis: The reasons warranted by the law as grounds for judicial decision are a subset of all otherwise relevant reasons consisting of those on which judges are authorized to act. They are justificatory reasons, not the ad hominem reasons that animate ordinary and transformative political contests. The radical critique,

61 See §§ 2.1, 7.1 and following.
62 See Unger, *The Critical Legal Studies Movement*.

which denies the liberal distinction between law and politics, rests on two now apparent errors. One is the belief that, when the law fails to dictate the result in a case deductively, anything goes. A major burden of the good faith and permissible discretion theses is to show that this is not so; deductive indeterminacy of results is not a license for judges to do whatever they can get away with in the political context. The other is the genetic fallacy of thinking that, because the law emerges from a clash of interests, it is fantasy to think it would constitute a coherent and morally justified whole, as required by political liberalism. A coherent and morally justified whole is required only if determinacy of results is required and, furthermore, the results in all cases must be morally justified, as some natural law theories affirm. The good faith thesis denies that political liberalism requires either determinacy of results or a moral justification for results to be lawful. With the latter point we enter territory to be explored in subsequent chapters. We will look in Chapter 6 at whether determinacy of results is required by the nature of law, as distinct from political liberalism; we will then consider in greater depth the relationships between law, politics, and morals.

5.4. CONSTRAINT AND CHARACTER

We should, however, first pause to address an objection that may have been developing in readers' minds. In Chapter 4, we distinguished between reasons for action that depend for their normativity on a person's desires and those that depend on an independent standard of conduct. In this chapter, we distinguished more generally between reasons that motivate (cause) a person to act and those that justify action. The question may arise: If the law latches onto neither a person's desires nor other motivations within a person's psyche, how could it provide *reasons for action?* Must not the good faith thesis, having declined to rely on desires or other motivations, face the classic philosophical problem of accounting for how norms, however intelligible in the abstract, might move a person to action?

5.4.1. *Motives*. The classic problem is a difficult one for any moral or legal theory.[63] There seems to be a dilemma. On one hand, as a theory excludes desires and other motivations within the psyche, it tends to lose any causal connection with action. Some causal connection, however, seems to be implied by the idea of a reason for action. On the other hand, as the theory connects norms with the motivating aspects of the psyche, it tends to gain the causal connection only by diluting its normative function. It seems a crucial function of law, in particular, sometimes to require people to take actions that they positively do not want to take. The law may not be effective if it must connect causally with a person's independent motivations, but it may not guide conduct at all if it remains abstract and aloof from those same motivations.

Duncan Kennedy's existentialist/phenomenological account of judging illustrates the first horn of the dilemma in informative detail.[64] Kennedy imagines himself to be a federal district court judge with strongly liberal activist political commitments, deciding a case involving a labor strike. He thus adopts the practical standpoint of a judge (though perhaps incompletely). Kennedy supposes that a bus company hires nonunion drivers to operate its buses when its regular drivers go on strike. Without otherwise disrupting activities in the area, the strikers lie down in the street outside the bus station to prevent the buses from passing. They are arrested on the first day and charged with disturbing the peace and obstructing a public way, but they return each day

63 For a recent philosophical treatment, see Christine M. Korsgaard, "Skepticism About Practical Reason," *Journal of Philosophy*, 83 (1986): 5–25.

64 Duncan Kennedy, "Freedom and Constraint in Adjudication: A Critical Phenomenology," *Journal of Legal Education*, 36 (1986): 518–62. For similar ways of rooting legal constraint in self-interested motivations, inspired by Holmes, see Richard A. Posner, *The Problems of Jurisprudence* (Cambridge: Harvard University Press, 1990), pp. 194–5, 223–4; Frederick Schauer, "Formalism," *Yale Law Journal*, 97 (1988): 509–48, at 530–48.

to replay the scenario. The buses run, but only on an unpredictable schedule. The bus company seeks an injunction against the union tactic.

Kennedy's first impression, imagining himself to be Kennedy, J., is twofold. He thinks the law will prohibit the union from denying management use of the means of production with substitute labor during a strike. Due to his liberal activist political commitments, however, he does not believe management should be allowed so to operate the means of production. The latter instinct generates what Kennedy calls "how-I-want-to-come-out," producing a clear conflict between Kennedy, J.'s political objective and the law as imagined on first encounter. Kennedy describes how Kennedy, J. would work the legal materials in a concentrated effort to find a way to come out how he wants to come out. He labors to manipulate the law to find a legal way to deny the owner's request for an injunction – delay, a technical snag, an implied contract making the union a part of ownership, an analogy to the right to picket, and a First Amendment ban on prior restraints. Many possibilities seem to him too implausible to get him where he wants to go. Others look promising after the expenditure of some effort, but fade with further study. (This suggests that the law may not be infinitely manipulable.)

A main point of Kennedy's exercise, and a valuable one, emphasizes the effects of allocating effort to one line of legal inquiry or another. One never knows, Kennedy suggests, whether with more work an abandoned legal argument would have panned out or the one that prevailed would have faded. One never knows whether an abandoned argument would have prevailed had the press of the docket not required a curtailed deliberation. It may be added, moreover, that the initial political instinct to deny management use of the means of production during a strike also is open to revision during the judge's encounter with the law. Few judges will have thought out their views on the specifically relevant labor policy with as much intensity or under as great a burden of responsibility as when deciding a case.

For present purposes, the important aspect of Kennedy's exercise lies in the basic concept of the exercise itself: A conflict between how-he-wants-to-come-out and the perceived requirements of the law requires him to work hard to justify legally coming out how-he-wants-to-come-out. The bind is real. Kennedy, J. acknowledges that he might not be able to get there; he might have to grant the bus company's request for an injunction despite his political convictions. What generates the experience of this bind? Why not lie about the facts or the law, denying the injunction just to let the union have its way until an appeal can be prosecuted and won? A federal judge, with lifetime tenure, could get away with that. In what way does the law constrain Kennedy, J. from a disingenuous effort to further his prior political commitment?

Kennedy offers an explanation that ties the constraint of the law directly into the motivational structure of Kennedy, J.'s psyche:

> My model of constraint is that people (me as a judge) want to back up their statement of a preference for an outcome (the workers should not be enjoined) with an argument to the effect that to enjoin the workers would "violate the law." We can't understand how this desire to legalize my position constrains me without saying something about why I want to do it.
>
> First, I see myself as having promised some diffuse public that I will "decide according to law," and it is clear to me that a minimum meaning of this pledge is that I won't do things for which I don't have a good legal argument. . . .
>
> Second, various people in my community will sanction me severely if I do not offer a good legal argument for my action. . . . [B]oth friends and enemies will see me as having violated a role constraint . . . and they will make me feel their disapproval.
>
> Third, . . . [b]y developing a strong legal argument I make it dramatically less likely that my outcome will be reversed.
>
> Fourth, by engaging in legal argument I can shape the outcomes of future cases. . . .
>
> Fifth, . . . [w]hat I do in this case will affect my ability to do

things in other cases, enhancing or diminishing my legal and political credibility. . . .

Sixth, . . . I would like to know for my own purposes how my [ethical] position looks translated into [legal argument].[65]

Note that the second through sixth reasons for trying to legalize the position involve personal desires that are independent of the law. Kennedy, J. wants to avoid the disapproval of his social sets, to avoid the embarrassment of being reversed by the boss, to wield the power of setting a respected precedent, to enhance his personal power for future cases, and to satisfy his curiosity. As a descriptive matter, some of these motivations probably do move judges at times. The point here, however, is conceptual. Kennedy's concept of constraint requires a close connection between offering a legal justification for the decision and these self-interested motives within the judge's psyche. Judicial duty would operate unevenly. The legal justification is conceived as an instrument for Kennedy, J. to pursue ends determined by his prior personal goals and political commitments.

Note also, however, that the first of the reasons for Kennedy, J.'s effort to legalize his position does not involve a self-interested motive. Rather, it involves a promise to "decide according to law" and therefore involves the judicial duty to uphold the law. Kennedy omits to say explicitly what motivates Kennedy, J. to want to keep the promise and fulfill the duty. There are two interpretations. Perhaps he means that the second through sixth reasons, in addition to motivating the search for a respectable legal justification, also moti-

---

65 Kennedy, "Freedom and Constraint," at 527–8. I interpret the sixth point as a matter of intellectual curiosity. It could mean that the judge starts with a hunch and tests it against the law. There is nothing objectionable in that so long as the judge is ready to give the hunch up if the opinion "won't write." See Alvin B. Rubin, "Does Law Matter? A Judge's Response to Critical Legal Studies," *Journal of Legal Education*, 37 (1987): 307–14, at 311. Compare Joseph C. Hutcheson, Jr., "The Judgment Intuitive: The Function of the 'Hunch' in Judicial Decision," *Cornell Law Quarterly*, 14 (1929): 274–88, at 285–7.

vate the keeping of the promise to uphold the law. In that case, however, the promise would collapse into the other motivations; it would be superfluous to the general point about constraint. Legal constraint would require a motivational structure of pertinent desires within the judge's psyche. On this view, the law constrains when and only when abiding by the law serves the judge's personal and political interests.

This is an implausible understanding of practical constraint and probably is not Kennedy's. In his presentation, the oath of office stands independently of the self-interested motives. More important, the legal duty to uphold the law is crucial to connect the self-interested motives with the effort to legalize the political position. Why would various people in Kennedy, J.'s community sanction him severely for failing to offer a good legal argument? Because he will thereby have failed to do his legal duty, which they think he ought to do. Similarly, the appellate court will reverse if he fails to do his duty. Other people will be influenced by his view of the strikers' actions only if they think it was formed within the authority of the law, and not as editorial opinion. Kennedy, J.'s prestige will be enhanced because the members of the legal community respect judges who play by the rules. In sum, the motivational reasons offered by Kennedy generate the effort at legal justification only because Kennedy, J. operates within a legal community that *takes seriously the judicial duty to uphold the law*. The constraint of the law, even on Kennedy's view, does not get going without accepting the normativity of judicial duty at least as a conventional rule practiced within the legal community.[66]

Moreover, once we accept the necessity of legal duty to the explanation of legal constraint, the motivational structure of

66 That is, adapting H. L. A. Hart's famous view of social rules, there must be general conformity with the judicial duty to uphold the law, with deviations subjected to criticism by members of the legal community, while those who criticize deviations for noncompliance are not themselves criticized. See H. L. A. Hart, *Concept of Law* (Oxford: Clarendon Press, 1961), pp. 54–60, 110–14; chap. 8, note 4.

the judge is rendered unnecessary. We would say simply that Kennedy, J. is constrained by his duty to uphold the law, as expounded by the good faith thesis. He would thus be constrained to act on reasons warranted by the law as grounds for judicial decisions, and not on excluded reasons. Among the excluded reasons would be the judge's own prior political convictions (Kennedy, J.'s initial desire to find a way to deny the bus company's request for an injunction), his fear of criticism by his friends and enemies, his instincts to husband and enhance his personal power, and his intellectual curiosity. Conceptually, it seems that a legal constraint operates, if at all, independently of these personal characteristics. The self-interested motives might in practice support *or undermine* faithfulness to the law, depending on the circumstances. For example, a judge might gain a coveted appointment to a higher court by pandering with lawless action to a powerful political constituency that enjoys the President's favor. If legal constraint means anything, however, such a judge is constrained by the law just the same. He is not permitted to pander to further his ambitions, and he should be criticized severely for eluding the constraints of his office. Accordingly, self-interested motives are not among the conditions under which the law constrains (in the practical sense of "constraint").

5.4.2. *Character.* Rejecting any necessary tie between legal constraint and self-interested motives, however, does not solve the problem for the good faith thesis. A judge may understand both the judicial duty to uphold the law and the law he has a duty to uphold. The question might remain, Why should he do it? The way to an answer lies in distinguishing the question for judges from the general philosophical question in moral theory. Judges are not, or are not supposed to be, just like the ordinary person (if there be one). They are selected carefully and ostensibly in accordance with a cluster of criteria. Certain of the criteria are highly controversial, especially for appointments to important federal courts. Among the uncontroversial criteria, however, are those pertaining to the judicial character of a candidate. To a large extent, the sometimes thick politics of appointments operate only among candidates who have passed the test of judicial character. A reasonable answer to the pending question can be found in the link between the law and judicial character.

Character may be understood simply as a person's distinctive ensemble of dispositions to act in habitual ways in various circumstances. Dispositions of character are like the disposition of salt to dissolve in water; they constitute a person's character even when they have no immediate occasion to become evident behaviorally. They may not, however, be quite so automatic. A person may, on reflection, act contrary to a disposition. Dispositions of character are not wired into our genetic makeup. Neither are they made up on the spot. Dispositions are conditioned and cultivated over a lifetime, evolving as a person gains distinctive experiences and, it is hoped, wisdom. Some dispositions are cultivated in one's professional activities. For lawyers, professional dispositions depend on the legal culture, which may provide a good environment for growing judges. Emphasis may be placed on the virtues of good judgment, attention to detail, patience, independence, honesty, initiative, a capacity to see several sides to an issue, and persistence.[67]

Judges should be selected in part because they display these virtues of a good lawyer and something else besides. Many lawyers, when confronted with a rule of law, are disposed to see only the loopholes and manipulations to which it is susceptible, adopting a cynical attitude toward the law. (Kennedy, J. approaches the law this way, as if he had a client and were engaged in vigorous advocacy.) Other lawyers, by contrast, are disposed to look for the point or value of the law and try to make it work for their clients and for their

---

67   See, for example, Anthony T. Kronman, "Living in the Law," *University of Chicago Law Review*, 54 (1987): 835–76. In some parts of the current practice in the United States, however, it seems that the professional "virtues" involve a contrasting list: aggressiveness, competitiveness, loyalty, minimal scruples, and strategic savvy.

communities. The latter cultivate a disposition highly valued in judicial selection proceedings. The critical standard – the one implicit in public debate – places great value on a candidate's track record of law-abiding conduct, scrupulous honesty, personal integrity, and community service, evidencing a settled disposition to continue those habits as a matter of character.

A legal standard does not motivate its own compliance. That would be nonsense. Nor does it work when and only when it serves the personal and political interests of a judge to follow it. If that were so, our judicial selection criteria should emphasize the second to sixth motivations identified by Kennedy. That would be absurd. Rather, a legal standard latches onto a judge's disposition to follow the law. The law thus moves a judge to act as indicated only in conjunction with a preexisting feature of the judge's character, one that is conditioned and cultivated over a lifetime within a legal culture. With respect to other subjects of the law, the basic philosophical problem remains, for there is no reason to suppose that the general population has a comparable disposition of character. The problem is far less severe in a theory of judging because the population of judges is, or should be, atypical in a crucial respect.

To summarize, it is only the authorization chain interpretation of the Rule of Law that is required in a constitutional democracy. The Rule of Law is best understood to require practical constraints on judges, constraints that restrict a judge's legal reasons for action within an authorization chain. Judges, we hope, are disposed by character to fulfill their duty to uphold the law so conceived. When this is so, the law can guide their conduct effectively as required by democratic political theory.

Chapter 6

Philosophies of law

6.1. DETERMINACY AND THE NATURE OF LAW

A further group of possible objections to the good faith thesis looks to certain philosophical understandings of the nature of law. Four otherwise very different philosophies claim that, among its central features, the law necessarily determines results. If this were so, judges could fulfill their duty to uphold the law only by reaching the results determined by the law. The determinacy condition would be a part of what judicial duty requires conceptually, and the idea of law-governed discretion would be a confusion. As we shall see, however, none of these four philosophies supplies adequate grounds for an account of the law that would render the good faith thesis pointless. Judicial duty should be understood shorn of the determinacy condition. Judges can fulfill their duty to uphold the law by exercising discretion in good faith. There is nothing essential about the law that renders discretion impermissible.

6.2. RULES, BY DEFINITION

Some readers might think that the law by definition consists only of rules and that rules by definition dictate results. The good faith thesis clearly would have no point were these a sound pair of propositions. They constitute, however, an assertion of determinate-formalism by fiat and do not need yet another refutation. In contemporary discussions in

166

American legal theory, the model of rules serves mainly as a foil against which other theories of law can be contrasted and, more insidiously, as an implicit standard defining what a successful theory of law would have to establish.[1] Occasionally, a writer might paint opposing views into a determinate-formalist corner as a rhetorical move to discredit them without good argument. Surely, however, there is no a priori reason to believe that the law could, does, or should consist only of rules that dictate results. It might be thought that, because the law guides conduct, it should determine the specific conduct required by the law. The alternative possibility is that the law guides conduct by changing a person's reasons for action.[2] A further argument is needed, but no academic theorist at present is willing to defend that conclusion.[3] No constructive theorist should cater to critics who use such an undefended alternative as the standard of criticism. Consequently, the determinacy condition cannot at present be derived from a definition of law as determinate rules.

6.2.1. The framework of rules. Most contemporary philosophers of law nonetheless agree that rules are a distinct and

1 See, for example, Stanley E. Fish, *Doing What Comes Naturally* (Durham, N.C.: Duke University Press, 1990) [criticized in Steven L. Winter, *"Bull Durham* and the Uses of Theory," *Stanford Law Review*, 42 (1990): 639–93]; Joseph William Singer, "The Player and the Cards: Nihilism and Legal Theory," *Yale Law Journal*, 94 (1984): 1–70 [criticized in John Stick, "Can Nihilism be Pragmatic?," *Harvard Law Review*, 100 (1986): 332–401]; Peter Westen, "The Empty Idea of Equality," *Harvard Law Review*, 95 (1982): 537–96 [criticized in Steven J. Burton, "Comment on 'Empty Ideas': Logical Positivist Analyses of Equality and Rules," *Yale Law Journal*, 91 (1982): 1136–52].
2 See §§ 2.2 and following.
3 Perhaps the strongest contemporary supporter of a model of rules is Frederick Schauer, whose views on "presumptive positivism" place him far from determinate formalism. See Frederick Schauer, "Formalism," *Yale Law Journal*, 97 (1988): 509–48; Frederick Schauer, "Rules and the Rule of Law," *Harvard Journal of Law & Public Policy*, 14 (1991): 645–94. For criticism, see "Symposium on Law and Philosophy," *Harvard Journal of Law & Public Policy*, 14 (1991): 616–852. See also Antonin Scalia, "The Rule of Law as a Law of Rules," *University of Chicago Law Review*, 56 (1989): 1175–88.

necessary part of the law. Few agree either on what rules are, or on what role rules play, by contrast with other legal standards. In my view,[4] legal rules can be usefully distinguished from other legal standards – mainly principles and policies – because they have certain structural functions in a mature legal system. They do not, however, necessarily dictate results in adjudication. Important implications follow from distinguishing between the several roles of rules in adjudication. In particular, it will be seen, certain currently prominent legal theories present law as a deeply conflicted enterprise, opening the door to political conflict in adjudication over the basic terms of social life. These theories, however, depend on an underdeveloped and unsound view of rules. Understanding that rules serve a framework function and provide reasons, not necessarily results, makes it possible to think of the law, if not as a fully coherent scheme, at least as a scheme whose inherent conflicts are not so disturbing.

The framework function involves two formal dimensions of legal guidance by rules in adjudication. On the first formal dimension, rules attach practical legal consequences to the membership of a particular case in a class of cases designated by the rule.[5] The form is that of antecedent and consequent ("when . . . then . . ."). For example, the negligence rule provides that "when a defendant harms another person or property by breaching a duty to exercise due care, which breach is a cause-in-fact and proximate cause of damage, then he shall compensate the victim in money damages." That is a rule of law because it attaches a practical legal consequence – the defendant shall pay compensatory damages – to any case that is a member of the designated class of negligence cases. In this respect, its form is common to all rules.[6]

4 For an earlier version of this line of thought, see Steven J. Burton, *An Introduction to Law and Legal Reasoning* (Boston: Little, Brown & Co., 1985), pp. 41–82.
5 Ibid., p. 68 ("rules refer to abstract cases and do not themselves supply the particularities that are needed to decide a problem case").
6 See Richard A. Wasserstrom, *The Judicial Decision* (Stanford, Calif.:

Moreover, the form of a rule has distinctive functions: It helps lawyers and judges to identify common starting points for reasoning in a case, to locate the relevant legal materials, and to formulate issues that can be joined intelligently. More important, a court is also guided by a complex series of such rules to order legally authorized remedies. These are good reasons for judges to start and end with the rules though other resources are employed on the way. Plaintiffs, accordingly, bear the burden of invoking a legal rule that, if applied, will get them where they want to go. In principle, lawful judicial decisions affirm or deny the application of a legal rule to a case. These formal functions, however, do not require that rules suffice to dictate results.

On the second formal dimension, rules often mandate the order in which a series of legal questions must be taken up and answered in a legal decision-making procedure. For example, we must ask whether the defendant in a tort action was under a legal duty before we ask whether the duty was breached, and we must ask whether the duty was breached before we ask whether the breach of duty was a cause-in-fact and proximate cause of harm to the plaintiff. Such a conceptual ordering is helpful in legal deliberations because, in principle, different sets of reasons should bear on each question in turn. It is confusing and can be capricious to relitigate the question of duty under the rubric of cause-in-fact or to relitigate the cause-in-fact issue under the rubric of harm. Different principles and policies bear on each finding, and the rules keep them from wandering without direction into every legal question. It is possible, for example, for a defendant to be under a duty not to discharge a firearm unsafely on the basis of general public safety principles. On the basis of common standards of reasonable conduct, he may have breached that duty by firing it into the air. He has not com-

Stanford University Press, 1961), pp. 36–8 (legal rules or laws "could be put into the form of hypothetical imperatives in which the antecedent designated a particular kind of relationship, activity, or person, and the consequent designated the legal consequences that ought to follow from the occurrence or presence of the antecedent").

mitted an actionable tort, however, unless someone was hurt, which is likely to depend on evidence of physical events. The requirement that the breach cause harm to the plaintiff reflects principles of responsibility that should not be slighted in a tort action no matter how much conduct like the defendant's should be deterred. Thus, rules ensure that every legal question need not turn into a judgment of general public policy on the totality of the circumstances.

On the substantive dimension, legal rules and other standards may provide reasons for one or another legal classification of a case in the framework established by the formal dimensions. Attention now is focused on the membership of a particular case in a class of cases designated by the antecedent of a legal rule. The antecedent may contribute a reason for one or another legal classification based on the ordinary meaning of the words.[7] Other legal standards may contribute supporting and competing reasons. For example, there could be a principle or policy on negligence providing simply that "all persons should use due care for the safety of other persons and property." Such a standard can be useful when interpreting many different legal rules by providing reasons for one or another legal classification. Principles, however, do not attach a practical legal consequence to the classification or fix an order for taking up legal questions. Principles have legal implications mainly when they contribute reasons for or against the classification of a case in a class of cases designated by the legal rules. Rules form the basis of legal claims and authorize remedies in relation to legal claims. Both rules and principles may contribute reasons bearing on the lawful classification of a case.

The framework function of legal rules seems integral to the concept of a legal system. Legal rules can perform this cluster of functions, however, without determining the scope of their own applications. That is, they need not determine the

---

7 See Burton, *Law and Legal Reasoning*, pp. 68–77. See also Michael S. Moore, "A Natural Law Theory of Interpretation," *Southern California Law Review*, 58 (1985): 277–398, at 301–13; Schauer, "Formalism," at 520–35.

membership of any particular case in a class of cases designated by a legal rule, even after finding all relevant facts. It is necessary in adjudication both to identify the available legal classes and to classify cases in an orderly way grounded in the legal materials. Distinguishing these dimensions makes it clear that rules are distinct because only they designate the unifying classificatory apparatus that gives the law its systemic quality.

6.2.2. The determinacy of rules. Legal theorists often claim that rules by definition determine single correct results but that the law consists of rules together with other standards. The vestige of determinate-formalism in the definition of a rule has serious untoward consequences. If rules serve a comprehensive framework function and also dictate results, other legal standards would be superfluous in adjudication. It is obvious, however, that principles and policies also play important roles. Therefore, it might seem, determinate rules and other standards are in deep jurisprudential conflict because there is no room for both kinds of standards. Accordingly, following Dworkin, it might be thought that law is an essentially contested concept within which conceptions of law based on a model of determinate rules (or determinate conventions) vie with incompatible conceptions of law as a matter of principle.[8] Or, following the early Duncan Kennedy, it might be thought that the availability of other standards in the legal materials gives judges a political choice in any case to follow the applicable rule or to follow a standard, generating pervasive and stubborn indeterminacy.[9] Such visions of deep and recalcitrant conflict in the law are not attractive because they open the door to an uncontrollable kind of politics. Fortunately, both visions lose all point when we understand that rules need not dictate results.

8 See Ronald Dworkin, *Law's Empire* (Cambridge: Harvard University Press, Belknap Press, 1986), pp. 90–6.
9 Duncan Kennedy, "Legal Formality," *Journal of Legal Studies*, 2 (1973): 351–98; Duncan Kennedy, "Form and Substance in Private Law Adjudication," *Harvard Law Review*, 89 (1976): 1685–778.

The idea that rules, as distinct from other legal standards, must dictate results probably stems from the jurisprudence of Roscoe Pound.[10] It made its most influential appearance, however, in the unpublished teaching materials on "The Legal Process" by the Harvard law professors, Henry Hart, Jr., and Albert Sacks.[11] Hart and Sacks were careful, when defining "rule" narrowly for their purposes, to recognize that the term also signifies any proposition of law:

> The most precise form of authoritative general direction may conveniently be called a *rule*, although this term is often used much more broadly to signify a legal proposition of any kind. In the narrow and technical sense in which the term is here used, a rule may be defined as a legal direction which requires for its application nothing more than a determination of the happening or non-happening of physical or mental events – that is determinations of *fact*. An example would be the fifty-mile-an-hour speed statute earlier mentioned.[12]

Dworkin's early view of rules was similar but much less cautious:[13]

> Rules are applicable in an all-or-nothing fashion. If the facts a rule stipulates are given, then either the rule is valid, in which

10 Roscoe Pound, *An Introduction to the Philosophy of Law* (New Haven, Conn.: Yale University Press, 1922), pp. 56–60. Cardozo and Holmes had written that the law is generally determinate but also has gaps in which judges must legislate, if only "interstitially." In speaking of the law, however, they did not distinguish rules and other standards as Pound did, and as has lately become commonplace. Benjamin N. Cardozo, *The Nature of the Judicial Process* (New Haven, Conn.: Yale University Press, 1921), pp. 113–15; Southern Pacific Co. v. Jensen, 224 U.S. 205, 221 (1917) (Holmes, J., dissenting).

11 Henry M. Hart, Jr., & Albert M. Sacks, *The Legal Process: Basic Problems in the Making and Application of Law*, tent. ed. (Cambridge, Mass.: Harvard Law School, 1958), pp. 155–60.

12 Ibid., p. 155. See also Lon L. Fuller, *The Morality of Law* (New Haven, Conn.: Yale University Press, 1964), p. 106 ("law is the enterprise of subjecting human conduct to the governance of rules").

13 The Hart and Sacks materials probably were especially influential on Dworkin's work. See Vincent A. Wellman, "Dworkin and the Legal Process Tradition: The Legacy of Hart & Sacks," *Arizona Law Review*, 29 (1987): 413–74.

case the answer it supplies must be accepted, or it is not, in which case it contributes nothing to the decision.[14]

Kennedy followed Dworkin's definition,[15] and legions have followed Dworkin and Kennedy. But Hart and Sacks, in their recognition that "rule" could signify a legal proposition of any kind, were closer to the mark.

Rules should be distinguished from other standards on the basis of their distinctive framework functions, not their determinacy. To see why, consider first a significant ambiguity in the idea of determinate rules. To dictate results, a legal rule must have both determinate content and determining force. That is, it must both identify a single action and require the judge to perform that action. Analytically, the distinction between content and force stems from the formal statement of a legal rule:

It is the law that, when [a factual situation occurs] then [a specified action should be taken].

As with other general propositions of law,[16] the content is signified by the unitalicized phrases, which represent some part of the law of the relevant legal system. The content,

---

14 See Ronald Dworkin, *Taking Rights Seriously* (Cambridge: Harvard University Press, 1977), pp. 24, 36. Rules are not discussed in Dworkin's later work and his account of easy cases no longer invokes such a conception of rules. For criticism of Dworkin's early treatment of legal rules, see Joseph Raz, "Legal Principles and the Limits of Law," *Yale Law Journal*, 81 (1972): 823–54 (H. L. A. Hart's references to legal "rules" can encompass what Dworkin calls "principles" as standards with only prima facie force); Joseph Raz, "Legal Principles and the Limits of Law," in *Ronald Dworkin and Contemporary Jurisprudence*, ed. Marshall Cohen (Totowa, N.J.: Rowman & Allanheld, 1983): 73–87, at 81–6 (postscript added to republication omitting Part I). For Dworkin's reply, see Dworkin, *Taking Rights Seriously*, pp. 72–80; Dworkin, "A Reply by Ronald Dworkin," in *Ronald Dworkin and Contemporary Jurisprudence*: 247–300, at 260–3. See also note 17 below.
15 Kennedy, "Legal Formality," at 355 n. 10. See also Kennedy, "Form and Substance," at 1687–701 (treating formal realizability of a rule as the pole of a continuum).
16 See § 2.2.1.

without more, is merely informative because it only identifies a generic situation and links it to an idea of a legal consequence. The distinctive force of the law, if any, stems from the italicized phrase. It presses a judge to take the indicated action in fact when the requisite facts materialize, all else being equal.

Legal force is of two kinds. It may be the force of a single legally required result, as Dworkin and Kennedy treat all legal rules. This will be called "result-determining force." Or it may be the force of a reason to be weighed against other reasons, as Dworkin treats principles. Distinguishing rules on the basis of their determinacy makes sense only if rules must have both determinate content and result-determining force. A great many rules do in fact have a determinate content linked with result-determining force in many cases. For example, few people face a hard legal question whether to file an income tax return. Probably most people face determinate federal income tax liability in most years. The number of content-determinate rules increases infinitely if we include all the things that clearly are not "income" as the term is used in the Internal Revenue Code of 1986, as amended. In adjudication, each case involves a plethora of legal issues. By far the lion's share are resolved with no difficulty whatever.

Rules, however, also can have determinate content with only the force of a reason, leaving the rule indeterminate with respect to results.[17] In *Riggs v. Palmer,* discussed

17 For example, a typical rule of law provides that damages for the breach of a building contract by the builder are measured by the cost of completing the project as promised, but if completion would involve "unreasonable economic waste," then damages are measured by the difference in value between what was promised and what was received. *Restatement of Contracts* § 346(1) (1932). Such a rule does not obviate the need to weigh legal reasons stemming from each of the rule's branches to decide whether there would be "unreasonable economic waste." To call rules like this "standards" or "principles" would be to reduce the number of rules drastically, and probably to lose their valuable framework function. In my experience, few legal rules are applied mechanically whenever they are relevant.

above,[18] the statutory rule had determinate content because, through its ordinary meaning, it unquestionably generated a reason for the property to descend to the murderer-grandson. In the event, however, it did not have result-determining force because it did not carry the day due to weightier considerations of principle. That does not imply that the rule counted for nought. It need imply only that it did not have sufficient force, on the facts of the case as a whole, to determine the result. Rules can guide conduct by serving the framework function and providing determinate reasons for action even when they do not dictate results.[19] Reasons stemming from rules can be overridden by more forceful reasons stemming from other kinds of standards.

When Dworkin stipulated that the answer supplied by a valid rule must be accepted or else "it contributes nothing to the decision,"[20] or Kennedy asserted that, by definition, a judge either follows a rule or it "is no longer in force,"[21] the implication is that a rule must have result-determining force because a judge must act as it indicates regardless of other considerations. Their criticisms of law as a model of determinate rules are impressive, if you accept this view of rules, because cases like *Riggs* are not renegades.[22] One need not, however, accept their view of rules, the consequent distinctions between rules and other standards, and the implicit invitation to disregard the rules. The better explanation of *Riggs* is that the statutory rule had determinate content without result-determining force. The rule supplied a reason for one decision to be weighed against competing reasons that blocked the application of the rule. Rules, principles, and policies all can have determinate content without result-determining force.

This understanding of rules has important consequences

18　See § 2.3.1.
19　See §§ 2.2 and following.
20　See note 14 and text accompanying above.
21　Kennedy, "Legal Formality," at 355 n. 10.
22　See, for example, Schauer, "Formalism," at 515–19.

for American legal theory. Dworkin and Kennedy each claim that the law is deeply conflicted in its jurisprudence, leading to understandings of law and adjudication as but another arena for political struggle. For Dworkin, law is a concept that permits rival conceptions, such as conventionalism, pragmatism, and his favored law as integrity, which treats the law as a matter of principle instead of rules. These three main conceptions implement rival political visions and generate rival theories of adjudication. Dworkin can favor law as integrity, however, only because he would evaluate the rivals by his own conception of law as interpretation, which is but a more abstract version of law as integrity itself. In his empire, there is no common denominator from which the alternatives can be compared intelligently by a judge; the pertinent choice is between deeply conflicting visions of the good society. Similarly, for Kennedy (at least in his earlier writings), the law consists of rules and standards that invoke, respectively, a politics of individualism and a politics of altruism. Again, there is no common ground for preferring one rival over the other in any case. The law is seen as deeply conflicted because it contains rules and standards in fundamental contradiction. Only politics can determine the choice of forms within which to adjudicate cases.[23]

These influential claims of deep and unavoidable conflict are mistaken. A workable system of legal standards cannot indicate that a judge must issue a judgment for both the plaintiff and the defendant on the same legal question; only one action is possible as the result in a case. Given this fact, Dworkin's and Kennedy's pictures of deep conflict each emerge inexorably from three premises. First, presuppose the necessary framework function of rules. Second, stipulate that rules must dictate results. Third, call attention to the fact that other standards may override the rules. Given these three premises, only one inference is possible: Rules and other standards must stand in deep conflict. If rules are nec-

---

23 Kennedy, "Form and Substance." See also Pierre Schlag, "Rules and Standards," *UCLA Law Review*, 33 (1985): 379–430.

essary in law and must dictate results, other kinds of standards must be superfluous. But other standards are not superfluous. So they must contradict the rules, forcing a choice in any case of conflict on grounds outside the law. It might seem coherent to suppose only that law is a matter of principles instead of rules or rules instead of principles, or that standards are available to justify results opposed to the rules in almost any case.

By contrast, rejecting the idea that rules necessarily dictate results allows rules to serve the framework function and to provide content-determinate reasons for judicial action. Other standards can supply supporting or competing reasons, in relation to those supplied by a rule, without requiring a judge to do the impossible. Legal standards of all kinds can provide reasons for a judge to decide different ways, leaving the outcome to discretionary deliberations as contemplated by the good faith thesis. There is no contradiction or deep conflict between rules and other standards when they are distinguished on the basis of their functions, not their force. Furthermore, there is no deep opposition between a jurisprudence of rules and a jurisprudence of principles or other standards. With no need to take sides on a pervasive jurisprudential issue, the law can be understood as an enterprise that need not be just another arena for political combat.

A cautionary note: The claim here that rules do not necessarily dictate results is carefully circumscribed as a conceptual claim. Rules might contingently dictate results in practice for three main reasons.[24] First, a rule may provide a reason for an action and exclude all other reasons or all conflicting reasons, thereby dictating the outcome of legal deliberations as a practical matter. The law requiring all residents with more than a specified income to file an income tax return comes close to that ideal. Second, an authoritative priority rule might give determining force to one of two conflict-

---

24 See also R. Kent Greenawalt, "How Law Can be Determinate," *UCLA Law Review*, 38 (1990): 1–86.

ing rules by ranking their weight in advance and excluding competing considerations. Statutory rules are thus subordinated to the rules in the U.S. Constitution. Third, a rule may have predominant weight according to the prevailing interpretive conventions within the legal community. It might not be illogical to claim that the First Amendment protects, from an injunction against the union tactic, striking bus drivers who lie down in the street outside the bus station to prevent management from operating the buses. But it just won't wash, and everyone knows it. Normatively, rules with effective determining force may be highly desirable for many reasons in many circumstances – when the predictability of the law is especially important and reasonably achievable, when the purpose of the law is only to coordinate an activity fairly, or when the law seeks to encourage reliance and someone has reasonably relied on its determinacy. Rules without determining force may be desirable in other circumstances. (No claim is made here that the present mix of rules in American law is appropriate or desirable.)

In sum, the good faith thesis denies both that the law consists only of rules and that an essential property of rules is that they have both determinate content and result-determining force. It also rejects recent suggestions that rules and other standards contradict each other or that rules can be treated as mere rhetoric, having no role to play in a legal system. Legal rules play a crucial role by designating the classificatory apparatus and often by ordering the legal reasoning in a case. They may play a further important role, along with other standards, by providing reasons for a legal classification. A sound jurisprudence of rules, however, provides no grounds for insisting on a determinacy condition for judges to fulfill their legal duty to uphold the law.

6.3. HART'S CONCEPT OF LAW

H. L. A. Hart supposes a determinacy condition in his treatment of judicial discretion. He holds that judges often have discretion as a consequence of his doctrine of the rule of recognition and the vagueness and open texture of legal standards.[25] To clarify, consider a conceptual model of the adjudicatory process in four steps: (1) judges have a duty to uphold the law of their legal system; to perform their duty, judges must (2) identify the laws of their system, (3) interpret those laws, and (4) apply those laws by issuing a ruling or order accordingly. The determinacy condition restricts the bite of judicial duty to cases in which the law identified at the second step, including laws of interpretation, is sufficient fully to determine the outcome at the fourth step. Judges have discretion when the corpus of law thus identified is indeterminate. For Hart, "the law" consists *only* of legal standards identified by criteria contained in a legal system's rule of recognition. Stubborn indeterminacy in that law therefore requires judges to go outside the law for resources needed to reach some decisions. Hence, the doctrine of the rule of recognition, because it so severely restricts the law, is a possible source for the determinacy condition.

Hart's philosophical claims about indeterminacy and judicial discretion should be understood in the context of his method and goals. Hart's method seeks to elucidate the concept of law by giving the conditions under which various uses of the concept, represented by statements, are valid.[26]

25   "[I]n any modern legal system there must be many occasions where the settled law fails to dictate a decision either way, so that if courts have to decide such cases they must exercise a limited 'interstitial' law-making power, or 'discretion'."
H. L. A. Hart, "Introduction," in *Essays in Jurisprudence and Philosophy*, ed. H. L. A. Hart (Oxford: Clarendon Press, 1983): 1–18, at 6. See also H. L. A. Hart, *The Concept of Law* (Oxford: Clarendon Press, 1961), pp. 120–32 (discussing core of settled meaning and penumbra of uncertainty); H. L. A. Hart, *Essays on Bentham* (Oxford: Clarendon Press, 1982), p. 161 (implicit principles are not law because they do not dictate results). See also Joseph Raz, *The Authority of Law* (Oxford: Clarendon Press, 1979), pp. 67–8, 70–7, 90–7, 180–209 ("The sources thesis requires that the way conflicts of reasons are to be resolved is also determined, to the extent that it is legally determined at all, by social facts. Such facts are also legal sources").
26   Hart, *The Concept of Law*, pp. 1–17; Hart, "Definition and Theory in Jurisprudence," in *Essays in Jurisprudence and Philosophy*: 21–48, at 21; Hart, "Introduction," at 1–6. See also Neil MacCormick, *H. L. A. Hart* (Stanford, Calif.: Stanford University Press, 1981), pp. 12–19.

For example, there are statements of legal rules: "It is the law that residents of the United States shall pay taxes as required by the Internal Revenue Code of 1986, as amended." The conditions for asserting this truly may be called the *grounds for identifying general propositions of law*.[27] There are also statements of concrete legal rights, duties, powers, and permissions; for example, "it is the law that Costello has a right to $100 from Abbott." The conditions for making such statements truly may be called the *grounds for judicial decisions*. Speakers of the legal language, Hart believes, presuppose such conditions in their ordinary discourse when making such statements. The philosopher's job is to make explicit the conditions left implicit in ordinary legal discourse.

Giving grounds for identifying general propositions of law, as Hart does in his principal works on law,[28] is part of a general theory of legal systems, one that would be true, if at all, of all possible legal systems. He starts with a statement of a general proposition of law. He then looks for the conditions under which such a statement could be used in legal discourse without encountering significant criticism, passing as valid law in the legal practice. He claims that the practice of officials when they identify the law reveals the existence of a rule of recognition for any legal system. That rule contains the system's criteria of legal validity. Accordingly, a general condition for identifying valid legal rules is satisfaction of the rule of recognition's criteria of legal validity.[29] A particular rule of recognition may contain criteria specific to a legal system, such as consistency with the Constitution of 1787, as

27 As Jules Coleman pointed out, the problem of identification involves both an epistemic and a semantic dimension. Jules L. Coleman, "Negative and Positive Positivism," *Journal of Legal Studies*, 11 (1982): 139–64. Unless otherwise noted, this text refers to the semantic dimension.

28 See Hart, *The Concept of Law*, pp. 97–107. See also Joseph Raz, *The Concept of a Legal System*, 2d ed. (Oxford: Clarendon Press), pp. 187–203; Raz, *The Authority of Law*, pp. 37–162; Joseph Raz, "Authority, Law and Morality," *The Monist*, 68 (1985): 295–322.

29 Hart, *The Concept of Law*, pp. 97–107.

amended. However, the content of a particular legal system's rule of recognition is not a part of Hart's general theory of legal systems.[30]

Hart's method may be accepted for purposes of the present discussion, but his goals differ materially from those of a practical understanding of adjudication. Judges identify general propositions of law and also interpret and apply them, producing judicial decisions. A practical understanding of adjudication focuses on the grounds for judicial decisions. For two reasons, these grounds need not be coextensive with the grounds for identifying general propositions of law. First, the different kinds of propositions represent different uses of the concept; evidently, they are deployed properly under different conditions within a legal practice.[31] Second, almost no one believes any longer that particular judicial decisions are deduced from general propositions of law together with straightforward findings of fact, even in easy cases.[32] A legal system must therefore provide judges with interpretive resources, like purposes, in addition to general legal standards. Such resources are not general propositions of law in Hart's terms: We do not say, *"it is the law that* a statute prohibiting vehicles in the park shall be interpreted to further the safety of pedestrians in the park." Nonetheless they are a part of the legal materials properly consulted by judges to aid their deliberations.

Despite the widespread impression to the contrary, Hart did not present a theory of adjudication in Chapter 7 of *The Concept of Law*.[33] The relevant passage should be read only as

30 By contrast, restrictions on the rule of recognition are made by Raz's sources thesis. See Raz, *Authority, Law and Morality*.
31 For example, general propositions of law are asserted by legislators and treatise writers in the absence of the facts in a particular case. Particular propositions can be advanced only after the congeries of facts in a case have materialized or are imagined.
32 See Lochner v. New York, 198 U.S. 45, 76 (1905) (dissenting opinion of Holmes, J.) ("[g]eneral propositions do not decide concrete cases").
33 See also H. L. A. Hart, "Problems in the Philosophy of Law," in *Essays in Jurisprudence and Philosophy*: 88–120, at 98–109. See also Joseph Raz, "Dworkin: A New Link in the Chain," *California Law*

a response to a possible counterargument to his larger treatment of legal rules. The thesis of the book is that legal systems generally are unions of primary rules of obligation with secondary rules of recognition, change, and adjudication. Chapter 7 is introduced as a defensive move against the possible objection that "any elucidation of the concept of law in terms of rules must be misleading."[34] In Chapter 7, accordingly, Hart sought only to show that rules had enough punch to serve the functions assigned to them by his principal thesis, without endorsing determinate-formalism.[35] Hart was well aware that problems of rule application were a "wider topic."[36] Similarly, in the famous 1958 debate with Lon Fuller,[37] Hart's discussion of adjudication was a response to a possible counterargument to his main thesis about the separation of law and morals.[38] Moreover, Hart's views would appear uncharacteristically incoherent if the rule of recognition were thought to provide criteria for identifying all the grounds for judicial decisions. The rule of rec-

Review, 74 (1986): 1103–19, at 1107 ("[a]ll [the rule of recognition] is meant to do, is to identify which acts are acts of legislation and which are the rendering of binding judicial decisions").

34 Hart, The Concept of Law, p. 120.
35 Ibid., p. 149 ("it is indeed a necessary condition of a legal system existing, that not every rule is open to doubt on all points").
36 Ibid., p. 119. See also p. 124 (to characterize the criteria of relevance and closeness in analogies would be to characterize whatever is specific in legal reasoning); p. 144 ("[m]uch indeed that cannot be attempted here needs to be done to characterize in informative detail . . . the varied types of reasoning which courts characteristically use in exercising the creative function left to them by the open texture of law in statute or precedent").
37 Lon L. Fuller, "Positivism and Fidelity to Law: A Reply to Professor Hart," Harvard Law Review, 71 (1958): 630–72; H. L. A. Hart, "Positivism and the Separation of Law and Morals," Harvard Law Review, 71 (1958): 593–629.
38 Hart's subsequent comments on legal reasoning have been comments on the work of others, not a positive contribution of his own. See Hart, "Introduction," at 6–8; H. L. A. Hart, "Problems in the Philosophy of Law," at 106–8; H. L. A. Hart, "American Jurisprudence Through English Eyes: The Nightmare and the Noble Dream," in Essays in Jurisprudence and Philosophy: 123–44, at 132–41; H. L. A. Hart, "1776–1976: Law in the Perspective of Philosophy," in Essays in Jurisprudence and Philosophy: 145–58, at 152–8.

ognition does not validate as law the purposes both Hart and Fuller regard as important resources for legal interpretation,[39] or the implicit principles both Hart and Dworkin find to be ingredients of judicial decisions.[40] His theory of legal systems offers just one restriction on a theory of adjudication: Nothing counts as a part of the law that judges have a duty to uphold unless it is a general proposition of law identified by the criteria contained in the legal system's rule of recognition.[41]

This restriction is mistaken. A well-known risk in developing general theories of legal systems is the ethnocentric mistake of treating features of one's own legal system as necessary or central features of all legal systems. A converse risk is

39 See Fuller, "Positivism and Fidelity to Law"; Hart, "Introduction," at 7–8.
40 Hart, *Essays on Bentham*, p. 161 (courts characteristically exercise discretion by "promoting those moral values or principles which the existing law can be regarded as instantiating"). From Hart's point of view, however, Dworkin's early criticisms on this score, which challenged the doctrine of the rule of recognition for failing to capture such principles, are not greatly bothersome. See Dworkin, *Taking Rights Seriously*, pp. 14–45. For arguments that the rule of recognition can capture principles, see Coleman, "Negative and Positive Positivism"; David Lyons, "Principles, Positivism, and Legal Theory," *Yale Law Journal*, 87 (1977): 415–35; E. Philip Soper, "Legal Theory and the Obligation of a Judge: The Hart/Dworkin Dispute," *Michigan Law Review*, 75 (1977): 473–519. Moreover, using an ordinary language method, we do say, "*It is the law that* an automobile manufacturer is liable for negligence to a buyer injured by its product." The conditions warranting such a statement should elucidate the concept of law as it is used in general propositions of law. We do not say, "*It is the law that* no man shall profit by his own wrong." Nor do we say, "*It is the law that* the courts will not allow themselves to be used as instruments of inequity and injustice." Two of Dworkin's principal examples of principles are thus not a part of "the law" in its relevant use for Hart's general philosophical purposes. Dworkin, *Taking Rights Seriously*, pp. 23–4.
41 Hart had good reason to restrict his concerns. The interpretive resources provided by the legal materials probably vary too much from one to another legal system for them to be captured by a general theory of the kind he sought. Studies of adjudication usually claim to account only for a family of local legal practices. Dworkin, for example, considers only the grounds for judicial decisions in Anglo-American legal practice. Dworkin, *Law's Empire*, p. 102.

the cosmopolitan mistake of treating the features that are a necessary part of the law in all legal systems as the only features of law, properly conceived, for all purposes. There is no imperial warrant for a general theory of legal systems to confine the law that judges have a duty to uphold in one legal system to that which it must have in common with all legal systems. The concept of law is also used when announcing judicial decisions and may, in that use, comprehend a wider range of legal materials. A judge who "consults the law" does not consult only general legal rules. He or she consults the full range of legal materials, including precedents, implicit principles and policies, and the conventions of the legal community. These interpretive resources generally do not supply result-determining legal standards to resolve vagueness, ambiguity, or truncation in a general legal rule, or to mediate between competing legal rules. Rather, they augment the general rules by providing a constellation of additional legal reasons needed to classify a problem case in a class of cases designated by a legal rule.

The legal rules identified at the second step of the above model[42] are those serving the framework function necessary in all mature legal systems. In that function, legal rules might be the connection that ties legal systems together in general within a project like Hart's. Within a practical understanding of adjudication, however, such a concept of law is too meager to do the job. The law identified at the second step in adjudication might consist of legal rules, understood in their framework function. In addition, the wider range of legal materials, including the content of legal rules, may guide interpretation and application by admitting and excluding reasons for judicial action without necessarily determining results. The admitted reasons will be weighed as contemplated by the good faith thesis. Consequently, the doctrine of the rule of recognition does not ground the determinacy condition in a theory of adjudication.

---

42 See text following note 25 above.

6.4. THE RIGHT ANSWER THESIS

The right answer thesis, as advanced by Ronald Dworkin, holds that the law in principle determines a single right legal result and that a judge's legal duty is to reach that result.[43] In terms of the four-step model of adjudication employed above, Dworkin agrees that judges are bound by the law only when the law identified at the second step determines the result (in principle). That is, he accepts or presupposes the determinacy condition. Dworkin's wide conception of the law so identified, however, enables him to claim that the law constrains judges in almost all cases by determining the right legal answer. In broad outline, Dworkin holds that moral principles of a certain kind are the law that judges have a duty to uphold. Principles of political morality, in particular, are the law when they pass a threshold requirement of "fit" with the legal practice of a community and are morally more appealing in justifying the state's use of coercion than any competitor that fits. The best interpretation of a flourishing legal tradition supports attractive principles that have incompatible implications in hard cases. Principles, however, have a property of weight, and some will be more weighty than others. The judge's duty is to act on the weightiest principles, overruling past judicial decisions that are mistakes in light of a judgment that shows the community's overall practice in its best light. Though a tie is possible, Dworkin thinks that the set of legal principles determines a unique legal outcome in all other cases.

If sound, Dworkin's thesis would challenge the good faith thesis because it entails the determinacy condition. If the law that judges have a duty to uphold determines right results, as Dworkin urges, then a judge's duty to uphold the law can be fulfilled only by reaching the results determined by the

---

43 For Dworkin's most complete argument on the point, see Ronald Dworkin, *A Matter of Principle* (Cambridge: Harvard University Press, 1985), pp. 119–45.

law. This would negate the permissibility of significant judicial discretion, depriving the good faith thesis of its point. To be sure, Dworkin rejects "semantic theories of law" – those that require determinate results as a consequence of the meaning of "law."[44] And he rejects interpretive conventionalism, which requires determinate results in order to settle expectations through the meaning of the words in which explicit rules are cast.[45] He does not, however, challenge the determinacy condition as such. He deploys the right answer thesis partly to show that it can be satisfied.

One reason for resisting Dworkin's right answer thesis, as a thesis about the lawful-making characteristics of a judicial decision, will be offered here. Dworkin's argument is centrally dependent on his conception of principles and, in particular, their property of weight.[46] He has not, however, written much specifically about the grounds of weight.[47] A claim that the law determines a single right answer would be sound only if the grounds of weight must be all among the grounds for law. Otherwise, *the law* would not determine a single right answer. Outcomes would be determined by the law together with something else.

Dworkin's right answer thesis seems to hold, accordingly, that the grounds for identifying abstract principles and weighing them are the same.[48] For example, he introduces

44 Dworkin, *Law's Empire*, pp. 31–46.
45 Ibid., pp. 114–50. Dworkin's conventionalist foil is but an interpretive version of the result-determining rules discussed in §§ 6.2 and following.
46 A relevant principle of law, by contrast with a rule as defined by Dworkin, is to be taken into account as a consideration inclining in one direction or another to some extent depending on its weight. Dworkin, *Taking Rights Seriously*, pp. 26–7, 71–80. Dworkin, more than anyone else, has built a jurisprudence on principles with weight.
47 Dworkin's early view was that weight depends on the amount of "institutional support" for a principle, as evidenced by the frequency of cases and statutes in which it figures. See ibid., pp. 14–45. For criticism of this idea, see § 2.3.2. Nothing to like effect appears in *Law's Empire*.
48 His works do not speak sufficiently to the point to be confident that Dworkin is deliberately committed to a position on the question.

Law's Empire as an exploration of the grounds for "propositions of law," which consist of

> all the various statements and claims people make about what
> the law allows or prohibits or entitles them to have. Proposi-
> tions of law can be very general – "the law forbids states to
> deny anyone equal protection within the meaning of the Four-
> teenth Amendment" – or much less general – "the law does
> not provide compensation for fellow-servant injuries" – or
> very concrete – "the law requires Acme Corporation to com-
> pensate John Smith for the injury he suffered in its employ last
> February."[49]

Without distinguishing between general and concrete propositions, Dworkin observes that "[e]veryone thinks that
propositions of law are true or false (or neither) in virtue of
other, more familiar kinds of propositions"[50] – the grounds
of law. So it seems that the grounds for abstract and concrete
legal propositions are the same.

This understanding of Dworkin's position is confirmed
when Dworkin's heroic judge, Hercules, decides a hard case,
in which competing legal principles indicate incompatible
outcomes. According to Dworkin, the grounds of law are fit
with the historic legal practice and justification in political
morality, which are treated as siblings for the most part within the general search for the best interpretation. In the hard
case, however, fit and justification lose their parity, with fit
folding into justification.[51] Competing principles within the
best general interpretation then may "require some nonarbitrary scheme of priority or weighting or accommodation . . . that reflects their respective sources in a deeper
level of political morality."[52] In the event, Hercules concludes
abruptly without giving any reason: "I believe that though

49 Dworkin, *Law's Empire*, p. 4. See also pp. 109–11 (distinguishing
    grounds and force of law, excluding the latter from consideration).
50 Ibid.
51 Ibid., pp. 257, 263.
52 Ibid., p. 269.

the impulse behind each of the two principles is attractive, the second is more powerful in these circumstances."[53] Dworkin thus draws a distinction between the shallow level of political morality used to identify abstract legal propositions and the deeper level used for weighing them when they compete. The nature of the deeper level, and thus the grounds of weight, are left unexplained and mysterious.

There are two interpretations of this brief but critical passage. One is that the grounds of weight move from the law to a distinct political morality outside the law, which might provide the nonarbitrary basis that the right answer thesis requires. This, however, would be an unattractive interpretation because it merely pushes the problem of weight back one step. In hard cases, the "deeper level of political morality," too, will generate competing reasons for assigning weights; the competing reasons will need to be weighed. A move to morality, or to any other extra-legal standards, enters a regress that can be stopped, at any point, only by weighing the then-identified reasons more or less as indicated by the good faith thesis. There is no reason to enter the regress at all. We can stop it after identifying the reasons warranted by the conventional law as grounds for judicial decisions, however competitive they might be in a hard case.

The second interpretation is that the "deeper level of political morality" somehow is among the grounds of law. Dworkin would not enter a regress, which is probably why Hercules stops giving reasons when he reaches his final judgment on weight. Dworkin must keep the grounds for weighing principles among the grounds for them to be law: To repeat, the right answer thesis cannot be maintained if the grounds of weight are different from the grounds for identifying abstract legal propositions. On the second interpretation, Dworkin's right answer thesis poses a challenge to the good faith thesis. For reasons given above,[54] the good faith thesis denies that all the grounds of weight are among the

---

53 Ibid., p. 271.
54 See § 2.3.2.

grounds for identifying the law. Rather, it claims distinctively, the congeries of reasons in a case are the grounds for weight, reflecting the dependency of legal standards on the facts of a case for their actual normative force and, more important, on the mix of legal reasons for the weight of any one of them.

The good faith thesis is superior because the weights of legal reasons do change in the play of principles invoked by the facts of a case. Weight is not fixed as a property of abstract principles because no legal principle prevails over another whenever they compete. Nor is it plausible to suppose that the scheme of legal principles as a whole fixes weights for each legal reason for all possible congeries of reasons arising in all possible worlds.[55] Absent such a supposition, taken on faith or merely assumed as an a priori truth about law, it is hard to imagine how a deep level of political morality could contain a nonarbitrary basis for the variance of weight with the congeries of reasons in a case. Because the weight of any one reason depends on the congeries of reasons, the law cannot determine all weights in advance and therefore cannot determine results in principle. Judges have discretion because the mixtures of facts that can materialize at bar are so variable.

It might be argued in reply that the difference here is trivial. Within adjudication, the only law that matters is the law that is relevant to the case. The relevance of any law depends on the existence of facts that invoke it in the case. Normative force and weight, however, have their source in the abstract normative standard – not in the plain fact, which is inert. So, it might be concluded, the grounds of weight turn out to be in the abstract legal standards after all, subject only to the presupposed requirement that they be relevant in the case.

55 Within a Dworkinian framework, such an understanding might come only at the cost of either abandoning the right answer thesis or jettisoning the law that gives at least some settled precedents special weight even when they are mistaken. See S. L. Hurley, "Coherence, Hypothetical Cases, and Precedent," *Oxford Journal of Legal Studies*, 10 (1990): 221–51, at 244–51.

It may help to clarify the idea that weight is grounded in the congeries of reasons in the case. The weight of a reason does not have its source only in the abstract legal standard that is a component of that same reason. In a case like *Riggs*, the mere fact that the grandson killed his grandfather is a reason for not allowing him to inherit based on the principle of respecting a testator's autonomy: We have some confidence that, had the grandfather known he would die by his grandson's hand, the grandfather would not have made the grandson his heir. There is an additional reason for not allowing the grandson to inherit, however, if he killed to prevent a change in the will. That is a legal reason because, by the familiar maxim, a court should not allow the grandson to profit as intended by his own wrong. Crucially, the additional reason has weight in its own right *and also enhances the weight of the reason based in the principle of respecting a testator's autonomy.* The grandfather in the latter situation had formed an intent to disinherit the grandson and was prevented by the grandson from formalizing it. By contrast, suppose that the grandfather was terminally ill and suffering. The grandson claims to have assisted in a suicide, though it might have been a mercy killing. Now, perhaps, the weight of the reason based in the maxim declines. The weight of the reason based in the testator's autonomy is diluted if it was a mercy killing and dissipates if it was assisted suicide.

The weight of one reason – that the grandson killed the testator – thus varies depending on the other reasons in the case. Consequently, it would be misleading to say that all the grounds of weight are among the grounds of law as though, having identified all abstract legal standards within the corpus of law, the right answer in almost every possible case thereby has been determined in advance. That, as I understand it, is what the right answer thesis must claim if it is to negate judicial discretion and thereby render the good faith thesis pointless. The permissible discretion thesis is a more plausible alternative. It allows that two or more alternative decisions may be *lawful* in the same case. From a critical standpoint, unhampered by any duty to uphold the law, one or another may be the right answer. But as a practical matter within judicial duty, it is also important that the decisions all be lawful.

The good faith thesis should be preferred mainly because it provides suitable places for the congeries of legal reasons in a case among the grounds for weight and for the ebb and flow of the weight of legal reasons from case to case. The good faith thesis better takes into account the fact that, from the judicial standpoint, a judge's duty is to decide specific legal questions arising in a case that has materialized. It does not confuse the grounds of weight with the grounds for identifying abstract legal standards, thereby conflating the legal status of a principle with its force in a particular judicial decision. The good faith thesis respects the distinctive feature of adjudication as a process for settling particular disputes under law, thereby distinguishing judges from legislators and moral philosophers.

6.5. SEMANTIC NATURAL LAW

The philosophy of Michael Moore suggests yet another way of grounding the determinacy condition due to the nature of the law.[56] Moore's jurisprudence, however, dovetails imperfectly with the good faith and permissible discretion theses. These theses concern the conditions under which a judge fulfills the judicial duty to uphold the law – the lawful-making characteristics of a judicial decision. They do not directly concern the conditions under which a judicial decision is morally right, which is Moore's philosophical interest.[57]

56 Moore, "A Natural Law Theory of Interpretation"; Michael S. Moore, "Precedent, Induction, and Ethical Generalization," in *Precedent in Law*, ed. L. Goldstein (Oxford: Clarendon Press, 1987); Michael S. Moore, "The Interpretive Turn in Legal Theory: A Turn for the Worse?," *Stanford Law Review*, 41 (1989): 871–957. See also Michael S. Moore, "Moral Reality," *Wisconsin Law Review* (1982): 1061–156; Michael S. Moore, "The Semantics of Judging," *Southern California Law Review*, 54 (1981): 151–294.
57 Michael S. Moore, "Three Concepts of Rules," *Harvard Journal of Law & Public Policy* 14 (1991): 771–96, at 793. See §§ 7.1 and following.

Nonetheless, Moore's semantic natural law approach might establish that legal results are metaphysically determinate. If this were so, the judicial duty to uphold the law would require a judge to reach the results thus determined. This, in turn, would entail the determinacy condition due to the nature of the law that judges have a duty to uphold.

Based on recent developments in semantics,[58] Moore argues that laws refer to real kinds of things that have essential natures. For example, a statute that uses the word "death" could be understood to refer to whatever it is that death really is, even when the statute contains a specific definition treating "death" according to conventional or instrumental understandings.[59] Following an old statutory definition of death, a person whose brain function has ceased, but whose cardiac and respiratory functions have not ceased, may not be deemed dead. If our best current theory about what death really is defines it as the cessation of brain function, however, a judge might be under a duty to find that the person is dead despite the old statutory definition (or a more current convention to the same effect). Death might be a real kind of thing – a "natural kind" – about which we have better or worse scientific theories. The statute might refer to *that kind*, which might have an essential nature. All else being equal, the proper applications of the statute might be naturally determinate even when our knowledge of them is indeterminate.[60] According to Moore, the statutory definition is supposed to be but one theory about what death really is. An interpreter should interpret according to the best theory he or she can muster now, even when conventional under-

---

58 See generally Saul A. Kripke, *Naming and Necessity* (Cambridge: Harvard University Press, 1972); Hilary Putnam, "The Meaning of Meaning," in *Mind, Language and Reality*, ed. Hilary Putnam, 2 vols. (Cambridge: Cambridge University Press, 1975) 2: 215–71.

59 Moore, "A Natural Law Theory of Interpretation," at 322–38.

60 Even when all else is not equal, Moore believes that each relevant factor has a "correct weight," and that they can be combined to produce "the correct decision." He does not elaborate on the assertion. Moore, "A Natural Law Theory of Interpretation," at 370–4; Moore, "Three Concepts of Rules," at 793–4.

standings all go the other way. Additionally, Moore believes that there is a moral reality containing "moral kinds," to which moral terms in legal rules refer in like manner. Some legal words, moreover, refer to "functional kinds," which operate comparably.[61]

Accepting this theory of interpretation, however, requires surmounting some tall hurdles. The first hurdle is the metaphysics, which are hard for most lawyers and judges to take seriously despite a recent revival of interest among professional philosophers.[62] This is not the place to engage in the kind of philosophical argument necessary to address the metaphysics completely. Two quick points, however, justify doubt insofar as the argument involves nonnatural kinds and is derived from Hilary Putnam's original work.[63]

61 Moore classifies the terms in rules as terms referring to natural kinds, moral kinds, artifactual kinds, functional kinds, and legal kinds. He applies his realist semantics to natural kinds, moral kinds, and functional kinds, is doubtful about the existence of artifactual kinds (like "sloop"), and declines to apply his semantics to legal kinds. Moore, "A Natural Law Theory of Interpretation," at 322–8, 328–33, 300 n. 39, 301 n. 44; Moore, "Precedent, Induction, and Ethical Generalization," at 206; Moore, "The Interpretive Turn in Legal Theory," at 881–90. Professor Brink apparently would go further than Moore and treat all terms in legal rules according to the same semantic theory. See David O. Brink, "Legal Theory, Legal Interpretation, and Judicial Review," *Philosophy and Public Affairs*, 17 (1988): 105–48, at 116–21. For criticism, see Stephen R. Munzer, "Realistic Limits on Realist Interpretation," *Southern California Law Review*, 58 (1985): 459–75; Dennis M. Patterson, "What Was Realism?: A Reply to David Brink," *Canadian Journal of Law and Jurisprudence*, 2 (1989): 193–5.

62 The cold response to metaphysical realism by legal scholars is explored in Moore, "The Interpretive Turn in Legal Theory"; Note, "Relativistic Jurisprudence: Skepticism Founded on Confusion," *Southern California Law Review*, 61 (1988): 1417–509 (by Heidi Hurd).

63 In Kripke's version of realist semantics, a word first gets associated with a physical kind of thing historically, when someone dubs a particular thing with the word. He argues that there is a causal chain from the dubbing to current usage. The word consequently designates rigidly, in all possible worlds, the kind of thing instantiated by the original. Thus, he argues, we use "tiger" to refer to the same kind of thing that everyone has referred to by that word since the original dubbing. Kripke, *Naming and Necessity*, at 91–7, 116–29, 134–44. Moore makes no mention of an original dubbing. It is doubtful whether everyone since an original dubbing has referred to the same

According to Putnam, a natural kind of thing has a "hidden nature" that is the same in all possible worlds. Thus, he argues plausibly, water is H_2O in all possible worlds.[64] Semantic natural law supposes that moral concepts also have a hidden nature. But it is hard to imagine what the counterpart to H_2O would be. A recent effort to explain it seems self-refuting: "Just as water *is in fact* H_2O . . .wrongness *is in fact* cruelty; and culpability *is in fact* voluntariness."[65] In addition, how could this realist theory of moral kinds make sense in relation to possible worlds where the beings had moral interests very different from our own? In a world without scarcity, for example, property would be radically unlike what it is in our world.[66] Closer to home, a moral requirement of respect for the person forbids all cannibalism in our culture. There have been cultures, however, in which eating the body of a defeated enemy warrior was an act of respect. A moral principle of respect for persons can be valid universally while its instances vary too radically for moral kinds to have essential natures in all possible worlds.

Another hurdle is the view that legal standards, or many of them, in fact refer to features of an independent reality and that judges have a duty so to interpret them, regardless of the conventional understandings of authoritative lawmakers, law interpreters, and practicing lawyers. One thus might accept the general semantic position for purposes of discussion and yet demur. Even if the metaphysics were correct, it would not follow that the law of a community refers to a moral and functional reality. After all, metaphysical questions are obscure and perennially controversial. A main function of the law in a community is to provide a practicable framework for living that avoids endless debates over the basic terms of existence. Accordingly, judges

kind of thing with words like "blameworthy," "respect," "duty," and "good," much less "security interest" or "corporation."

64   Putnam, "The Meaning of Meaning," at 223–35.
65   See Heidi M. Hurd, "Sovereignty in Silence," *Yale Law Journal*, 99 (1990): 945–1028, at 1001–2 (emphasis in original).
66   I thank Hilary Putnam for raising these questions in conversation.

should coordinate their decisions. We should hesitate before turning them into solitary metaphysicians by slighting this function and the practical epistemic difficulties.

A main alternative is to believe that legal terms designate classes of cases, created and interpreted conventionally (even though some coincide with independently existing kinds of things). That is, a statutory term like "security interest" or "corporation" may designate the class of situations in which there is a security interest or a corporation in law in our legal world. That class, however, might have no existence independent of our conventional practices and dispositions and therefore no existence wherever those practices are absent. If so, the membership of a case in that class would depend on conventional criteria.[67] A judge's duty might be to decide in accordance with the relevant conventions even when they are not congruent with a convention-independent reality (in which case a judge might properly be criticized on realist grounds[68]). Reality would not then ground determinacy of legal results.

Thought experiments will not resolve the dispute between metaphysically realist and conventionalist understandings of the reference of legal terms. Intuitive reactions to hypothetical examples vary in a way that denies either side a dispositive ground. Furthermore, for every example of a term that might operate as the realist supposes (like "death"), there is another example that seems to operate as the conventionalist supposes (like "security interest"). The realist can argue that legal terms of art (like "security interest") are just instances of a more general kind of thing (like "property"), or he can conjure up new entities to avoid the objection.[69] The conventionalist, however, has several replies. Even terms like "death" are used by legislators conventionally in a culture that has not taken moral realism seriously for many decades. Since they bear responsibility

67 Burton, *Law and Legal Reasoning*, pp. 125–64.
68 See §§ 7.1 and following.
69 See Moore, "The Interpretive Turn in Legal Theory," at 881–90 (proposing that legal terms of art refer to "functional kinds").

and have authority as lawmakers, their words should be interpreted in a way that they would recognize as theirs. Politicians on Capitol Hill do not deal their way to moral reality; we should not deem their deeds to be something other than *theirs*. Moreover, a judge's oath to uphold the law is understood by appointing authorities and almost everyone else to refer to the conventional law, conventionally understood. Requirements of democracy, separation of powers, predictability, notice, and equal treatment under law counsel against breaking the law free of the conventional understandings of its implications. The operative law of a community simply does not require a judge, even prima facie, to reach decisions that perhaps no one else thinks are the correct legal decisions.

On the conventionalist account, the judge's legal duty is to interpret the law in accordance with the social practices and dispositions of the relevant interpretive community even when the result does not conform to moral reality.[70] There are three reasons for this. First, morality permits a wide variety of solutions to many social problems. Conventional selections within the permitted range are embodied in laws that cannot be interpreted in the semantic natural law style because the laws refer to local practices, like the recordation of real property titles on a race, notice, race-notice, or Torrens basis.[71] The rules in such cases employ legal terms of art that would refer, so to speak, to "legal kinds," which even Moore declines to countenance.[72] Surely the conventional theory of interpretation should then be employed. Once legal terms of art are admitted, it is an open question how much of the law

70 See Chap. 2, notes 1, 38, 55.
71 This view encompasses, for example, the important idea of law as a solution to coordination problems (and more). See generally Finnis, *Natural Law and Natural Rights* (Oxford: Clarendon Press, 1980), pp. 231–51; Edna Ullman-Margalit, *The Emergence of Norms* (Oxford: Clarendon Press, 1977), pp. 74–93; Leslie Green, "Law, Coordination and the Common Good," *Oxford Journal of Legal Studies*, 3 (1983): 299–324; Gerald J. Postema, "Coordination and Convention at the Foundations of Law," *Journal of Legal Studies*, 11 (1982): 165–203.
72 See note 61 above.

consists of such terms, including terms that also have moral or other uses but are specially defined in statutes or by precedent. Second, morality requires or prohibits some solutions, in which case the law, interpreted conventionally, might get it wrong. In that case, the judge's *legal* duty, I will argue in the next chapter, is to uphold the conventional understanding of the law whether or not the legal system is generally just. The loyal and dutiful judge in a wicked legal system is fully complicit in its wickedness and deserves to be criticized, perhaps harshly. That judge's *moral* duty may be to resign or to engage in disobedience from the bench, throwing monkey wrenches into the works at every opportunity. The moral duty is not to put a moral gloss on evil laws, pretending them to be better than they are and serving as an apologist for evil. Third, morals serve as the ground from which one evaluates the law, criticizing it when it is morally deficient, while the law remains a matter of convention.[73] Retaining a conventional conception of the law permits moral criticism to be more thorough. Moral criticism should not be hampered by the words used by lawmakers in their legal pronouncements.

A semantic natural law theorist might reply that the question is more pertinent and harder when the judge believes that the conventions get it wrong on some particular legal question in a generally just legal system. It could be argued that the judge should follow his or her own convictions and correct the error for the sake of justice. This might be Moore's position,[74] though it must surmount another hur-

---

73 For example, Hart, *The Concept of Law*, at 181–207; Hart, "Positivism and the Separation of Law and Morals," at 594–600; § 7.2.1. The importance of both law and morals is affirmed by both legal positivist and natural law philosophers. See, for example, John Finnis, *Natural Law and Natural Rights*, pp. 351–6. It is a common and serious error to suppose that legal positivists generally seek to *supplant* morals with law.

74 Moore holds that a judge should never allow himself or herself to be an instrument of immorality. See Michael S. Moore, "Authority, Law, and Razian Reasons," *Southern California Law Review*, 62 (1989): 827–96, at 859–73. See Chap. 7.

dle. The metaphysics of law cannot support a determinacy condition within a practical understanding of adjudication without passing through an epistemic filter. It serves no practical purpose to insist that legal results are metaphysically determinate if members of the legal community can readily disagree about an outcome, using all lawyerly skill in good faith, upon full adjudication of a case.

Moreover, excluding epistemic considerations is not justified because epistemic humility can be a reason for judicial action as a practical matter. Consider a judge who is required to rule on whether an attorney in bankruptcy can secure his or her own fee by taking a security interest in personal property of the bankrupt client. The problem is significant when the attorney will be advising on the conduct of the business and have the ability to give preferential treatment to the assets in which the attorney is interested, disadvantaging the interests of other creditors. The attorney's duties are fairly clear in such a case. There is nothing wrong in principle with taking the security interest along with a duty to treat all assets under liens on an equal footing. The judge, however, might worry about the conflict of interest. He or she knows that preferential treatment of assets can take subtle forms and be hard to discover and prove. Those epistemic concerns are reasons for the judge to hold that no attorney in bankruptcy can take a security interest to secure the legal fee. They are reasons of legal policy, not principle, which properly can change the outcome to guard against foreseeable error.[75]

When "doing philosophy," it may be appropriate to separate epistemic from metaphysical questions and to treat the important philosophical questions in their metaphysical aspect. When a judge is on the bench, by contrast, a sharp separation is not justified. The judge can be a committed moral realist and have confidence in his or her lonely moral judgments. The accretion of human judgments and conventions that we ordinarily call "the law," however, fend off

75 I thank Elizabeth Warren for the example.

error when the legal system is generally just. Any judge is at least as fallible as the conventions of the legal community. Fallibility counsels deference to the collective judgment of the legal community reflected in its interpretive conventions. Such coordination, with its check on judicial self-righteousness, seems highly desirable to say the least.

A conventionalist theory of legal interpretation does not require the determinacy condition. It need not deny that there is a reality consisting of real kinds of things or even that a moral reality grounds sound moral criticism of the law in principle. It does deny that legal rules generally refer to convention-independent kinds of things and that judges should interpret the law apart from the interpretive conventions of the legal community. Even if semantic natural law got its metaphysics right, it would not generate an adequate ground for regarding law-governed discretion as a confusion. Like so much legal theory, semantic natural law focuses on the results in cases and the relation of the law to those results. It provides no persuasive arguments for dismissing the good faith thesis's claim that the law provides reasons for judicial decisions, not necessarily results.

To summarize Part II, the main objection to the good faith thesis is that the idea of law-governed discretion is a confusion because judges have no legal duties when the law is indeterminate. This objection depends in many different ways on the determinacy condition – the claim that a judge can fulfill the judicial duty to uphold the law only if the law determines one correct result in each case and the judge reaches that result. The determinacy condition, however, is not self-evidently sound; it requires justification. We have reviewed the most prominent grounds for defending the determinacy condition – epistemic grounds involving logical positivism or empirical pragmatism, political grounds involving the claims made by the law or "liberal legalism," and philosophical grounds involving the jurisprudence of rules, the theory of legal systems, Dworkinian interpretation, and semantic natural law. All have been found wanting. To be sure, rejecting a limited number of possible grounds does not establish that the determinacy condition is ungrounded. However, this discussion should stimulate explicit debate in place of the confusing and distorting implicit role the determinacy condition plays in much American legal theory. For now, the arguments suffice to justify rejecting the determinacy condition and embracing the permissible discretion thesis. The idea of an authorization chain gives us good reason to hold that judicial discretion is compatible with legitimate adjudication in a constitutional democracy.

Part III

Law, morals, and politics

Chapter 7

Legal and moral duties

7.1. DOING JUSTICE

A different kind of objection to the good faith thesis – one not based on the determinacy condition – charges that it requires blind obedience to the conventional law when it claims that a judge acts in bad faith by relying on moral reasons excluded by that law from the grounds for a judicial decision. A judge's general moral duties, it might be argued, require that justice be done in each case because morality is sovereign over the conventional law. When that law fails to produce the just result, considerations of justice should prevail. The judge might thus be duty bound to change the law or, if necessary, to manipulate the legal rules and the facts of cases as necessary to get to the morally right result. The good faith thesis, it might be charged, is objectionable because it requires judges to allow themselves to be used as instruments of injustice.

The good faith thesis allows that law and morals will provide conflicting guidance to judges whenever the applicable law is unjust and the reasons showing it to be unjust are excluded from judicial deliberations. The law often excludes general reasons of political morality – the special moral constraints imposed on public officers when they are exercising official power. Judges, in particular, are at the end of an authorization chain that significantly constrains their reasons for official action. The good faith thesis consequently holds that a judge acts in bad faith *toward legal duty* if he or she acts on reasons not warranted by the law as grounds for judicial decision. In some circumstances, however, judges may be morally obligated to do that. Perhaps surprisingly, a judge can do the morally right thing, all things considered, and at the same time be in bad faith toward legal duty.[1]

7.2. CONFLICTS OF LAW AND MORALS

Conflicts between law and morals occur because legal and moral propositions have distinct grounds. The sets of legal and moral propositions consequently can (and not uncommonly do) differ, producing divergent and conflicting guidance. In this respect, however, the good faith thesis is not distinctive. H. L. A. Hart and Joseph Raz, for example, hold that the rule of recognition provides the criteria for identifying general propositions of law. The rule of recognition is a social rule that exists only within a contingent social practice. It commonly requires reference to historical lawmaking acts (such as the enactment of a rule by a legislature). Since those acts are done by humans who may act mistakenly or corruptly, the set of legal propositions might overlap the set of moral propositions only partially or conceivably not at all. A principal point of Hart's and Raz's legal positivism is to facilitate clear moral criticism of the law in force in a community. Ronald Dworkin also allows for divergence between law and morals. The law for him is the best interpretation of a historical practice. The practice in some community might lend itself to no interpretation that is morally acceptable, but still might be "law" in a less than flourishing sense.[2] Even in a flourishing legal practice, the best interpretation of the law

1 As will be seen, the distinction here between legal and moral duties does not track the one criticized in Ronald Dworkin, *Law's Empire* (Cambridge: Harvard University Press, Belknap Press, 1986), p. 135 (discussing semantic theory that the phrase "legal rights" should not be used to describe rights people have in virtue of consistency in principle).
2 Ibid., pp. 101–8. See also Steven J. Burton, "Ronald Dworkin and Legal Positivism," *Iowa Law Review*, 73 (1987): 109–29.

might be less than ideal.[3] A decision in accordance with the best interpretation of the legal practice thus may differ from a wholly moral decision, which would not be so hampered by historical and institutional accidents.[4]

Consider the case of a trial judge charged to decide a claim of sex discrimination based on a statute (Title VII) that the claimant interprets to require comparable pay for comparable worth in public employment. Assume that the judge – call her "Rachel, J." – is firmly convinced that comparability is the morally correct principle and a reasonable interpretation of Title VII under the circumstances. The most recent precedent of the court of appeals above her, however, held that Title VII did not require comparable pay for comparable worth. It held further that an employment practice is not unlawful if the rates of pay reflect market rates and there is no intentional discrimination.[5] Left free of precedent, Rachel, J. undoubtedly would sustain the claim of gender discrimination. This trial judge believes that morality and her own interpretation of Title VII require her to grant relief to the plaintiff. Legally speaking, however, she should reject the claim.[6] The rule of stare decisis requires her to follow a precedent that precludes her from granting that relief.

Rachel, J. faces conflicting guidance from law and morality. The law provides her with two reasons for rejecting the claim – reasons based on the rule of stare decisis and the precedent. Morality, as she sees it, provides her with two reasons for vindicating the claim – reasons based directly on the

3 Dworkin, *Law's Empire*, pp. 400–13.
4 For new and novel natural law theories that take a different view, see Heidi M. Hurd, "Challenging Authority," *Yale Law Journal*, 100 (1991): 1611–77 (arguing that law has theoretical, not practical authority); Donald H. Regan, "Authority and Value: Reflections on Raz's *Morality of Freedom*," *Southern California Law Review*, 62 (1989): 995–1096 (same). John Finnis would not deny the existence of conflicts as described in the text. See John Finnis, *Natural Law and Natural Rights* (Oxford: Clarendon Press, 1980), pp. 351–70.
5 See AFSCME v. Washington, 770 F. 2d 1401 (9th Cir. 1985) (Anthony Kennedy, J.).
6 California State Employees' Assoc. v. California, 724 F. Supp. 717 (N.D. Cal. 1989) (Hall Patel, J.).

principle of comparable pay and on the statute as interpreted in light of that principle. Rachel, J.'s first inclination could be to try resolving the conflict by balancing her legal and moral reasons. But it is not so simple. Having identified the four reasons, her legal duty to uphold the law requires her to restrict her deliberations to the reasons warranted by the law as grounds for judicial decision. The reasons dependent on the comparable pay principle are excluded from legal consideration. The upshot of her legal deliberations then gives the content of her legal duty. The competing moral reasons give the content of a distinct moral duty, assuming her view to be correct.

Rachel, J. might think that her legal duty should be balanced against her moral duty, possibly permitting her to vindicate the plaintiff's claim despite the unhelpful precedent. On reflection, however, she may question whether legal and moral duties can be balanced against each other. Legal and moral duties may be incommensurate – ineligible for the same scale at all. Balancing requires a comparison of the weight of each consideration, which is a function of the force of the underlying normative standard in the circumstances. A legal reason is a plain fact that matters due to a conventional legal standard that is a product of fallible and often compromised human decisions. It has no necessary moral force because no one need follow the mistaken opinions of others, and there is no obvious reason why a decision like the precedent should be repeated if it is morally faulty. A genuine moral reason, by contrast, is a fact that matters due to a moral standard that is independent of human conventions. The most widely accepted human conventions can be criticized soundly with a valid moral standard. The force of such moral standards, however, cannot be tempered by conventional legal standards. Morality governs what Rachel, J. should do in the end, all things considered. So Rachel, J. will either have to find another way of regarding the conflict or come up with a more sophisticated understanding of balancing when law and morals yield conflicting guidance.

There are three other ways to regard the conflict. First, for

judges, law could trump any independent moral considerations in all cases. This "role morality" would seem to require blind obedience to the law. Given the sorry history of
unjust laws, it is not an attractive resolution of the problem.
Second, morals could trump law in all cases, rendering the
conventional law superfluous when it is inaccurate in relation to morals. As will be seen, this implausible way rests on
an analytical mistake. The third way introduces the idea that
lawmakers might have the normative power to issue genuine
moral reasons, at least for some persons. This approach
leads to a reconsideration of the idea of balancing legal and
moral duties. We speak of such balancing, I will suggest,
only on the assumption that a judge has a moral duty to obey
the law. If this were so, the conventional law would fill in the
content of a moral duty, rendering the two kinds of reasons
commensurate. Morality would retain its supremacy, but
conventional law would not be superfluous. As will be seen,
there would also be an important place for considerations of
justice in adjudication.

7.2.1. Role morality. The most common argument supporting the view that, for judges, law trumps morality appeals to
an idea of role morality. This argument supposes that Rachel,
J.'s legal duties may diverge from her moral duties in the way
supposed by the good faith thesis. Unlike that thesis, however, role morality implies that the duties of the judicial role
supplant any contrary moral duties. The argument is that,
"as a judge," a person is subject to a different set of obligations than "as a person."[7] The obligations of a judge center
on the duty to uphold the conventional law, which guides
Rachel, J.'s conduct in place of morality. A judge who takes
role morality seriously may feel duty bound to reach unjust

7 The argument is better developed in the context of a lawyer's ethics,
   where it serves as a favorite foil. See generally David Luban, *Lawyers
   and Justice: An Ethical Study* (Princeton, N.J.: Princeton University
   Press, 1988); William H. Simon, "The Ideology of Advocacy: Procedural Justice and Professional Ethics," *Wisconsin Law Review*, 1978
   (1978): 29–144, at 39.

results whenever the conventional law so requires because the judicial role excludes any counterweight of any kind. Role morality casts the oath of judicial office as a "devil's compact."[8]

There are two problems with this common argument. First, as Serena Stier made clear in an analogous context,[9] our obligations do not attach to us as different persons when we function in different social roles. We remain the same person when we function as lawyer, judge, businessperson, parent, and so forth. Persons, however, act for various reasons in various circumstances.[10] Our roles are among the circumstances in which we act. The fact that one is functioning as a judge can make a moral difference to one's obligations, as the fact of a red light can require a motorist to stop or the fact of a promise can give rise to special obligations on the promisor. The plain fact that a person acts as a judge is inert; no moral obligation follows directly. There may, however, be a principle of morality that gives the social role, or its incidents, that moral significance. As will be seen below, there are good grounds for holding that judges have a moral duty to uphold the law independently of their legal duty to do so.[11] That duty need not, however, supplant competing moral duties in the way supposed by the role morality argument.[12]

Second, the role morality argument may be thought to rest on a common misunderstanding at the jurisprudential level. This is the view that legal positivism, as a theory of law, separates law from morals completely and privileges law over morals.[13] If so, a judge's legal duty would supplant any

8   Duncan Kennedy, "Freedom and Constraint in Adjudication: A Critical Phenomenology of Judging," *Journal of Legal Education*, 36 (1986): 518–62, at 555–7.
9   Serena Stier, "Legal Ethics: The Integrity Thesis," *Ohio State Law Journal*, 52 (1991): 551–609, at 560–4.
10 See § 2.2.1.
11 See § 7.3.
12 See § 7.4.
13 See, for example, Simon, "The Ideology of Advocacy," at 39 (discussing the role morality of lawyers).

contrary moral duties. To my knowledge, no major legal theorist currently takes this view. The leading legal positivists, H. L. A. Hart and Joseph Raz, do not. As Hart made clear, the legal positivist's claim is not that law and morals bear no connections. Rather, it is that law and morals bear no necessary or conceptual connections. Thus, as Hart put it,

> What both Bentham and Austin were anxious to assert were the following two simple things: first, in the absence of an expressed constitutional or legal provision, it could not follow from the mere fact that a rule violated standards of morality that it was not a rule of law; and, conversely, it could not follow from the mere fact that a rule was morally desirable that it was a rule of law.[14]

For a legal positivist, the law and morals may and commonly do bear many contingent relationships.[15] Thus, the law and morals may overlap, as in the law against child abuse. For many legal positivists, the law may incorporate morals, as may the Cruel and Unusual Punishments Clause of the Eighth Amendment. The law may leave discretion with an official together with a permission to employ moral criteria of judgment, as does the good moral character requirement for admission to the bar. Furthermore, *good* law satisfies moral requirements. Civil disobedience may be justified on moral grounds. Hart wrote:

> What surely is most needed in order to make men clear sighted in confronting the official abuse of power, is that they should preserve the sense that the certification of something as legally valid is not conclusive of the question of obedience, and that, however great the aura of majesty or authority which the official system may have, its demands must in the end be submitted to a moral scrutiny.[16]

14 H. L. A. Hart, "Positivism and the Separation of Law and Morals," *Harvard Law Review*, 71 (1958): 593–629, at 599. See also H. L. A. Hart, *The Concept of Law* (Oxford: Clarendon Press, 1961), pp. 181–207.
15 See, for example, Jules Coleman, "Negative and Positive Positivism," *Journal of Legal Studies*, 11 (1982): 139–64.
16 Hart, *The Concept of Law*, p. 206.

For thoughtful legal positivists, morality surely has the up-
per hand in cases of conflict. Consequently, the role morality
argument lacks a sound basis insofar as it is supposed to rest
on a legal positivist philosophy.

7.2.2. Inaccurate rules. Another common way to understand
Rachel, J.'s situation starts with the observation that general
rules, like the rule of stare decisis, are pervasively inaccurate.
The background assumption is that morals trump law whenever they conflict.[17] For various reasons, any legal rule (as
stated) may be over- and underinclusive with respect to the
(morally) right results in possible cases.[18] In some cases, the
rule applies when the result required by the rule is not just
(overinclusiveness). In other cases, the rule does not apply
by its terms even though the case is indistinguishable from
those it governs (underinclusiveness). For example, Rachel,
J. might think that the rule of stare decisis is justified, for the
most part, because the law should be stable, predictable, and
consistent. She might think also that the rule of stare decisis
unquestionably applies so that the precedent controls her
decision in the case before her. This case, however, is one in
which she believes the rule of stare decisis requires her to
follow a mistaken precedent.[19] In her view, therefore, it is
overinclusive with respect to the just result.

Rachel, J. might feel that she is in a deep dilemma present-
ing her with only two choices: She can follow the law or the

17 For example, Duncan Kennedy, "Legal Education as Training for Hi-
    erarchy," in *The Politics of Law*, ed. David Kairys (New York: Pantheon
    Books, 1982): 40–61, at 47 ("There is never a 'correct legal solution'
    that is other than the correct ethical and political solution to that legal
    problem").
18 Duncan Kennedy, "Form and Substance in Private Law Adjudica-
    tion," *Harvard Law Review*, 89 (1976): 1685–778, at 1687–701.
19 Inaccuracy can be measured with respect to a higher order of positive
    law (the Constitution rather than a statute), to the background justifi-
    cation of the rule (the purpose or rationale of statutory provision), or
    to morality simpliciter (the wrongfulness of gender discrimination).
    For this discussion, the baseline against which a rule is inaccurate is
    left unspecified because the arguments work the same way
    regardless.

morality that tells her what justice requires in the case. Some of those who are quick to find bottomless jurisprudential or political conflict in the law might see the question in these terms. The choice can seem to depend simply on whether one accepts the legal positivism underlying the role morality argument or believes that a moral law prevails over all inconsistent conventional laws. The two kinds of norms seem to generate incommensurate reasons, which cannot in any meaningful way be balanced against one another. Accordingly, since the jurisprudential dispute is of such long standing, it may seem to produce stubborn indeterminacy at the levels of law and jurisprudence. Rachel, J.'s choice consequently might seem to be political because it would depend on whether she values fairness to female employees over the efficiency of supporting employer autonomy or identifies politically with empowered or disempowered groups.

The problem of inaccurate rules is most pressing when two popular assumptions are made – that the law consists of general rules as stated and that these rules have both determinate content and result-determining force.[20] Were both assumptions valid, there could be no discretion for judges to avoid unintelligent and unjust decisions in any case governed by the law. For reasons given in Section 6.2, however, the good faith thesis rejects both assumptions. When rules are reconceived as propositions that provide legal reasons, rather than necessary results, judges have discretion to avoid blind obedience to rigid rules. They can weigh all relevant legal reasons with reference to the pertinent background justifications and act more intelligently than the popular academic caricatures would suggest. Turning to this conception of rules does not dissolve the problem of conflicting legal and moral duties. Rather, the reconceptualization of rules suggests that the problem is not pervasive in the law, as some would suggest. Even so, it is no less difficult when it occurs.

The problem of conflicting duties seems to lead into politi-

20 Kennedy, "Form and Substance," at 1687–701.

cal conflict because the issue is framed in an inappropriate way. The usual framing confuses two distinct issues. The rule of stare decisis provides, let us say, "It is the law that lower court judges must follow higher court precedents." In Rachel, J.'s view, the content of the rule is overinclusive in the case because it requires her to follow a mistaken precedent. That overinclusiveness might be a reason for her to disapprove of the general rule in a legislative or critical context. Perhaps, for example, the rule of stare decisis should have a limited exception when a lower court judge thinks there has been a mistake, to recycle questions back to the higher court until they say they really meant it. Rachel, J., however, is not in a legislative or critical context and has no legal power to make a new rule. It is not open to her to pick and choose among the conventional laws according to her moral convictions, depriving the law of its systemic quality. The law binds judges in a package deal or not at all.

Analytically, the judicial duty to uphold the law does not latch onto the content of a particular law. Rather, it latches onto the (usually unstated) prefatory phrase, "It is the law that," which represents the rule's legal status. The legal status, however, is not prone to be over- or underinclusive. It can be the locus of falsehood, as when what follows in fact is not the law. It might not control what a judge should do when the law applies by its terms, as when other laws provide exceptions, excuses, or justifications, or when overriding moral considerations justify disobedience. The judicial duty to uphold the law, however, operates in a content-independent manner.[21] Rachel, J.'s duty to uphold the law requires her to uphold all laws *because they are laws*. The problem of inaccurate rules is not central for her because only the content of a law can be inaccurate with respect to the just result in a case. Regardless of any inaccuracy in the scope of the rule's application, the rule of stare decisis tells her to follow the precedent.

---

21 On the idea of content-independence, see H. L. A. Hart, *Essays on Bentham* (Oxford: Clarendon Press), pp. 254–61.

Moreover, a legal rule's force for the judge does not depend on whether its content or implication coincides with the independent requirements of morality. If it did, the coincidence requirement would imply that the conventional law is superfluous to what Rachel, J. should do; all normative guidance would stem from morality. Judicial power, however, should not be so disconnected from the official law that judges may nullify any unjust law, as the Supreme Court may nullify any unconstitutional law. Judges should have no such reigning power in a democratic society under the Rule of Law.

7.2.3. Normative powers. Both the role morality and inaccurate rules arguments lead to unsound conclusions. Focusing on a stark choice between law and morals, however, neglects a variety of more sophisticated alternatives. Two alternatives set the stage for the approach taken by the good faith thesis. Both involve the important role of normative powers, which enable one person to change another person's reasons for action.[22] For example, when one businessman promises to ship a quantity of widgets "to be set by the buyer" within agreed limits, the buyer is given a normative power to determine what the seller's duty is. Before that power is exercised, the seller has no reason to ship any particular quantity of widgets to the buyer. After it is duly exercised, the seller has a reason to ship the set amount. Similarly, to give a rough overview, Rachel, J.'s duty before the precedent had been decided would have been to follow her own interpretation of Title VII in an appropriate case. The higher court in the precedent, however, might have exercised a normative power, reflected in the rule of stare decisis, and thereby changed her reasons for action in the case. Only if one is prepared to deny that Rachel, J. has any duty to uphold the law, or that the rule of stare decisis is law binding on lower courts, can one hold

---

22 On normative powers, see Hart, *Essays on Bentham*, pp. 243–68; Joseph Raz, *Practical Reason and Norms* (London: Hutchinson, 1975), pp. 98–104.

that the precedent is not a reason for Rachel, J. to decide against her independent judgment.

If the rule of stare decisis does generate a reason, Rachel, J.'s deliberations should change due to the higher court's decision. Her legal and general moral duties consequently may diverge and conflict. She will then face squarely the question whether she should follow the precedent or her own morally infused if questionable interpretation of Title VII. It will help to look in detail at how the legal status of the rule of stare decisis affects Rachel, J.'s reasons for action. There are two main approaches, both of which suggest parts of the approach taken by the good faith thesis.

The first approach focuses on the lawmaking authority. It suggests that a lawmaker's normative power is, if anything, a fully moral power. Rules made in the exercise of that power thus would be fully moral rules albeit made by humans and would change a judge's reasons for action, supplanting any independent benchmark of right action. If the law thus provides her with moral reasons and also excludes all otherwise relevant reasons, Rachel, J.'s only moral reasons would be those provided by the law. Her legal duty could not be contrasted meaningfully with another duty, and there would be no problem of incommensurate reasons. Alternatively, rules made by a legitimate lawmaking power might not exclude other reasons but only provide additional moral reasons with special weight.[23] Again, there would be no problem of incommensurate reasons because legal reasons would be a kind of moral reason and could be balanced against other kinds of moral reasons.

This approach asserts that the lawmaker's power is a moral power that generates legal rules with necessary moral force. It stands in need of a supporting argument at its starting point: The normative power might be only a legal power with contingent force. It is highly implausible, however, to

23 Stephen R. Perry, "Second-Order Reasons, Uncertainty and Legal Theory," *Southern California Law Review*, 62 (1989): 913–94; Stephen R. Perry, "Judicial Obligation, Precedent and the Common Law," *Oxford Journal of Legal Studies*, 7 (1987): 215–57.

suppose that there is an argument adequately supporting the broad conclusion that any lawmaker's normative power is fully moral; indeed, it is hard to imagine what such an argument would look like. The mere fact that one person or group – even a supreme court or a democratically elected legislature – announces a view about what other people should do is not a reason for them to do it. They should do it if they consented to follow that kind of guidance, or if the guidance coincides with what justice requires, or on any number of other grounds for establishing the law's legitimate authority and a moral obligation to obey the law. It is unlikely, however, that any ground of political obligation generates a moral obligation for all persons to obey all laws just because they are laws.[24] Moreover, looking to the duties of persons addressed by the lawmaker is to turn toward the second approach.

As Joseph Raz puts it, a lawmaker's power over reasons for action might be a moral power only *from the legal point of view*.[25] That is, the law might provide legal reasons indistinguishable from moral reasons to those who take up the standpoint of an ideal law-abiding citizen, who obeys the law howsoever it requires obedience. The law, in Raz's view, does not allow a general justification for disobedience based in political morality.[26] Excuses and justifications for disobedience are limited by the law to those based in specific legal doctrines, like the criminal law of self-defense or necessity. For those who do not take up the legal standpoint, legal reasons on this approach differ from moral reasons only because their force is contingent. The law *claims* to have full

24 See, for example, R. Kent Greenawalt, *Conflicts Between Law and Morals* (New York: Oxford University Press, 1987), pp. 47–203; Joseph Raz, *The Morality of Freedom* (Oxford: Clarendon Press, 1986), pp. 70–105; A. John Simmons, *Moral Principles and Political Obligations* (Princeton, N.J.: Princeton University Press, 1979); M. B. E. Smith, "Is There a Prima Facie Obligation to Obey the Law?," *Yale Law Journal*, 82 (1973): 950–76.
25 Raz, *Practical Reason and Norms*, pp. 170–7; Joseph Raz, *The Authority of Law* (Oxford: Clarendon Press, 1979), pp. 132–45, 153–9.
26 Raz, *The Authority of Law*, pp. 233–7.

moral force, providing fully moral reasons for action for all its subjects, but the law cannot determine whether this claim is valid. Rather, the validity of the claim – the legitimacy of the law's authority – depends on considerations of political morality. Accordingly, the law cannot require anyone to take up the legal standpoint. One may do so because one self-identifies as a good citizen in the community or decides to respect the law because it is generally just. Obligations to obey the law, however, will vary among persons because there is no general prima facie obligation to obey the law because it is law.[27]

The second approach is like the first insofar as it treats legal reasons as having a moral kind of content. Unlike the first, it refuses to give legal reasons any necessary moral force because the lawmaker has a moral power only from the legal standpoint. In Razian terms, Rachel, J.'s task is to decide whether she is or should be committed to the legal standpoint and therefore to giving legal reasons moral force in her deliberations. Her decision does not depend directly on any general moral authority of lawmakers or on the legal status of a rule. The law cannot lift itself up by its bootstraps here. Nor does it depend only on whether Rachel, J. subjectively identifies as a good citizen in her community or decides to respect the law.[28] Rather, her decision depends also on considerations of political morality that might or might not ground a more general moral duty for all judges, including Rachel, J., to obey the law as such.

Criticism of the first approach suggests helpfully that we should turn from the moral status of the lawmaker to the moral duty of the judge. The second suggests that we should look for a moral duty that attaches to judges just because they are judges within a legal system. There would be no problem of incommensurate legal and moral reasons if Rachel, J. were under such a moral duty. The conventional law itself would have no necessary moral force. However,

27 For the culminating expression of Raz's views, see Raz, *The Morality of Freedom*, pp. 23–109.
28 Ibid., pp. 88–105.

that law would supply the content of her moral duty to uphold the law: If (1) Rachel, J. is under a moral duty to follow
the law; and (2) the law requires Rachel, J. to follow the
precedent even if it is mistaken; then (3) Rachel, J. is under a
moral duty to follow the precedent even if it is mistaken. So
the law, together with the moral duty, would supply fully
moral reasons in her judicial deliberations. These moral reasons would be fully commensurate with any other relevant
moral reasons, including those for believing the precedent to
be mistaken or the law to be unjust.

The full reasoning is elided when we say that the law has
moral force for judges. Nonetheless, the analysis suggests
that legal authorities may have the moral power to change
Rachel, J.'s reasons for action, and she may be obligated to
take up the legal standpoint. If so, the problems of role morality and inaccurate rules dwindle in importance because
judges would have a moral obligation to uphold the law
because it is law. To determine if she is bound by this duty,
Rachel, J. must review the grounds of political obligation to
see if she is under a moral duty to obey the law, including the
rule of stare decisis that might bind her to follow the precedent.

7.3. A MORAL DUTY TO UPHOLD THE LAW

At least two grounds support the existence of a moral duty
for all judges to uphold the conventional law.[29] The first, and
most obvious, is consent. Recent work in political philosophy has made it apparent that, notwithstanding the standard lore of American government, all citizens do not con-

---

29 A third ground for a judge's moral duty to uphold the law might be
the duty to uphold just institutions, developed by John Rawls. John
Rawls, *A Theory of Justice* (Cambridge: Harvard University Press,
Belknap Press, 1971), pp. 333–42. Such a duty would have no force,
for example, requiring a judge to uphold the old Jim Crow laws in the
Southern states. One should be wary of assuming that the laws currently in force are not similarly unjust in ways as yet unappreciated.
For this reason, I decline to add this third ground for a judge's moral
duty.

sent to be governed by the laws of the United States.[30] Current generations are not bound by the consent of the founding generation to the Constitution and most laws made thereunder. Few people perform any voluntary act that expressly or impliedly manifests informed consent to obey all laws.[31] A judge, however, undertakes to uphold the law when taking the oath of office. Judges are in no way compelled to undertake the duties of judging, typically having more than sufficient education and assets to make a genuine choice. They surely know what they are doing, having had a notable career in the practice of law at the time of appointment. The argument for a consent-based moral obligation for all judges to obey the law is strong.

The second and related ground for a judge's moral duty to uphold the law is entrustment. All judges consent to obey the law when taking the oath of office. In a polity committed to the Rule of Law, the public and appointing authorities reasonably and foreseeably rely on the judge to do so from the moment the oath is taken. Independent of consent, the judge as public servant has a relational obligation to fulfill the public's reasonable expectations. The judicial office is not an asset of the judge's own. It is a public asset to be used only for conventionally understood public purposes. Unlike ordinary citizens wielding their own powers, a judge qua judge consequently has a moral obligation not to act opportunistically. She must obey the laws that manifest the purposes for which the judicial power is conferred. Moreover, the law shaping the power of the judge is generally understood to be predominantly the law set forth in the Constitution, the United States Code, the Administrative Code, the common law, and analogous sources of state law. Even if that

---

30 Sources cited, note 24 above.
31 Voting has no such significance, and surely the many people who vote for a losing candidate or do not vote at all cannot reasonably be deemed to consent. Attempts to imply consent from other common acts, like a citizen's continuing residence in the territory, fail both because such acts are not generally understood to carry such legal significance and because, for many persons of limited means, they are not voluntary in fact.

law might in some cases be overridden for weighty moral reasons, few indeed would argue that it carries no moral weight for a judge.

The legal duty to uphold the law is independent of the corresponding moral duty. Unlike the consent- and entrust-ment-based moral duty to uphold the law, a judge's legal duty is grounded in the conceptual truth that judges within a legal system have a legal duty to uphold the law of that system.[32] We simply cannot conceive of a legal system that did not hold its judges to such a duty. In negating that duty, a legal system would lose its systemic quality and the prac-tical effectiveness needed for it to be in force in a pluralistic society; the law would be hard-pressed to serve its coordinat-ing and social guidance functions. The content of the two duties is the same: They each require a judge to decide cases on the basis of legal reasons and only legal reasons, accord-ing to the good faith thesis. Most important, however, the force of each duty is different. The force of the legal duty necessarily is only a legal force; that is, a judge's legal duty to uphold the law generates a conclusive answer to the ques-tion, "Legally, what should the judge do?". The outcome of good faith legal deliberations informs the judge of the con-crete content of the legal duty. From the legal standpoint, if there were any practical point to it, we might say that the outcome of legal deliberations has absolute legal force. Un-less so qualified as to be mainly of academic interest, how-ever, the legal duty as such should be understood to gener-ate no moral force whatever. By contrast, the moral duty to uphold the law generates a genuine moral force that is nei-ther absolute nor conclusive. It leaves to further delibera-tions whether the act prescribed by the law must be done.

To elaborate, we might say to an ordinary citizen – call him "Michael" – that he ought to perform some act "according to law" or "legally speaking." That informs him of what his legal duty is. It does not follow that he should indeed per-form that act. Michael may not have even a prima facie moral

32 See § 2.1.

obligation to obey the law because it is law; even if he has such an obligation, it may be overridden by independent moral considerations. For example, a legal rule might provide that all motorists should stop on encountering a red traffic light; Michael encounters a red traffic light; Michael's legal duty is to stop. The relevant norm is thus a proposition of law, and the outcome informs him of his legal duty, leaving it open whether Michael indeed should stop. When Michael encounters a red traffic light at a deserted intersection at 3:00 A.M. on a clear moonlit morning, while rushing his pregnant wife to the hospital in labor, his legal duty nonetheless is to stop (unless conventional law contains a general defense of necessity). His independent moral duty, however, is otherwise. On balance, Michael should not stop. There is a difference between concluding that "legally, Michael should stop" and that "Michael should stop."

In the case before her, there seems little doubt that, according to the law, Rachel, J. should follow the precedent. The question whether she should act as required by stare decisis, however, has no wholly legal answer: It depends on the moral force of the law for her. It might be that she should seize on a pretextual distinction between the precedent and the case before her, deciding to redress the perceived gender discrimination in her case and hoping that second thoughts by the appellate court or the burden of appealing will leave her decision standing. The law can claim to exclude general considerations of political morality from a judge's deliberations, but it cannot ultimately do so because morality is the prevailing guide to proper conduct for anyone, including judges within their professional role.

However, for the two reasons given above, a judge has both legal and moral duties to uphold the law. The two duties have the same content, but not the same grounds or the same moral force. They also have distinct functions. The moral duty is crucial if the law is to generate genuine reasons for action. The law does so by supplying the content of the moral duty, giving the conventional law derivative moral force for all judges. The legal duty is crucial if we are to

220

identify the content of the moral duty to uphold the law as something distinct from a general and unfocused moral obligation to act properly. The law makes a difference to what a judge should do, morally speaking. The "two duties approach" helps to see how that can be so.[33]

7.4. ALL THINGS CONSIDERED

We now draw back to see a bigger picture. The good faith thesis does not claim that the law is always just or that judges should never disobey it. The crucial claim is that, when judges do disobey the law, they should know that they are doing so, they should think clearly about the justification for doing so, and they should do so only if disobedience is morally justified in the end, all moral reasons considered. This requires a clear and distinct understanding of what the law is in a case, independent of all reasons of political morality not warranted by the law as grounds for judicial decisions. A judge can achieve such an understanding through good faith *legal deliberations*, supposing neither that the law must satisfy the determinacy condition nor that the outcome of legal deliberations requires the indicated action unqualifiedly. Reasons of political morality excluded by the law may enter *judicial deliberations*, in one way or another providing the grounds for opposing unjust laws.

Judicial deliberations have two major components, which we can call legal and moral deliberations. (They do not, however, correspond to the two duties to uphold the law.) By "legal deliberations," I mean the identification and consideration of legal reasons under a legal duty to uphold the law or, what amounts to the same thing under a different description, of (some) moral reasons specifically under the moral duty to uphold the law. Legal deliberations by judges are

33 A consequence of this approach is to allow the duties of judges and citizens to diverge from one another. I thus part company with Raz's "service conception of authority" without at this time elaborating an alternative political theory. See Raz, *The Morality of Freedom*, pp. 38–69.

221

understood more simply as deliberations involving a subset of moral reasons admitted to judicial deliberations by virtue of the conventional law. For example, one can have a legal duty to drive on the right side of the road, as required by statute. Furthermore, one can have a moral duty to uphold the law, which duty is filled in by the law prescribing right-side driving. That is, if morality requires one to follow the law, and the law requires one to drive on the right side of the road, then morality requires one to drive on the right side of the road, all else being equal.

"Moral deliberations" involve all relevant moral reasons; they are not necessarily dependent on the conventional law. General moral obligations depend on principles of critical political morality in any of several versions. These principles, broadly speaking, may be consequentialist or nonconsequentialist, libertarian, utilitarian, liberal, communitarian, or perfectionist in character. It does not matter for present purposes as long as the relevant reasons can be balanced together on the common dimension of their normative force. That is, the relevant reasons all have normative force, and these forces are commensurate despite differences in kind.

How can a judge's legal and moral deliberations be integrated in a larger judicial deliberation? It makes sense to think of legal and moral deliberations nested within a larger judicial deliberation, with the outcome of legal deliberations subject to override by the outcome of moral deliberations. This is but a way of saying that the outcome of legal deliberations has less than absolute moral force. Rachel, J.'s judicial deliberations do not end with the conclusion of her legal deliberations, which were confined to Title VII and the precedents. Her moral duty to act rightly counsels her to grant relief on the gender discrimination claim, producing a conflict of legal and moral duties for her. The outcome of the legal deliberation is a moral reason for her because a judge has a moral duty to uphold the law, based on consent and entrustment. Good faith legal deliberations supply the content of her moral duty to uphold the law, which counsels her to reject the employee's claim. This moral duty can be bal-

anced against her moral duty to act rightly in a final deliberation resulting in action.

It might be thought that the good faith thesis loses its
point if general considerations of political morality, having
been excluded by the law, thus enter judicial deliberations
and ultimately might guide the judge's conduct. It might
seem that there is no need to distinguish legal deliberations
pursuant to a legal duty to uphold the law, and no need for a
moral duty to do the same thing. There might be a quandary.
If general considerations of political morality are excluded, a
judge must obey the law blindly. Justice then has no part to
play in judicial deliberations, which seems implausible. If
such considerations are included, however, there might be
no reason for distinguishing legal deliberations based on
legal reasons considered in good faith.

It is too simple, however, to think in terms only of whether
or not moral considerations enter judicial deliberations. Judicial evaluation of the law does not vitiate the good faith
thesis though it allows into judicial deliberations moral reasons not warranted by the law. The matter can be clarified
once we distinguish the two most general components of the
final decision about what to do, all things considered.

When viewing the judicial decision as a moral decision,
and a fortiori when viewing it as a legal decision, there are
distinct and important places for both legal and moral deliberations because they involve different sets of reasons. In our
example, the outcome of legal deliberations, and therefore
the content of the moral duty to uphold the law, do not
depend on the reasons that ground Rachel, J.'s moral conviction favoring the comparability principle – justice and fairness. The legal outcome depends on the reasons warranted
by the law as grounds for judicial decisions – chiefly the
authority of the recent decision by the higher court in the
jurisdiction. Rachel, J.'s reasons for favoring the comparability principle belong on the other side of the balance
because they ground criticism of the law (as elaborated by
the higher court). The outcome of good faith legal deliberations may indicate what a judge should do apart from any

specific moral duty; general considerations of political morality include the moral values of a Rule of Law, which may
require a judge to follow the law. The integrity of the legal
deliberations should be preserved to reach a clear understanding of the content of a judge's moral duty to uphold the
law, even though the outcome of legal deliberations does not
determine proper action unqualifiedly. The integrity of the
moral deliberations should be preserved to provide a basis,
grounded in political morality, for overriding the law when
disobedience is justified.

Popular understandings of the natural law slogan, *An unjust law is not law,* suggest otherwise. If law and morals bear a
necessary connection, and if that connection involves, as a
necessary condition for being part of the law, a requirement
that a norm be morally permissible, it would follow that an
unjust law is not valid and should play no role in judicial
deliberations. Popular understandings of legal positivism's
reaction against any such connection seem to insist that
judges obey the law uncritically in all circumstances, even
when they find themselves complicit in evil. Neither understanding is attractive (or consistent with a careful reading of
the leading traditional writers). Moreover, it may be inad-
visable thus to locate the problem in the grounds of law. That
permits only one of two consequences: A law either is or is
not valid law and accordingly does or does not establish
what the judges must do. The rich texture and difficulty of
the judicial burden may thus be obscured. For one thing, the
judge's trouble is likely to be most acute when the applicable
law is just in general but not as applied in the case. For
another, the limitation to two consequences follows from the
determinacy condition. Again, it is more fruitful to unpack
the law's grounds, content, and normative *force* so that a
fuller range of alternatives can be considered.

The idea of distinct legal and moral deliberations helps to
foster both clarity and appropriate critical attitudes. For example, the law can have both positive and negative moral
force in a way that has concrete practical implications for a
judge's conduct. A moral duty generates a reason that is

224

always a reason to do the act specified by the relevant moral norm. If a moral norm requires Michael to operate his vehicle safely, Michael simply has a reason to operate his vehicle safely. In this respect, a legal duty is the same within a legal deliberation and, when the law is morally permissible, within a moral deliberation. Morally proscribed laws, however, may generate a moral reason to *oppose* the act specified by the relevant legal norm. The laws of apartheid were not only invalid as moral reasons for action by citizens; they were reasons to take action in opposition. The law is too important to the moral quality of social life for morality only to take it out of consideration. Accordingly, when the law is wicked, the final deliberation on its critical side reverses the polarity of the law's force.

Judges, no less than the classic subjects of civil disobedience, might sometimes have a duty to oppose the acts prescribed by wicked laws. A judge might engage in active opposition by proposing reform or writing a critical opinion while upholding the law, making new law judicially when that is within her lawful power, recusing herself or resigning from the bench, or engaging in disobedience or revolution from the bench. Which, if any, way of opposing the law would be in order would depend on further circumstances and prudential considerations. In a generally just legal system, occasions for judicial disobedience will be rare. The judge's moral duty to uphold the law will have great weight in order to secure the benefits of systematic law – social coordination and guidance, fairness, equal treatment, and the other advantages of a Rule of Law. In a generally unjust legal system, however, one hopes that judges will throw more than a few well-placed monkey wrenches into the works. A rule of evil law is only the worse for its efficiency.

Great and undue confusion sets in, impairing the quality of judicial deliberations, when reasons belonging only on one side of the balance are allowed also to shape the competing alternative.[34] There are times when judging is hauntingly

34 A reason of political morality might be warranted by the law and thus

hard because the judge on balance should act lawfully, at the same time believing that act to be morally wrongful but for the law. Though I do not agree with Rachel, J. on the morality of comparable worth, I think that she is in that situation.[35] She should not be taken off the hook by counting her moral convictions twice – once when giving content to her duty to uphold the law and again when deciding what to do, all things considered. Legally required action might have untoward consequences, as when a judge is required by the Fourth Amendment to release a hated criminal in politically heated circumstances. Or a legally required act with good consequences might be intrinsically wrongful, as when general deterrence considerations justify jailing a person who was not culpable in proportion to the sentence. The democratic political process might produce law that takes the rightness path or the consequentialist path when the unfettered judge more properly would go the other way. Significantly, the judge's moral duty to uphold the law can tip the balance in favor of the law's solution to the dilemma even when the law is mistaken. General Rule of Law values can have the same effect.

In this scheme, judges in all good faith toward both their legal and moral obligations can find their actions vulnerable to trenchant critical claims, exposing the harm done to the litigants and others with similar interests. Prudential considerations can lead a judge to apply an evil law in a case without protesting by writing a critical opinion. The press of a crowded docket may leave no time to engage in full moral deliberations or to write a critical opinion; doing the right thing in a minor case may harm one's credibility for doing greater good elsewhere. Even a critical opinion does not alter

go into legal deliberations, producing the content on one side of the balance, and also be taken into account qua moral reason on the other side.

35 Judge Marilyn Hall Patel, who decided the case on which the illustration is based, agreed. See California State Employees' Assoc. v. California, 724 F. Supp. 717 (N.D. Cal. 1989).

the fact that the judge who nonetheless upholds an evil law is acting wrongly according to her unfettered moral judgment.

There are two ways to respond to trenchant criticism. One, and probably the more common, is to deny the critical claim and to defend what one has done out of a psychological need for self-justification. This can be done in anticipation or with hindsight. It commonly may involve allowing reasons of political morality, not warranted by the law as grounds for judicial decision, to lead to an identification of something as law when it is not, or to an interpretation of the law requiring a result that it does not, to avoid facing the tragic choice between evils. For a judge, that is bad faith toward her moral duty to uphold the law and toward herself. The result is an act of disobedience to the law, however clever the lawyerlike rationalizations might be, and however unlikely it might be that the deception will be discovered. Having engaged in false rationalizations to deny and defend what one has done in one case, moreover, a judge seems likely to form beliefs with undue staying power, distorting perceptions, understandings, and legal reasonings in future cases. The psychological mechanisms of denial and defensiveness are well known to have such costs in private life. In addition to the private costs to the judge, they probably also have public costs to the quality of the judge's professional performance.

The alternative is to acknowledge frankly a trenchant critical claim and to take a moral loss akin to the many kinds of emotional losses that pepper life. Judges at times may need to grieve and forgive themselves morally even when they would do the same thing again in the same circumstances. Some such candid personal process seems necessary at times to clear away cobwebs and continue with a clear view of the immediate scene. There are no guarantees in life, and surely none in the law, that all will work out coherently so that no such moral losses need be suffered unless deserved. Martha Nussbaum provides a larger context for this thought:

That I am an agent, but also a plant; that much that I did not make goes towards making me whatever I shall be praised or blamed for being; that I must constantly choose among competing and apparently incommensurable goods and that circumstances may force me to a position in which I cannot help being false to something or doing some wrong; that an event that simply happens to me may, without my consent, alter my life; that it is equally problematic to entrust one's good to friends, lovers, or country and to try to have a good life without them – all these I take to be not just the material of tragedy, but everyday facts of lived practical reason.[36]

Confronting and taking moral losses seems the better alternative, for the sake of justice. There is no easier way to lose sight of justice than to get lost in opportunistic or defensive lawyerly rationalizations.

36 Martha Craven Nussbaum, *The Fragility of Goodness* (Cambridge: Cambridge University Press, 1986), p. 5.

Chapter 8

The politics of good faith

8.1. POLITICAL MOTIVATION

The motive for endorsing any practical understanding of adjudication must be a political one. To avoid misunderstanding, however, we should be careful to distinguish two things this might mean. A political motive can seek to advance one's own desires and interests, as when it turns on beneficial or harmful consequences of a proposal for one's favored political groups or causes. Alternatively, it can seek to endorse a good proposal for reasons of political morality, which is aimed at the good of all persons. In jurisprudence, the latter kind of politics should be the grounds for endorsing a proposal. The consequences of a proposal affecting various groups depend far more on the substantive content of the law than on the ethical standards of judging under it, if it depends on the ethics of judging at all. More important, the integrity of adjudication as a distinct legal institution is especially important. The winners of democratic political encounters (in the first sense) encase their victories in the law. The job of judges is to implement that law. The long-term implications of transforming adjudication into another arena for political contests are troubling: We should hesitate before depriving the political victors of their victory and thereby blunting the point of engaging in politics in the first place. One can only speculate how a society would resolve its important disagreements were political avenues turned into dead ends.

The attraction of the good faith thesis lies in its promise, if implemented, of sustaining a good judicial practice in a democratic society like the United States. What constitutes a "good" judicial practice depends on a normative political vision that is interested in the quality of adjudication under law in a constitutional democracy in the long term. It can be so interested while it is disinterested as between the groups and causes that contend with each other as a matter of current everyday politics, where the quality of adjudication is rarely a live issue. The politics of the moment should not drive a theory of adjudication. Politics can shift in unpredictable ways over time; for example, an expansive federal judicial role was far more appealing to liberals in the 1960s than it is today. Adjudicatory practices, once institutionalized, tend to be more stable. Consequently, our longer-term interests in sound basic institutions should be the more salient.

Any evaluation of a proposal for adjudication depends on assumptions about the political context in which judges operate. One can take an existing political system for granted or provide the context by developing a complete political philosophy. The following discussion will assume the existing political institutions and traditions in the United States. The goals of the good faith thesis are practical, not utopian; accordingly, the thesis should be useful to judges and those who seek to understand judges under present and foreseeable circumstances. The mere existence of the U.S. political system does little to vouch for its justice. It is possible that the context for evaluation is unjust in a way that would counsel rejection of the good faith thesis together with radical political change. I do not think this is the case, but will not tackle the broader political questions within the scope of this project. We should understand a tradition well before we reject it. We question nothing effectively when we question everything at once. Everything should be open to question in turn, and answers as always should be endorsed pending further thought and argument.

8.2. LAW AND POLITICS

Members of the critical legal studies movement and others have launched aggressive attacks on the distinction between law and politics implicit in the good faith thesis. Broad questions, such as whether law and politics are distinct, have a way of glossing over many specific issues, producing avoidable confusion. The specifics may not lend themselves to glib political slogans, like the popular critical assertion that "law is politics." But there are important differences between adjudication, log-rolling on Capitol Hill, and protests in the street. The specifics may help us understand what we are after with a fitting intellectual complexity.

For example, one might endorse a thesis requiring judges to uphold the law, as distinct from power politics. This in no way involves doubt that the endorsement may be politically motivated, or that the law requires certain political conditions for its effectiveness, may be made by power politics in democratic and administrative processes, is influenced in operation by power imbalances among litigants, and often has profound consequences for the relative power of various social groups. Nor does it deny that, descriptively, judges sometimes decide important cases on improper political grounds or that judges should rely on some kinds of political grounds, especially when they have legitimate lawmaking power. One can understand the law to have political content at its core as long as the political values in the law are distinguished from those outside it. Within the good faith thesis, the judicial duty to uphold the law requires that the grounds of judicial decisions be sufficiently legal for judges to decide cases without recourse to moral or political reasons not warranted by the law as grounds for judicial decisions. So the specific issue would be whether the special status of the politics we signify by "law" is politically justified in the first instance.

The legal tradition in the United States predominantly manifests the politics of individual liberty in a representative

231

democracy. As I understand it, three basic features of traditional democratic theory bear directly on the role of the courts. First, the pluralism hypothesis assumes that, within the populace at large, there are any number of competing views about the good society in general and the substantive content of the law in particular. Call these views "primary principles of political morality." Second, the democratic principle holds that individuals should be free to develop their respective views about the good life and the good society and to advance their views through political activity in fair and representative processes of government. To avoid deadlock, the clash of plural views in the political process will often produce laws that represent a compromise of competing views rather than a total victory for any competitor's primary principles. Third, the Rule of Law requires courts to settle disputes by interpreting and applying the laws enacted as the outcome of the political process, whether or not the laws represent morally sound dispute resolution according to a judge's primary principles.

In this framework, the grounds of judicial decisions in principle may be legal in the following sense. In the political process, individuals and their political representatives have political reasons based on their primary principles for advancing various views about the good society. Broadly speaking, these may be both interest-oriented reasons generating "public choice" politics and principles of political morality generating "public interest" politics.[1] Pluralism and the need to live together imply political deadlock unless primary principles are qualified in the give and take of politics. Fair legal standards, as a corporate whole, should contain fragments of almost everyone's primary political principles. They also should encompass many secondary or tertiary views held by a large part of the polity. It is not crucial that anyone agree with all the results of the political process. In a

1 See generally James M. Buchanan & Gordon Tullock, *The Calculus of Consent* (Ann Arbor, Mich.: University of Michigan Press, 1962); *The Theory of Public Choice*, ed. James M. Buchanan & Robert D. Tollison (Ann Arbor, Mich.: University of Michigan Press, 1984).

pluralistic society, in any practicable system, everyone will lose a few. It is crucial that the legal and political system as a whole respect the most basic rights and interests of all significant groups and contain open avenues of legal change.[2] It is also crucial that the reasons justifying the laws that emerge from the political process deserve the respect of dissenters. In part for this reason, a justificatory public political discourse is important even when the relevant political actors are motivated by less than lofty goals.

Judges should not rely on their own primary principles because they are of a kind appropriately advanced at the start of a political process involving much give and take. Judges have custody of the legal standards that emerge from the clash of primary principles.[3] For a judge to recapture the opportunity to advance the interests of oneself or groups one favors, or to advance one's ideal view of the good society as such, is bad faith and a breach of the judicial duty to uphold the law. Thus, in principle, a judge is supposed to decide cases on the basis of the compromised standards that emerged from the political process. These standards should be in the long-term interests of all because of how they came to pass, though their content may disadvantage one subgroup or another to some extent.

It may be objected that the traditional approach neglects the social structure in which law and politics operate. That social structure manifests a serious maldistribution of education, wealth, and power. Consequently, it may be argued, the primary principles that favor disempowered people receive short shrift in the political process; to limit judges to the outcome of that process guarantees that the judicial power will be used at times as an instrument of further in-

2 See Steven J. Burton, *An Introduction to Law and Legal Reasoning* (Boston: Little, Brown & Co., 1985), pp. 199–214.
3 The common law, of course, is made by judges subject to legislative correction. It would be fictional to claim that the legislature acquiesces in all common law made by judges. The common law is made in such a piecemeal fashion, and at present is so qualified by numerous statutes, that it is unlikely to represent anyone's comprehensive view of the good society.

justice. The objection has a superficial appeal, but is problematic on reflection. I assume no one would argue that there is never distinct law binding on judges unless and until there is a just distribution of resources in the society. That would narrow the concept of law to the vanishing point, as though there could be no law until there is no disparity between haves and have-nots. Without such an argument, however, it is hard to see the ground of the objection. The objection appeals to fine convictions favoring a more egalitarian distribution, but it proves too much to suggest that a less egalitarian distribution cancels the law in a society. Energy should be directed, rather, to the content of the laws to secure a more just distribution than to the abandonment of good faith adjudication under law. The distributive deficiencies of the current social structure are glaring. The available alternatives to good faith adjudication, however, look much worse when viewed in light of the sorry history of governmental overreaching. They tend to involve nothing less than abandonment of the Rule of Law insofar as the law seeks to confine the power of government officers.

Two key consequences of the traditional conception of proper adjudication are that the law is conceived to be conventional and prone to partial indeterminacy of results. Conventional law depends on human lawmaking acts, paradigmatically including the acts of ratifying a constitution or enacting legislation. It also depends on sufficiently convergent practices and dispositions among members of the legal community on legal questions to sustain a largely coordinate practice of legal interpretation. The idea of convention need not be confined to a clear express agreement that settles expectations uncontroversially in advance of a dispute. That would leave a huge area of indeterminacy because foresight is so limited, and language is so unusable apart from practice. Conventions can consist also of the convergent practices and dispositions of the members of a community, manifested on appropriate occasions for action and criticism.[4] Lawyers

4 For elaboration, see Burton, *Law and Legal Reasoning*, pp. 94–144,

and judges turn out to agree on too many concrete legal
questions, and would agree on many more if asked, for their
legal views to involve either express conventions only or a
mere reflection of the diverse primary political views in the
society.[5] The best explanation of such agreement is that the
convergent dispositions of the legal community can provide
answers to specific legal questions even when they have not
previously had occasion to become manifest. Such conventions, however, do not erase all indeterminacies.

The conventional and at times indeterminate character of
law poses a central problem for the Rule of Law, conceived
within the political framework summarized above. Put simply, it is often hard to understand how the compromised,
truncated, and partly indeterminate corpus of law can be
interpreted and applied by judges without recourse to primary principles of a general political sort. Allowing such
principles to enter legal deliberations as grounds for judicial
decision, however, would defeat a main purpose of the Rule
of Law, which is to privilege the outcome of the pluralistic
political process over any judge's or litigant's primary principles. Rather than serving the political process, judges act-

204–14. In my view, Hart's theory of social rules erred by insisting that
a norm could not exist in a community unless there was a general
convergence of behavior within the group that is repeated by most of
the group when occasion arises. H. L. A. Hart, *The Concept of Law*
(Oxford: Clarendon Press, 1961), pp. 54–60. Hart probably underestimated the extent to which, descriptively, the rules of a group might be
manipulated or avoided in practice, producing less convergent behavior than he might desire. Rules nonetheless may exist because they
must be manipulated or steps taken to avoid them, even when such
moves are often successful. What Hart treated as the disposition to
criticize deviations from a rule seems far more important than a general
convergence of behavior.

5   See also Chap. 2, note 1. For example, someone as far from the mainstream as Duncan Kennedy claims that "[v]ast parts of the whole system of rules have, for me, intuitive legitimacy. . . . It's endlessly the
case that the judge's approach to the problem strikes me as intelligent
and that the judge comes up with a rule which, when I think about it,
strikes me as a good idea for the very reasons he gave for it." Address
by Duncan Kennedy, Association of American Law Schools Annual
Meeting (January 7, 1986).

ing on primary principles seem like participants in the political tug-of-war but from a greatly privileged position: Their contributions have the force of law with little by way of effective political checks. At best, that seems unjustified. At worst, it invites oppression should one or another faction capture control of the judiciary or the legal community.

There are four familiar ways to respond to this classic problem. A conservative approach is to limit all legitimate adjudication to conventional law that yields determinate results. That preserves the Rule of Law, but only at the cost of so constricting the scope of adjudication that the courts are seriously hampered in their role of checking abuses of power by the other branches of government and powerful private actors. A Dworkinian response is to limit legitimate adjudication to law that yields determinate results in principle, but to redefine the law by abandoning its conventional nature. Substituting the primary moral principles that best explain and justify the historical legal practice, however, abandons the traditional Rule of Law as a serious constraint on a nonpolitical judiciary in a pluralistic democratic polity. It invites political efforts to capture the judiciary as a power favoring one or another political faction, as each judge would act on his or her own best interpretation with no obligation to coordinate with other judges.[6] A Hartian response is to treat the law conventionally and as determinate with respect to results, but to abandon the limitation of proper adjudication to questions governed by law. Allowing courts to exercise discretion on the basis of primary principles of political morality, not limited to those embedded in the law, also abandons the traditional Rule of Law whenever the law is indeterminate. Finally, a critical response is to abandon the conventional and determinate characteristics of law, liberating adjudication altogether from the constraint of the democratic tradition in the United States. Giving away the traditional store might possibly be acceptable in a utopia yet to be

6 See Frank I. Michelman, "Foreword: Traces of Self-Government," *Harvard Law Review*, 100 (1986): 4–77, at 76.

conceived and described for general consideration. It would be a drastic and dangerous step within the existing political system, unlikely to help the less powerful members of our society.

The good faith thesis takes none of the above approaches. As argued mainly in Chapter 2, it distinctively maintains that the law is conventional and that judges are constrained to interpret and apply it in all cases within their jurisdiction. Unlike the conservative approach, it abandons the determinacy condition by requiring valid legal reasons instead of results. It consequently broadens the scope of legitimate adjudication relative to that approach, allowing courts better to perform their checking functions. Unlike the Dworkinian approach, it requires judges to act in tandem and only on reasons warranted by the conventional law, gauging the weight of the reasons internal to the case and without recourse to general political morality. It narrows the scope of proper adjudication relative to Dworkin's view. The good faith thesis approves of a scope for adjudication similar to the Hartian approach, but unlike that approach it denies that judges should ever go outside the law for the grounds of judicial decisions. It brings judicial discretion within the Rule of Law. Of course, the good faith thesis is not sympathetic to the critical idea of junking the tradition, at least until a better practical alternative is well developed.

The political attraction of the good faith thesis stems from this vision of the role of proper adjudication in a constitutional democracy: It preserves the Rule of Law, allows a meaningful scope to adjudication, and constrains adjudication to the legal reasons invoked by the facts of the case before the court. Judges in good faith thus can check abuses of power by others even as they themselves are constrained by the law, understood conventionally with due respect for democratic politics. Democracy is a great political value to which judges should defer in the first place, whether or not its product pleases them. It may be fitting for judges to disrupt the works when the existing political context is seriously unjust. As long as judicial disobedience is not morally justified, however, judges should do their jobs in good faith as servants of the various democratic political processes within the Constitution, which itself is the result of a special and precious exercise of self-government.

8.3. IMPROPER BIAS

The Rule of Law is widely accepted among those who are active in the institutions that make up the U.S. political system. For many in the mainstream, this conventional defense of the Rule of Law consequently may seem unnecessary. Within intellectual circles, especially in American law schools, however, the Rule of Law is under sharp and widespread attack. It is claimed, in particular, that political liberalism is fraught with internal contradictions that render it incoherent and unworthy of respect.[7] This is not the place to engage in a thorough treatment of all the issues at stake, many of which involve unfortunate distortions of what liberalism encompasses. Some points, however, are seriously challenging with special relevance to adjudication. Accordingly, I have argued at length that the Rule of Law does not require determinacy of results on all legal questions, as critics and many supporters contend. I will consider here two claims that adjudication cannot in practice be depoliticized as required by the Rule of Law. One asserts that the neutrality

7 The starting point is Roberto M. Unger, *Knowledge and Politics* (New York: Free Press, 1975). One should be wary of characterizations of liberalism by critics whose hostility to it might lead them to mischaracterize it. For telling if overstated criticism, see William Ewald, "Unger's Philosophy: A Critical Study," *Yale Law Journal*, 97 (1988): 665–756. See also Ronald M. Dworkin, *Law's Empire* (Cambridge: Harvard University Press, Belknap Press, 1986), pp. 274–5 (critical legal studies' "accounts of liberalism begin and end in a defective account of what liberalism is, an account supported by no plausible reading of the philosophers they count as liberals"), 440–1 n. 19 [criticizing Mark V. Tushnet, "Following the Rules Laid Down: A Critique of Intepretivism and Neutral Principles," *Harvard Law Review*, 96 (1983): 781–827]; Owen M. Fiss, "Objectivity and Interpretation," *Stanford Law Review*, 34 (1982): 739–73 (advancing a liberal conception of rationality and objectivity by contrast with nihilism).

required of judges by the Rule of Law is not achievable in practice, that a judge's primary principles must enter judicial deliberations. The other asserts that the personal backgrounds and perspectives of individual judges so influence their judgments that the weight of reasons inevitably will be tainted.

8.3.1. Neutrality. Critical claims that the "law is not neutral" recently have proliferated among those who challenge the legal tradition, which is said to require that the law be neutral.[8] Roberto Unger probably led the recent parade of claims.[9] Since his early work, "[m]uch critical legal scholarship [has] consist[ed] of a series of complicated and erudite explanations of the idea that the law cannot be interpreted neutrally and thus that the law/politics distinction and the legitimating story on which the liberal state depends must inevitably collapse."[10] Writers in feminist jurisprudence recently developed the criticism further, often emphasizing the nonneutrality of laws that are neutral on their face and can be neutrally applied in a rational manner, but that operate discriminatorily in gender-biased social circumstances.[11] Writers in critical race theory offer a similar line of attack on the tradition, charging that the biased consequence of the practice manifests continuing racism.[12]

Some traditionalists do make neutrality central to their po-

8 For example, Joseph W. Singer, "The Player and the Cards: Nihilism and Legal Theory," *Yale Law Journal*, 94 (1984): 1–70, at 40–1 "[t]raditional theorists claim that law is, or should be, neutral").
9 Unger, *Knowledge and Politics*.
10 James Boyle, "The Politics of Reason: Critical Legal Theory and Local Social Thought," *University of Pennsylvania Law Review*, 133 (1985): 685–780, at 697.
11 For example, Martha L. Fineman, "Dominant Discourse, Professional Language, and Legal Change in Child Custody Decisionmaking," *Harvard Law Review*, 101 (1988): 727–74; Robin L. West, "Jurisprudence and Gender," *University of Chicago Law Review*, 55 (1988): 1–72, at 5–6.
12 See, for example, Richard Delgado, "Storytelling for Oppositionists and Others: A Plea for Narrative," *Michigan Law Review*, 87 (1989): 2411–41.

litical or legal philosophies. Herbert Wechsler famously called for neutral principles of constitutional adjudication, by which he probably meant impartial justificatory principles that favored no party due to the judge's identification with them or their cause.[13] Robert Bork called for judicial neutrality in the derivation, definition, and application of constitutional principle, by which he sought to exclude fresh value judgments by judges, choices not warranted by the constitutional text and history, and decisions influenced by a judge's sympathy or lack of sympathy to the parties in the case.[14] John Hart Ely in effect sought a kind of value neutrality by dismissing any constitutional theory that requires a court to make substantive value judgments.[15] Bruce Ackerman organized his theory of social justice in the liberal state around a neutrality requirement that prevents anyone from claiming authority because his conception of the good is better than anyone else's or because he is intrinsically superior to others.[16]

It should be apparent that "neutrality" is too abstract a concept to identify the specific issues being raised. Traditional thinkers surely do not argue that the legal and political system should be pervasively neutral according to all conceptions of neutrality. Robert Nozick points out, for example, that the law is not neutral toward rape.[17] No one, I hope, would argue that the law should be neutral in an appalling

13 Herbert Wechsler, "Toward Neutral Principles of Constitutional Law," *Harvard Law Review*, 73 (1959): 1–35; R. Kent Greenawalt, "The Enduring Significance of Neutral Principles," *Columbia Law Review*, 78 (1978): 982–1021.

14 See Robert H. Bork, *The Tempting of America* (New York: Free Press, 1990), pp. 146–53.

15 John Hart Ely, *Democracy and Distrust* (Cambridge: Harvard University Press, 1980), pp. 43–73.

16 Bruce A. Ackerman, *Social Justice and the Liberal State* (New Haven: Yale University Press, 1980), pp. 10–11. See also Ronald Dworkin, *A Matter of Principle* (Cambridge: Harvard University Press, 1985), pp. 181–204; John Rawls, "The Priority of Right and Ideas of the Good," *Philosophy and Public Affairs*, 17 (1988): 251–76, at 260–4.

17 Robert Nozick, *Anarchy, State, and Utopia* (New York: Basic Books, 1974), pp. 272–3.

way. Nor should it be neutral in an impossible way. John
Rawls's theory of justice endorses neutrality among conceptions of the good. It has been criticized for a bias encouraging
individualistic conceptions of the good, as opposed to those
more sensitive to the social structure within which one
lives.[18] Rawls grants, however, that the basic structure of a
just constitutional regime may have important effects and
influences on which conceptions of the good endure and
gain adherents over time. He regards neutrality of effect or
influence as impracticable and consequently no part of his
political theory.[19] To avoid overbroad claims about neutrality,
we should distinguish among specific neutrality claims along
two dimensions.

On one dimension, neutrality might be required at the
constitutional, legislative, or adjudicative levels. In the de-
sign of a basic constitution, neutrality might be required as
among permissible comprehensive conceptions of the good
life.[20] To implement this kind of neutrality, one might establish constitutional rights to protect everyone's liberty to pursue permissible happiness, as they see it, and procedural
checks to prevent any faction from capturing the governmental power consistently.[21] Citizens and their representatives might then be allowed to seek advantage for their conceptions of the good life in the legislative arena, subject to
the constitutional rights of others, in the expectation that
any such victories will be infrequent and fragmentary. The
outcome of the political give and take might then be laws
which should be interpreted by judges without exploiting
indeterminacies to the advantage of their own conceptions of
the good. For present purposes, we are concerned only with
the specific kind of neutrality required of judges at the adjudicative level.

18 See Joseph Raz, *The Morality of Freedom* (Oxford: Clarendon Press,
    1986), pp. 308–13, 348–57; Michael J. Sandel, *Liberalism and the Limits
    of Justice* (Cambridge: Cambridge University Press, 1982), pp. 154–74.
19 Rawls, "The Priority of Right," at 262–3.
20 See Ibid., at 260–4.
21 C. Rossiter, ed., *The Federalist* (New York: New American Library,
    1961), Nos. 10, 51 (James Madison).

On a second dimension, there are at least four kinds of neutrality that might figure in a discussion.[22] The first concept is one of scientific neutrality. The nineteenth-century scientific ideal held the scientific observer apart from the data so that the data would remain uncontaminated by any prejudices or other subjective distortions. The scientist's role was merely to record and report objective data – an untenable view of science in the twentieth century. No mainstream thinker to my knowledge claims that judges should similarly record and report neutrally. As Martha Minow recently put it, "[t]here is no neutrality, no escape from choice."[23] Judicial action or inaction has consequences that benefit some and harm others. There is nothing remarkable or objectionable in this.

A second concept of neutrality is value neutrality. Also derived from the scientific tradition, value neutrality holds that judicial decisions should not depend on values because values are inherently subjective and controversial. Bork, Ely, and other constitutional theorists seem to operate on this idea of neutrality when they criticize alternatives to their favored views just because the alternatives call for controversial value judgments, which are presumed to open the door to judicial shenanigans. However, the effort to develop a value-neutral theory of constitutional adjudication has failed.[24] Major legal and political philosophers have not endorsed this view, which is by no means essential to the democratic tradition. It is a hangover from the heyday of logical

22 For other efforts to disentangle the various conceptions of neutrality, see Andrew Altman, *Critical Legal Studies: A Liberal Critique* (Princeton, N.J.: Princeton University Press, 1990), pp. 72–7; Rawls, "The Priority of Right," at 260–4; Raz, *The Morality of Freedom*, pp. 110–17.
23 Martha Minow, "Foreword: Justice Engendered," *Harvard Law Review*, 101 (1987): 10–95, at 70.
24 See, for example, Paul A. Brest, "The Misconceived Quest for the Original Understanding," *Boston University Law Review*, 60 (1980): 204–38; Paul A. Brest, "The Fundamental Rights Controversy: The Essential Contradictions of Normative Constitutional Scholarship," *Yale Law Journal*, 90 (1981): 1063–112; Laurence H. Tribe, "The Puzzling Persistence of Process-Based Constitutional Theories," *Yale Law Journal*, 89 (1980): 1063–80.

empiricism, which lumped all value statements together as meaningless expressions of emotion.[25]

We can distinguish between different values only when we throw off that sorry legacy. The Rule of Law can treat the law as a value-laden set of reasons for action available to judges at the end of an authorization chain. Judges uphold the law when legal reasons, and the values implicated by them, are kept apart from nonlegal reasons and their associated values. Critiques of the law's alleged value neutrality, including most of the critical legal studies efforts, thus do not join issue with the political underpinnings of the good faith thesis.

A third concept of neutrality is political neutrality. Within a basic constitutional theory, this is the neutrality invoked when it is said that the structure of government should be neutral as among conceptions of the good. Despite common misunderstandings by critics,[26] this is not the same as value neutrality. Liberals, who are the main target of criticism, distinguish between the Good and the Right, requiring government to act, first, to secure the rights of all and only then to maintain neutrality among remaining permissible conceptions of the good life.[27] Government thus may rule out conceptions of the good life that involve unacceptable harm to others, as by outlawing pederasty, on the basis of value-laden rights. It may not, however, favor conceptions of the good that impede the rights of others, as by requiring everyone to keep or forbidding anyone from keeping the laws of Kosher. Government is neutral among conceptions of the good when such conceptions do not serve as grounds for governmental action. Within a theory of adjudication, therefore, political neutrality bars judges from giving as any part of a justification for a judicial decision that their own conception of the good life approves or disapproves of a party's conduct. Obviously, a Christian judge should not sentence a Jewish criminal defendant to more time in jail because the

25 See § 4.2.
26 See, for example, Singer, "The Player and the Cards," at 40–1; West, "Jurisprudence and Gender," at 6.
27 For example, Rawls, "The Priority of Right."

Jew does not live a Christian life. Such restrictions on judging are so accepted within contemporary judicial practice
that their practicability is hard to doubt.

The fourth concept of neutrality is legal neutrality. Many
traditionalists would claim that adjudication should be neutral with respect to the primary principles at play in democratic lawmaking processes. Rather than reconsider the clash
of values then at stake, judges should work with the legal
standards that resulted from the primary clash.[28] This, too, is
not a requirement of value neutrality in adjudication, nor is it
the same as political neutrality. Legal neutrality permits
judges to act on the values that serve as background justifications for the laws; these might include fragments of some
conceptions of the good when they prevailed within the political process. It does not permit them to act on the values
that lost out in the give and take of politics or to act de novo
on those that were truncated through accommodation and
compromise. Legal neutrality does not involve a distinction
between values and other things, but rather between legal
values and other values. Judges should act on legal values,
but not values outside the law's warrant.

When the various ideas of neutrality are disentangled, it is
apparent that sloganized criticisms that "the law is not neutral" are overbroad. The good faith thesis, for example, upholds neutrality only at the adjudicative level and only in
two specific senses: Judges should not justify their decisions
on the basis of their conceptions of the good life; they should
not act on primary principles of political morality as if there
had been no winnowing in the democratic lawmaking process. The good faith thesis does not claim that adjudication is
a value-neutral or scientific enterprise. It is not committed to
neutrality of any kind at the legislative and constitutional
levels. Critics of neutrality might be correct in disputing any
claim that the law is pervasively neutral according to all conceptions of neutrality. But would anyone defend that view?
Would anyone want the law to be neutral in all senses of

28 See Altman, *Critical Legal Studies*, pp. 76–7.

"neutrality"? The specific neutralities required by the good faith thesis can be achieved by judges acting in practice and, indeed, probably are being achieved to a large extent at this time.

8.3.2. "Perspectivism." A related possible challenge to the politics of good faith stems from a concern about the exclusionary effects of constraining judges to act only on reasons warranted by the law. The philosophy underlying this challenge claims that all of us construct our diverse realities through conceptual schemes influenced pervasively by our respective backgrounds and interests.[29] On this basis, it may be claimed that the law in particular constitutes an invented conceptual scheme representing the dominant perspective – that of empowered white males.[30] The dominant perspective is said to function as if its categories were true and immutable while other ways of constructing the world are denigrated.[31] Consequently, upholding the law excludes some groups from power unfairly. From an outsider's perspective, the good faith thesis might seem to require judges to think only within the dominant perspective by constraining them to act on reasons warranted by the law. This constraint, it

29 The starting point for such a challenge was expressed well by Professor Minow:

> What interests us, given who we are and where we stand, affects our ability to perceive. . . . The impact of the observer's perspective may be crudely oppressive. Yet, we continue to believe in neutrality.

Minow, "Justice Engendered," at 46. I take this to be the current stage in the development of a complaint that goes back to the legal realists' emphasis on the psychology of judging and perhaps to Nietzsche's perspectivism.

30 Ibid., at 65–70, 90. See also Ann C. Scales, "The Emergence of Feminist Jurisprudence," *Yale Law Journal*, 95 (1986): 1373–403; West, "Jurisprudence and Gender."

31 Minow, "Justice Engendered," at 73 ("[t]he more powerful we are, the less we may be able to see that the world coincides with our view precisely because we shaped it in accordance with those views"), at 85 ("[t]he Court's practice vividly demonstrates how fabricated categories can assume the status of immutable reality").

might be claimed, is politically unattractive because it would exclude the different perspectives of women and minorities in particular.

The most recently developed claim of this kind occupies a central place in feminist jurisprudence, which we will discuss primarily using the instructive versions offered by Professor Minow.[32] The key commitment of this approach to jurisprudence, as I understand it, is the use of gender as a fundamental category of analysis. Gender is supposed to generate distinct male and female perspectives from which different understandings of the world are constructed. A popular version in academic legal circles, stimulated by Carol Gilligan's famous psychological study,[33] suggests that men and women bring different perspectives to bear on legal and moral questions. Men tend to approach the world with a sense of separation from it and other people, generating an exclusive emphasis on individual autonomy, rational analysis using abstract categories, and impartial judgment. Women, however, tend to approach the world with a strong sense of connection with it and other people, generating a very different emphasis on caring, empathetic understanding of particular relationships in context, and mediated processing of disputes. Men and women, it is suggested, will bring their gendered perspectives into their jurisprudences, lawmaking, and judging. When powerful offices and academic posts are held predominantly by white men, as they have been historically, the legal tradition will reflect male ways of knowing, excluding the female.[34]

The implications of feminist jurisprudence do not go di-

32 The primary work is ibid. See also Martha Minow & Elizabeth V. Spelman, "In Context," *Southern California Law Review*, 63 (1990): 1597–652.

33 Carol Gilligan, *In a Different Voice* (Cambridge: Harvard University Press, 1982).

34 See, for example, Judith Resnik, "On the Bias: Feminist Reconsiderations of the Aspirations for Our Judges," *Southern California Law Review*, 61 (1988): 1877–944; Suzanna Sherry, "The Gender of Judges," *Law and Inequality*, 4 (1986): 159–69; West, "Jurisprudence and Gender."

rectly to the good faith thesis as a practical understanding of adjudication. They are more fundamental than that. If sound, a bid to include "female ways of knowing" in jurisprudence and adjudication calls into question, first, whether judges are under a duty to uphold the law and, second, whether the law they have a duty to uphold consists of anything resembling conventional law, including implicit principles. The very idea of a duty to uphold the law, conceived as a corpus of rules and other standards of conduct that warrant legal reasons, fits into the rationalistic "male ethic of justice." The "female ethic of care," by contrast, looks "to ways to maintain relationships among the protagonists, since for them the prominent moral concerns are not oppression or inequality, but 'disconnection or abandonment or indifference.' "[35] Moreover, "[t]hese alternative ways of conceiving moral problems . . . are different enough that subjects cannot orient themselves toward a given moral dilemma in one way without the other orientation being totally obscured."[36] Consequently, it would seem that a feminist ethic of care implies opposing the very structure of law as a matter of rights and duties bundled in general standards of conduct to be applied to facts impartially. The good faith thesis is vulnerable to this kind of feminist critique to the extent that traditional understandings of law and adjudication are generally so vulnerable.

In my view, feminist charges of wholesale gender bias in law, like critical claims that the law is politics and is not neutral, are often too sweeping to take adequate account of distinctions that should be made. For example, it is sometimes suggested that traditional ideas or ways of thinking should be rejected, or should be rejected by women, because they were originated or institutionalized by men. The fact that men supported a tradition when women had little influence is a reason to review the tradition for improper bias. It is not, however, a reason to find improper bias. To do so would

35 Minow & Spelman, "In Context," at 1607.
36 Ibid.

be to engage in a kind of ad hominem argument, involving the fallacy of thinking that the personal features of the author establish the merits of the work. It also invites a kind of gender feud reminiscent of failed politics. It is in Northern Ireland, for example, that nothing a Catholic does can be approved by a Protestant and vice versa. Such a vision of politics is hardly attractive.

I will not contest the other premises of feminism on which the jurisprudential claims depend, though I do not endorse them: I will assume for purposes of discussion that feminist tenets concerning the social construction of reality represent sound philosophy[37] and that the standard feminist description of male and female approaches to law and morals are sound psychology or useful metaphor.[38] Even so, we should distinguish between the content of the law, the characterization of facts in law application, and the form of adjudication under law.

The distinctions between adjudication, the law, and the facts are basic. Adjudication under law involves the identification, interpretation, and application of the law to the facts in a particular case. Its institutional structure is independent of the content of the law because one can easily imagine plugging any law into an adjudicatory process without altering its distinctive features. For example, courts in South Africa could identify, interpret, and apply the laws of apartheid in a manner identical to the way courts in the United States adjudicate under the Equal Protection Clause, though the inputs and outcomes are completely at odds. Adjudication thus can be neutral with respect to the content of the law. The facts again are a different matter. They consist of actions, events, and states of affairs in the empirical world, not normative propositions properly identified as law. It may be a fact that the manager of a municipal golf course denied entry

37 For a brief comment on the issue, see Steven J. Burton, "Foreword: Rhetoric and Skepticism," *Iowa Law Review*, 74 (1989): 755–9.
38 For criticism, see, for example, Margaret J. Radin, "The Pragmatist and the Feminist," *Southern California Law Review*, 63 (1990): 1699–726, at 1712–19.

to a black man solely because of his race. This can be so independently of whether the manager was thereby upholding or violating the applicable law. (No doubt one could come up with borderline examples hard to characterize as adjudication, law, or fact.)

The problem of improper bias can affect the content of the law, as the law of apartheid plainly suggests. Additionally, improper bias may infect factual premises on which a law's rationale depends. For example, a legislator may consider whether to require universities to provide equal athletic facilities for men and women within a general requirement of nondiscriminatory educational facilities. A male legislator might oppose such a proposal because he believes women do not enjoy vigorous sports; if that view prevails, the law might reflect prejudice by exempting universities from any such obligation. A belief that women do or do not enjoy vigorous sports, however, goes to a matter of legislative fact concerning women as a group; it is not the law. Rather, the law is the sports facilities exemption represented by a specific provision in the statutory text. It may be unjustified as a consequence of the prejudiced belief. The falsity of that belief may be a reason to change the law. There is nothing novel in this. As in the case of apartheid, the problem is in the content of the law, not its form, grounds, or force.

More relevant to adjudication, the problem of improper bias can arise also when judges characterize the facts in a case. The evidence does not come prepackaged in the categories of the law, but requires considerable sifting in litigation to develop a relevant understanding of what did happen. The sifting of evidence is guided at many points by one's general beliefs about how the world works, including beliefs about various classes of people. Stereotypical beliefs can generate inferences from the evidence to the finding of fact and thereby introduce improper bias in adjudication. For example, a judge may dismiss a woman's complaint of sexual harassment in the workplace because "the guys were just fooling around, affectionately giving her a hard time." Such a characterization of the facts is likely to be incomplete at best,

249

neglecting the very facts that ground a claim of gender discrimination under the relevant law.[39] This kind of bias, however, is not in the law or adjudication as such. Rather, it is in
the finding of facts. The general problem of improper bias in
characterizations of facts is a common concern, well known
to judges and litigators. Recent emphases on racial and gender discrimination call attention to specific instances of the
general problem.

Much feminist legal theory places an appropriate emphasis on these two kinds of bias. Laws that can be justified only
on the basis of prejudiced and erroneous factual assumptions are surely candidates for reform. To better understand
the facts when judging persons of different gender or race,
moreover, judges should listen extra carefully with an open
mind and without bias, to the stories of the parties. A practical understanding of adjudication, however, is not about
the content of the law or biased characterizations of facts.
Rather, it concerns how judges should act on the law given
the best factual understanding that they can muster. Some
adherents of feminist jurisprudence would go further, charging that gender and similar kinds of bias enter the very structure of adjudication under law.[40] This jurisprudential line of
thought might charge the good faith thesis with bias.

The main strategy of criticism probably would be a global
attack on the "male" abstraction of the thesis.[41] Many femi-

39 See Meritor Savings Bank v. Vinson, 477 U.S. 75 (1986) (hostile work
environment can be gender discrimination by employer, prohibited
by Title VII).
40 Minow, "Justice Engendered," at 65. See also Lucinda M. Finley,
"Breaking Women's Silence in Law: The Dilemma of the Gendered
Nature of Legal Reasoning," Notre Dame Law Review, 64 (1989):
886–910; Scales, "The Emergence of Feminist Jurisprudence."
41 See, for example, Radin, "The Pragmatist and the Feminist," at 1707
("[p]ragmatism and feminism largely share . . . the commitment to
finding knowledge in the particulars of experience"); Scales, "The
Emergence of Feminist Jurisprudence," at 1374 (describing the feminist theme of resisting "abstraction itself"); Robin L. West, "The Difference in Women's Hedonic Lives: A Phenomenological Critique of
Feminist Legal Theory," Wisconsin Women's Law Journal, 3 (1987):
81–145, at 90 ("[m]y methodological assumption is that the key to

nist legal scholars distrust abstraction because it is thought to
be a characteristically masculine way of seeing legal and moral issues, by contrast with the feminine "immersion in particulars." By "particulars," however, feminists should not be
understood to intend the classic metaphysical meaning. In
an influential article, for example, Minow recognized that
complete particularization is elusive: "[B]ecause our language is shared and our categories communally invented,
any word I use to describe your uniqueness draws you into
the classes of people sharing your traits."[42] Nonetheless, she
urged,

> Justice . . . is *not* abstract, universal, or neutral. *Instead*, jus-
> tice is the quality of human engagement with multiple per-
> spectives framed by, but not limited to, the relationships of
> power in which they are formed. . . .
>
> *Instead* of trying continually to fit people into categories,
> and to enforce or deny rights on that basis, we can and do
> make decisions by immersing in particulars to renew commit-
> ments to a fair world.[43]

As I and many others read it, this passage objected to the
form of the laws as general standards that designate classes
of cases and to adjudication as a matter of classifying cases in
the resulting legal categories on a reasoned basis. The objection is distinctively *jurisprudential* because it is not aimed
only at the content of the laws or the findings of fact in
judicial and other legal decisions. It is aimed at the basic
structure of adjudication and legal reasoning.

There are a number of objections to such particularism.
First, it is incompatible with justice, which if anything requires that similar cases be treated consistently. Judging consistency between different situations requires abstraction.

moral decision-making lies in our capacity to empathize with the pain
of others, and thereby resist the source of it, and not in our capacity
for abstraction, generalization, or reason").
42 Minow, "Justice Engendered," at 90.
43 Ibid., at 16, 91 (emphasis added).

Second, particularism undermines the normativity of law and morals by dispensing with any practical guidance to judges, leaving in place only an undeveloped and unhelpful reference to fairness or empathy. Third, overemphasis on the uniqueness of each person, act, and state of affairs tends to enervate critical judgment because we cannot consider *all* the particularities of a situation and come to a timely conclusion. Criteria for selection of relevant particularities, however, must be abstract. Fourth, particularism tends to hinder political action; things are what they are, but whether they are good or bad in any important way seems to require a claim that some kinds of knowledge are better than others, which again requires abstraction. Fifth, particularism suggests that language is useless in law because it fits people and situations into categories, calling into question whether notice even of the criminal law can be given to all governed by it. Sixth, it implies that apparent disagreement is a hoax because each person ultimately can be understood to respond to a situation only from his or her own idiosyncratic perspective. Seventh, it may fall into solipsism if everyone is held to construct his or her own reality. No one could with intelligible reason judge the conduct of another person. Eighth, it invites domination by dispensing with intelligible demands for justification by the more powerful actors in any setting.

Professor Minow, together with a coauthor, responded to some of these objections in a later work, shifting her focus from an "immersion in particulars" to "context."[44] She recognized the force of some of the objections. In particular, she accepted that feminists and others cannot reasonably reject all grounds for preferring one way of knowing and one set of judgments over others.[45] Moreover, she accepted that we cannot meaningfully talk without using categories,[46] and denied that contextualism means focusing on all possible features of a situation.[47] She argued that "the basic norm of

44 Minow & Spelman, "In Context."
45 Ibid., at 1625.
46 Ibid.
47 Ibid., at 1629.

fairness – treat like cases alike – is fulfilled, not undermined, by attention to what particular traits make one case like, or unlike, another,"[48] using general categories. Thus, Minow sought to "avoid the mistaken view that increased attention to specific circumstances undermines commitments to universal normative judgments."[49] Now, she believes, abstract "[p]rinciples such as equality, fairness, and freedom can be defended and even fulfilled in light of contextualized assessments of the limitations of particular rules."[50] Rules are more or less general. We can argue about degrees of generality and the relevance of specific circumstances.[51] In sum, she rejected "[t]he binary distinction between abstraction and contextualism"[52] found in feminist jurisprudence.

There are three instructive points to note about the movement of Minow's views. First, the evolution follows a logical line of development from the "immersion in particulars" supplanting general standards to an acceptance of general standards to be applied in light of the circumstances. A total immersion in particulars seems, most basically, to preclude reasoning and communication because they both require generalizations. To avoid dispensing with them, and thereby giving up any objection to base instincts and secret laws, it seems necessary at least to welcome reasoning by analogy, which operates on particular situations, drawing out similarities between discrete particulars. However, once one recognizes analogies between cases, it is but a short step to a full recognition that abstract categories are unavoidable in legal or other reasoning.[53] To say that two cases are alike in relevant respects simply is to say that they are members of

48 Ibid.
49 Ibid., at 1631.
50 Ibid., at 1632.
51 Ibid., at 1629–31.
52 Ibid., at 1628.
53 This is not to say, however, that abstract categories must be objective ontologically, immutable, implying human access to a view beyond human experience, ignorant of contingent particulars, or reified in a way that forecloses criticism of them. They can be conventional without being open to unconstrained revision.

the same class of cases, which may be designated by the words of a legal rule, principle, or other generalization. To distinguish two cases is to insist that they are not properly classified together.[54] Analogies are incomplete expressions of categorical reasoning, including legal reasoning from rules and other general standards of conduct.

The second point to note is the relationship of Minow's later views to the assumptions supporting the good faith thesis together with traditional thought about adjudication. As she now suggests, disagreements should center on degrees of generality in our legal standards and the focus and use of those standards:

> [T]he important question becomes which context should matter, what traits or aspects of the particular should be addressed, how wide should the net be cast in collecting the details, and what scale should be used to weigh them? Whether you prefer to be called a contextualist or a devotee of principled reason, you make choices about what features of context to address.[55]

I agree that the important questions concern the legal relevance of facts in the circumstances of action and the gauging of weight. With an acceptance of abstractions like rules and principles, the good faith thesis is not incompatible with the form of law and adjudication now advanced by Minow and others in feminist jurisprudence. As Minow suggests implicitly, the important questions concern the content of the premises in judicial reasoning. That is, the important questions concern the content of the law and the characterization of the facts, both of which may involve improper bias. The good faith thesis carries no brief in defense of existing laws or judicial habits in these respects. Criticism looking to reform of the law and judicial practice should be welcomed at all times. Criticism cannot proceed if it is limited to the facts made relevant by the law under evaluation. Critics of the law

54 Burton, *Law and Legal Reasoning*, p. 82.
55 Minow & Spelman, "In Context," at 1629.

properly look to the circumstances of action unconstrained by the criteria of relevance in the existing law. They operate from a critical standpoint, not the legal point of view.

Judges are not critics of the law when they judge cases. They are under a moral duty to uphold the law, which constrains the facts that count as legal reasons for them, well or badly as the case may be. We may disagree on what should be the law that judges have a duty to uphold. We may disagree on the proper interpretation of the law. We may disagree on the characterization of the facts in a case. But we should not criticize judges for doing the wrong thing when they fulfill their moral duty to uphold the law and disobedience would not be justified. Critics, too, bear ethical responsibilities. One of them is to criticize judges only for failing to act on the best of the available alternatives, as a practical matter, under the circumstances.

We need not disagree in a gendered way about the structure of law or adjudication. Perspectivism may seem attractive because it expresses the humility with which we all should regard the views we put forward. Those views may be improperly biased as a consequence of our backgrounds and interests. It may seem but a short step from recognition of that risk to a claim that any use of abstract categories implies a belief that what is said is true and immutable, leading to intolerance for the contrary views of others. Abstract beliefs, however, are not incompatible with a comparable humility, one that would eschew any belief that rules, principles, policies, and the structures of adjudication and legal reasoning, are imperialistic representations of the immutable truth. Rather, this kind of humility takes it for granted that every belief is *fallible*. It craves discussion of the grounds for believing something to be true or worthy of belief. It accepts criticism showing that the abstract belief is false or ungrounded, and it revises beliefs accordingly in an ongoing process. Humility based in fallibility denies, however, that among the general grounds for the truth of a statement is the gender or any other indelible characteristic of the author. It concerns what is said, not who said it, the motivation for saying it, the rhetoric in which it is said, or the consequences of the saying.[56] Moreover, humility based in fallibility denies that the prospect of revising a belief in light of new reasons itself is a reason to refrain from claiming that the belief is true. The ever present theoretical possibility of revision does not help to distinguish good reasons from bad ones within a practical understanding. Good reasons for action are objective, in the sense of impartial, without being features of a timeless heaven of juristic concepts of the sort sought by Langdell.[57]

In sum, the problems of perspectivism do not infect good faith adjudication under law although they may infect the content of the law and the characterization of facts. The good faith thesis does not treat the law as an immutable set of abstract categories to be applied in adjudication without sensitivity to the circumstances of action. It dispenses with such rigidity by abandoning determinacy of results and offering a practical understanding of the weight of legal reasons. The good faith thesis embraces judicial discretion within the Rule of Law. It does not, however, open the field to whatever strikes a judge's fancy or whatever plays to prior political commitments, as by abandoning any requirement of legal relevance. The good faith thesis sets a constrained but meaningful scope to the task of adjudication under law. Efforts to expel improper bias should be focused on the content of specific laws and judicial habits, not esoteric jurisprudential arguments about its form, objectivity, neutrality, determinacy, and generality.

8.4. THE FUTURE OF GOOD FAITH

The good faith thesis advances a view on the ethical standards judges should strive to satisfy and to which they should be held by serious critics. It seeks to influence the legal culture, which is shaped by the practice of approval

56 See § 1.4.2.
57 For the relevant idea of impartiality, see § 2.2.2.

and criticism, especially by members of the legal community. To be clear, there is nothing in the good faith thesis to guarantee that the present practice of adjudication is politically legitimate. My primary claim is a conceptual and normative one: Judicial discretion, when exercised in good faith, is compatible with the legitimacy of adjudication in a constitutional democracy under the Rule of Law. The practice of judging is better or worse at achieving good faith in different times and places. How well it is doing in any one time and place is an empirical question that can be investigated fruitfully only when the relevance and criteria of good faith have been made clear, and the determinacy condition has been laid to rest.

To some, the politics of good faith may seem to bear an especially weak relationship to the practices of law and politics we observe around us in the United States at the end of the twentieth century. The politics of good faith assume that law seeks to help us live well together, given our different and conflicting interests and values. To do this successfully requires a common ground on which to organize our social life as a practical matter. Judges most crucially, and all other members of the legal community to some extent as well, should serve the common ground as a matter of priority, resisting the temptation to exploit opportunities to take unjustified advantage in the interest of one or another primary political principle or interest. For judges, "good faith" is a way to mark the priority of the common ground over the play of personal and political loyalties. We may observe around us, however, many efforts to take advantage of the legal common ground of our society. We see efforts to capture the judiciary by making ideologically pure appointments and thus to control the common ground in the interests of one or another faction. We see efforts to transform the law through some kind of jurisprudential magic to produce what one or another subgroup would regard as politically correct results. The politics of good faith might seem unrealistic in a society riven by rivalrous politics.

This should not be surprising, though it is cause for con-

tinuing concern. The political common ground is like an economic commons that benefits the community only as long as
everyone acts with self-restraint.[58] Any one person, however, can be made better off by acting opportunistically in his
or her individual or subgroup self-interest if everyone does
not do so and thereby bring down the cooperative scheme
altogether. So some people will try in any case quietly to take
a piece of the common ground for themselves while continuing to benefit from the general scheme of order and justice
that prevails nonetheless. When too many get away with it,
the common ground may give way to a repellent kind of
politics that will strike most as a degeneration of the society.

We may unavoidably be living in a period of flight from the
common ground, as many people realign their priorities to
place the interests of the subgroups to which they belong, or
with which they identify, above the interests of the large
group to which we all belong. There may simply be centrifugal and centripetal periods in history, with good faith
most appropriate in the centripetal phase. We may be in a
centrifugal phase. No doubt the forces of racial, gender, eth-
nic, national, and religious loyalty are stronger on a global
scale today than they were a decade ago. If so, good faith
may seem to some but an idealist's dream, appropriate perhaps for a world we once tried to build, but now outmoded
as the world breaks up into yet smaller political groupings
engaged in nasty politics.

In my optimistic moods, however, I think that things are
not worse now than they were, often beneath the surface. Or
I hope that the worst of centrifugal politics in the United
States has passed or will pass soon, and that the future be-
longs to the centripetal forces that tend to bring us together –
all of us, under a reasonably just law, with due respect for
our differences. I do not know how that can happen without
a commitment to the politics of good faith or something similar.

58 See, for example, Garrett Hardin, "The Tragedy of the Commons,"
    Science, 162 (1968): 1243–8.

The politics of good faith emphasize understanding others as they understand themselves by looking to their reasons for action; these can be grasped only with regard for another standpoint in concrete circumstances. A practical understanding of another's standpoint does not imply any surrender of moral judgment. We each have our own reasons for action and are responsible for our own actions. The politics of good faith emphasize a vision of political disagreement in which we acknowledge and respect others' reasons even while we disagree with the results they reach.

I have tried to develop the idea of judging in good faith as a way of adapting for our times a most valuable strand in the American tradition. I commend it as a basis for judges and other officials to exercise restraint. I commend it as a basis for us all, through our practice of praise and reproach of judges, to maintain a shared ethic of good judging under law.

Table of cases

TABLE OF CASES

Index of names

263

Index of names

Purcell, Edward A., 8, 112
Putnam, Hilary, 21, 192–4

Radin, Margaret Jane, 141, 248, 250
Rawls, John, 26, 137, 141, 217, 240–3
Raz, Joseph, xvii, 6, 7, 28, 42, 46, 47, 49, 55, 63, 90, 100, 119, 120, 127, 138, 141, 151, 154, 173, 179–81, 204, 205, 209, 213, 215, 216, 221, 241, 242
Regan, Donald H., 63, 205
Resnik, Judith, 246
Richards, Richard F., 82
Roberts, Justice, 149
Rossiter, C., 241
Rubin, Alvin B., 11, 161
Ryle, Gilbert, 117

Sacks, Albert M., 7, 8, 172, 173
Sartorius, Rolf E., 9, 54
Sbisà, Marina, 38
Scales, Ann C., 27, 59, 245, 250
Scalia, Justice Antonin, xvi, 15, 44, 75, 123, 142, 154, 167
Schauer, Frederick, 4, 11, 63, 158, 167, 170, 175
Schlag, Pierre, 176
Schlegel, John Henry, 112
Searle, John R., 38
Sellars, Wilfrid, 118
Sherry, Suzanna, 246
Simmons, A. John, 151, 215
Simon, William H., 207, 208
Singer, Joseph W., 9–11, 136, 137, 149, 167, 239, 243
Sitz, Herbert, xvii
Smith, M. B. E., 40, 123, 151, 187, 215
Soper, Philip, 46. 49, 54, 90, 183

Spelman, Elizabeth V., 28, 246, 247, 252, 254
Steinbock, Bonnie, xvii
Stick, John, xvii, 27, 36, 167
Stier, Serena, xvii, 208
Sullivan, Charles A., 82, 132
Summers, Robert S., 8, 112

Tollison, Robert D., 232
Tribe, Laurence H., 19, 85, 242
Trubeck, David M., 5, 40, 128, 137, 146
Tullock, Gordon, 232
Tushnet, Mark V., 10, 19, 122, 140, 149, 238

Ullman-Margalit, Edna, 196
Unger, Roberto M., 4, 9, 27, 136, 139, 146, 156, 238, 239
Urmson, J. O., 38

von Hayek, Friedrich, 142, 148

Waldron, Jeremy, 37
Warren, Elizabeth, 132, 198
Wasserstrom, Richard A., 44, 120, 145, 149, 168
Watson, Alan, 137
Wechsler, Herbert, 8, 240
Weinrib, Ernest J., 4, 119
Wellman, Vincent A., 172
West, Robin L., 99, 239, 243, 245, 246, 250
Westen, Peter, 167
White, Justice Byron, 74, 81, 87–8
Winter, Steven L., 20, 27, 167
Wiseman, Zipporah Batshaw, 98
Wittgenstein, Ludwig, 18, 117
Woodworth, George, 133

Zane, John M., 149
Zimmer, Michael J., 82

Index of subjects

Abstraction, 27, 39n, 51–4, 55,
250–4. *See also* Particularism
Action threshold. *See* Deliberations, action threshold in
Actor's standpoint, 119–23. *See
also* Judicial standpoint
Adjudication. *See also* Deliberations; Good faith thesis; Judicial duty
distinguished from philosophy,
95, 198–9
and normative powers of lawmakers, 152–7, 213–17
practical understanding of, xv–
vi, 35, 53, 99–100, 109–10,
116–17, 117–24, 129, 147, 181,
229, 230, 250
role morality in, 207–10, 213,
217
structure of, 34, 250–1, 255
theory of, xv–vi, 181–3, 231, 243
Analogy, 40, 116, 253–4
Arbitrariness, 58, 137n, 144–57
Authority, hierarchies of, 8, 52,
78–81, 86–7
Authority, legal, 46n, 213–17
Authorization chains, 144–5, 152–
7, 165, 200, 203, 243

Background justifications. *See*
Good faith thesis, background
justifications in

Character, judicial, 46–7, 64, 93,
157–65

Client writ large, 129–32
Common ground, 33, 78, 79, 81,
256–8
Consent, 143–4, 150–2, 215, 217–
19, 222, 228
Constitutional theory, 77–81, 89,
95–6, 98
Constraint. *See also* Authorization
chains; Character, judicial;
Discretion, constraints on;
Desires; Judicial duty
causal, 44–5, 144–8, 157–63
contrasted with determinacy,
124, 141–65
generally, 61–2, 107, 124, 145–
65
on judges, xii–iii, 7, 8–12, 19–
20, 37, 38, 43–50, 56–62, 90–
3, 94, 114, 124, 135, 144–65,
185, 203, 235–6, 245, 255
logical, 27, 144, 149–52
practical, 49, 64, 124, 152–7,
162, 165
Conventionalism, 9, 36n, 57n,
68n, 80n, 86, 122–3, 178, 195–
9, 234–5n, 247
Conventions, defined, 57n, 234–
5n
Critical legal theory, 9, 14–34, 24n,
121, 135–65, 231–9, 243
Critical race theory, 18, 239

Deliberations. *See also* Discretion,
judicial; Good faith thesis;
Reasons for action

266

3356172R00160

Printed in Great Britain
by Amazon.co.uk, Ltd.,
Marston Gate.